NOW WHAT?

The Creative Writer's Guide to Success After the MFA

NOW WHAT?

The Creative Writer's Guide to Success After the MFA

Editor-in-Chief
Ashley C. Andersen Zantop, MFA

Ashley Andersen Zantop is group publisher at Capstone, Minneapolis, MN. She holds BAs in English Literature, Elementary Education (University of Michigan) and an MFA in Creative Writing (Fairfield University).

Editors
Michael Bayer, MFA

Michael Bayer is a fiction writer based in Pleasantville, NY. He holds a BA from the University of Rhode Island and an MFA from Fairfield University. He teaches at the City University of New York.

A.J. O'Connell, MFA

A.J. O'Connell is a Connecticut-based author. She holds a BA in International Studies from Trinity College in Hartford and an MFA from Fairfield University. She teaches journalism at Norwalk Community College.

Erin A. Corriveau, MFA

Erin A. Corriveau graduated from Fairfield University's MFA program with a concentration in creative nonfiction. She is the co-founding editor of Spry Literary Journal.

Adele Annesi, MFA

Adele Annesi is a Ridgefield, CT-based novelist and editor, and a professor of English with an MFA in creative writing from Fairfield University. She is co-founder of the Ridgefield Writers Conference.

Jean M. Medeiros, MFA

Jean M. Medeiros is an author, editor, auntie, Rhode Islander and owner of Medeiros Editing & Consulting, with an MFA in Creative Writing from Fairfield University and an MS from Johnson & Wales University.

Fairfield UNIVERSITY

Now What? The Creative Writer's Guide to Success After the MFA

Publisher: Michael C. White

Editor-in-Chief: Ashley C. Andersen Zantop

Editors: Michael Bayer, A.J. O'Connell, Erin A. Corriveau, Adele Annesi, Jean M. Medeiros

Cover and interior design: Kazuko Collins

Production and conversion: Danielle Ceminsky

Acknowledgements

Fairfield University and the Fairfield University MFA in Creative Writing program would like to thank Bonnie Cook, David Fitzpatrick, Meredith Kazer, Christine Koubek, Don Noel and Heather Zullinger for their generous donations to this publication.

The editorial team would like to thank the students, faculty, alumni and staff of the Fairfield University MFA in Creative Writing Program for giving so generously of their time, wisdom and craft to this project. You are a wonderful community.

Special thanks to Robbin Crabtree, Michael White, Elizabeth Hastings and Carolyn Arnold for their support in bringing this work to life.

For Peter and Alex. Your love and patience are a miracle. For my family, all of you, I'm so grateful to have you in my life. For my writing family, you keep me sane (and crazy) and writing. Thank you—ACAZ

For everyone who loves reading and writing. Also for Miguel, Jack, Eddy and Lola—MB

For my two guys: my amazing husband Tom, and for T.W., who will be born just as this book is launched. And for my writing group, The Barbarians, who keep me and my novel on track—AJO

For Ryan and Madden, my favorite guys in the world. For my incredible parents, family, and friends. For my literary mind link and my writing community. Thank you for bringing me this far and for keeping me going—EAC

I'm blessed by the support of my mother, Connie Keller and Wellspring Writers Workshop, the Ridgefield Writers Guild, and Fairfield University's MFA family of friends and faculty—AA

For Mary, my mom, my hero, you live on in our hearts. For all my family, with thanks for your love and support; Pat whose encouragement is endless; and the joys of Alex and Katie—JMM

CONTENTS

Map for the Weary Traveler
by Linsey Jayne

Chapter *1*

edited by Ashley C. Andersen Zantop

How Can I Use This? The Creative Use of Academic Requirements
by William Patrick

Strategy and the Reading List
by Jennifer Emerson

Your Journey Starts Here
by Adele Annesi

Chapter *2*

edited by Ashley C. Andersen Zantop and Erin A Corriveau

Your Literary Siblings: Engaging Your Alumni Community for
Lifelong Inspiration
by Michael Bayer

Contributors

Ashley C. Andersen Zantop

Ashley Andersen Zantop writes and edits fiction and nonfiction. She is group publisher and general manager of Capstone, one of the largest independent publishers of children's supplemental educational and trade titles and reading software. Andersen Zantop earned her MFA in creative writing from Fairfield University, degrees in English literature (AB) and elementary education (AB. ED) from the University of Michigan, Ann Arbor, Michigan, as well as teaching certificates (CERT K-5, CERT 6-8). Andersen Zantop founded and serves as co-president of the Fairfield University MFA Alumni Association.

Adele Annesi

Adele Annesi is an award-winning writer and editor. Adele crafts stories, columns and reviews for various journals, including *Southern Literary Review*, where she was managing editor. A co-founder of the Ridgefield Writers Conference, Adele received an MFA in creative writing from Fairfield University, and her flash fiction has been adapted for the stage. A professor of writing, Adele is completing a novel set in Italy.

Travis Baker

Travis Baker works as an adjunct professor of English at the University of Maine-Orono. His work has been published in *Spry Lit, Masons Road, Stolen Island, Hawk & Handsaw* and *The Maine Edge*, among others. His play, *One Blue Tarp* was named the 2013 Best in Maine in the Clauder New England Playwrights competition and is part of the Penobscot Theatre Company's 40th Anniversary Season.

credit: Jason Smith

Rachel Basch

Rachel Basch is the author of the novels *Degrees of Love, The Passion of Reverend Nash* and (forthcoming) *The Listener*. She teaches in Fairfield University's MFA program and in Wesleyan University's Graduate Liberal Studies Program.

credit: Tyler Sizemore

Michael Bayer

Michael Bayer writes fiction that explores darkness, crime and identity. He holds an MFA from Fairfield University, where he is co-president of the MFA Alumni Association, and teaches writing and communications at the City University of New York. Previously, he spent two decades working in corporate communications and public relations. He lives in Westchester County, New York, where his three Rhodesian Ridgebacks run the show.

Chris Belden

Chris Belden is the author of the novels *Shriver* (2013) and *Carry-on* (2012), as well as the story collection *The Floating Lady of Lake Tawaba* (2014). He is founder of the Ridgefield Writers Workshop, and co-founder of the Ridgefield Writers Conference. He has taught writing at Fairfield University, as well such less traditional venues as senior centers, soup kitchens and a maximum security prison.

Mark Berry

Mark is an airline pilot with an MFA from Fairfield University, the author of a memoir *13,760 Feet—My Personal Hole in the Sky* (with thirty-four companion songs) and two novels, a contributing editor for Airways magazine, and a former managing editor for Mason's Road literary journal. His work has also appeared in *4'33"*, *Aerospace Testing Int'l*, *AOPA Flight Training*, *BMW Owners News*, *Connecticut newspapers*, *Epiphany*, *ERAU EaglesNEST*, *Graze*, *LIFT*, *MilSpeak Memo*, *Port Cities Review*, *Rogue*, *So...Stories*, *The Stoneslide Corrective*, *The Story Shack*, *TARPA Topics*, *Under the Sun*, and *Write This*.

Lary Bloom

Lary Bloom is the author of eight nonfiction books and of the upcoming *Sol LeWitt: A Life of Ideas*, from Farrar, Straus and Giroux. He is a former columnist for the *New York Times*, the *Miami Herald*, the *Hartford Courant* and *Connecticut Magazine*. He is a book editor and cofounder of Praiano Writers, a workshop on Italy's Amalfi Coast. His website is www.larybloom.net.

Lisa Calderone

Lisa Calderone is a communications consultant and web designer, and the founding editor of Mason's Road, Fairfield University's online literary journal. Author of *How to Raise a Family & A Career Under One Roof* (Bookhaven Press, 1997), she built an author platform and online community for entrepreneurial parents from 1998-2005 that led to a spin-off book entitled *The Entrepreneurial Parent* (Tarcher/Putnam, 2002) with best-selling co-authors Paul and Sarah Edwards. She lives, works, and writes in Guilford, Connecticut.

Joseph R. Carvalko

Joseph Carvalko is an author and lawyer. His recent novel, *We Were Beautiful Once, Chapters from a Cold War* (Sunbury Press, 2013) was inspired by a trial he conducted. He also recently authored *The Techno-human Shell-A Jump in the Evolutionary Gap* (Sunbury Press, 2012). When not writing, he is an adjunct at Quinnipiac University School of Law, a member of the Community Bioethics Forum, Yale School of Medicine and a member of the Yale Technology and Ethics working group, and the ABA Section on Science and Technology, a jazz pianist and inventor with ten patents. Learn more at www.carvalko.com.

Abbey Cleland

Abbey Cleland writes fiction, TV, film, and promotional content for a variety of LA-based studios and independent clients. Since studying creative writing at The Ohio State University and The New School, she's optioned five romantic comedies, and earned an MFA from Fairfield University. Above all, Abbey believes in hard work, October baseball, and that in each of our daily lives, there's a delicious story to be told. Please visit: abbeycleland.com.

Bonnie Cook

Bonnie Cook teaches English and public speaking, and occasionally meditation, at Hudson Valley Community College. Her articles have appeared in *Integral Yoga Magazine, Potluck Pedagogy,* and *Academic Minutes.* Thirty years after obtaining an MA degree, Bonnie added an MFA in memoir from Fairfield University. She leads a writers' group, plays in a ping-pong league, is an avid swimmer and lives in an 1880s farmhouse at the edge of a wetland in upstate New York. Currently, she's writing poetry.

Erin A. Corriveau

Erin A. Corriveau is an emotional archeologist who graduated from Fairfield University's MFA program with a concentration in creative nonfiction. Her writing has been published in (em): *A Review of Text and Image, Revolution House, Lunch Ticket, Paper Tape, Shoreline Literary Arts Magazine, The Fall River Spirit,* and *RedFez.* She is the co-founder and editor of *Spry Literary Journal,* and is currently at work on a collection of linked essays. Her blog, Reinventing Erin, is her outlet for ruminating on the minutiae of everyday life.

Cisco Covino

Cisco Covino enjoys making pizza and riding his bike around Boston. He also enjoys being the art editor for *Spry Literary Journal.*

Alan Davis

Alan Davis's third collection of stories, *So Bravely Vegetative,* won the Prize Americana for Fiction. His other two prize-winning collections are *Rumors from the Lost World and Alone with the Owl.* Davis has received two Fulbright awards, a Minnesota State Arts Board Fellowship, and a Loft-McKnight Award of Distinction in Creative Prose. He also serves as senior editor at New Rivers Press, which is associated with Minnesota State University in Moorhead, where he's professor of English. He can be found on Facebook and LinkedIn.

Carol Ann Davis

Carol Ann Davis is the recipient of an NEA Fellowship in poetry and the author of Psalm and Atlas Hour, both from Tupelo Press. After directing the creative writing program at The College of Charleston and editing Crazyhorse for a decade, in 2012 she joined the writing faculty of Fairfield University. Recent work has appeared or is forthcoming in *Agni, The Southern Review,* and *Image.*

Alena Dillon

Alena Dillon is the author of the humor collection *I Thought We Agreed to Pee in the Ocean: And Other Amusings From A Girl Wearing Sweatpants*. Her work has appeared in publications including The Huffington Post, The Rumpus, Pithead Chapel, The Long River Review, and in all ten magazines of the Weston Magazine Group. She lives in New York with her husband. They wish they had a dog.

Rebecca Dimyan

Rebecca Dimyan has a BA in English from Boston University and a Master of Fine Arts in creative writing from Fairfield University. She is a writer, teacher, and food journalist. Her published work has appeared in *L'Allure des Mots*, the *Ampersand Review*, *The Fat City Review*, *eChook*, and The *Cupboard Magazine*. Rebecca teaches First Year Writing at Fairfield University.

Jennifer M. Emerson

Jennifer received her MFA in creative writing from Fairfield University in 2011. Her debut novel, *Dickens and the Whore*, was the basis for her MFA studies. A living history playwright and actress, Jennifer enjoys bringing history and literature alive in fun, fresh and believable ways. When her nose isn't stuck in a 19th century text, she probably can be found playing the harp or basking on the rocks of the nearest beach.

David Fitzpatrick

David Fitzpatrick grew up in Guilford, graduated Skidmore College in 1988, and received his MFA from Fairfield University in 2011. His memoir *Sharp: My Story of Madness, Cutting and How I Reclaimed My Life*, was published by HarperCollins in 2012. He's married to Amy Holmes, the incredible writer, photographer, and real estate research analyst. His writing can be found at *The Perch*, and *New Haven Review*. The two also offer speaking engagements. Their website is davidfitzpatrickbooks.com

Heather Frizzell

Heather Frizzell is a writer, teacher, and lover of fiction in all mediums. She earned a BFA in writing, literature, and publishing from Emerson College in 2007 and an MFA in creative writing from Fairfield University in 2011. She is currently at work on a young adult book series and also teaches college writing at Bunker Hill Community College. She lives in Boston, Massachusetts.

Stephanie Harper

Stephanie Harper received her Masters of Fine Arts in creative writing at Fairfield University with an emphasis in fiction in July 2012. Her work can be found in *The Montreal Review*, *Poetry Quarterly*, *Midwest Literary Magazine*, *Forever Buffs Insider*, and *Haiku Journal*. She served as fiction co-editor for *Mason's Road Literary Journal*. She lives in Denver, Colorado and is working on publishing her first novel.

Deborah Henry

Deborah Henry's debut novel, *The Whipping Club* was selected for *O Magazine's* July Summer Reading Issue and named to *Kirkus Reviews'* "Best of 2012." She is currently working on her next book. Visit her at www.deborahhenryauthor.com. She is an active member of The Academy of American Poets, a board member of Cavankerry Press and a patron of the Irish Arts Center in New York.

credit: Copyright:
Marion Ettlinger

Elizabeth Hilts

The author of four internationally bestselling humor books, Elizabeth Hilts earned her MFA in creative writing at Fairfield University. Formerly the editor of an alternative newsweekly and editorial director for direct mail companies, she is an adjunct professor at local colleges and universities. She is currently working on a memoir, a novel, and personal essays.

Linsey Jayne

Linsey Jayne received her MFA from Fairfield University. She has served as poetry editor for *Mason's Road*, as well as student editor for the *Bryant Literary Review* and the opinion section editor of *The Archway*, and is currently the co-founding editor of *Spry Literary Journal*. Linsey lives in Boston, Massachusetts, where she is currently at work on her first collection of poetry, entitled Idle Jive.

Lisa Diane Kastner

Lisa Diane Kastner is the former features editor for the Picolata Review and journalist for the Philadelphia Theater Review, among many other functions.

Meredith Wallace Kazer

Meredith Wallace Kazer, PhD, APRN, CNL, A/GNP-BC, FAAN is professor and associate dean at Fairfield University School of Nursing. She is the author of over one hundred nursing and health-related publications, including ten books.

Brooke Adams Law

Brooke Adams Law lives in New York with her husband, where she is finishing her first novel. She holds an MFA in fiction from Fairfield University and a BA in English from Vassar College. She continues to struggle with allowing her artist time to get out and play, but she's pretty sure there's meaning in the struggle all the same.

Phil Lemos

Phil Lemos writes the blog *Life in the Philloverse* and has published three short stories: "Let It Go", "BMW Supermodel" and "Upset of the Century." He has an MFA in fiction from Fairfield University and is working on a novel. You can follow him on Twitter.

Suzanne Matson

Suzanne Matson is the author of the novels *The Tree-Sitter, A Trick of Nature,* and *The Hunger Moon.* Her books of poems are *Durable Goods* and *Sea Level.* Her poems, short stories, and essays have appeared in *The American Poetry Review, Poetry, The Boston Review, Carolina Quarterly, Poetry Northwest, The Southern Poetry Review, The Harvard Review, Indiana Review, Mid-American Review, Shenandoah, The New York Times Magazine, The Boston Globe, Child, and The Seattle Times,* among others. She is a professor at Boston College and taught in the Fairfield MFA Program from 2011 to 2013.

Jean M. Medeiros

Jean M. Medeiros is a fiction writer, editor, auntie and Rhode Islander, with an MFA in creative writing from Fairfield University, an MS from Johnson & Wales University and a certificate in creative writing from the UCLA Extension Writers' Program, where she was also nominated for the Kirkwood Literary Prize. She owns Medeiros Editing & Consulting and has published fiction and non-fiction, including co-writing two legal manuals for the National Business Institute. She is crafting her second novel.

Pete Nelson

Pete Nelson lives with his wife and son in Westchester, New York. He got his MFA from the University of Iowa Writers' Workshop and has written both fiction and non-fiction for magazines. His WWII history, *Left For Dead* (Random House, 2002) won the 2003 Christopher award and was named to the American Library Association's 2003 top ten list. His novel, *I Thought You Were Dead* (Algonquin, April 2010) was named the Indie Next #1 Choice and reached the NEIBA Bestsellers List. He's currently working on his next novel.

A.J. O'Connell

credit: David Esposito

A.J. O'Connell is the author of two books: *Beware the Hawk* (2012) and *The Eagle & The Arrow* (2013), both published by Battered Suitcase Press. She got her start as an editorial assistant at *The Boston Herald,* worked for nine years as a reporter at *The Norwalk Hour,* and freelanced for various publications. Her creative work has appeared in various magazines and journals. Currently she teaches journalism at Norwalk Community College. She can be found at ajoconnell.com.

Ioanna Pettas Opidee

Ioanna Opidee has taught writing and literature at Fairfield University, University of Connecticut Stamford, University of Massachusetts Boston, and Florida Atlantic University. She has completed a novel and is currently working on a collection of essays.

Karen Osborn

Karen Osborn is the author of four novels: *Patchwork, Between Earth and Sky, The River Road*, and most recently, *Centerville*. Her awards include the 2013 Independent Publishers Award for Fiction and *The New York Times* Notable Book Award. Her poetry and short stories have appeared nationally in journals such as *The Southern Review, Poet Lore, Kansas Quarterly, The Centennial Review*, and *The Wisconsin Review*.

Steve Otfinoski

Steve Otfinoski received his MFA from Fairfield University in 2010. He has published more than 160 young adult books. Three of his books have been named Books for the Teen Age by the New York Public Library. He is also a playwright and teaches composition and creative writing at Fairfield University.

William Patrick

William Patrick's works have been published or produced in many genres: creative nonfiction, poetry, fiction, screenwriting, and drama. His latest book, *The Call of Nursing: Voices from the Front Lines of Health Care*, was published in July, 2013. *Saving Troy*, (2009), chronicles a year spent riding along with firefighters and paramedics. His memoir in poetry, *We Didn't Come Here for This* (1999), was published by BOA Editions, as was *These Upraised Hands* (1995), and a novel, *Roxa: Voices of the Culver Family*. More information is available at www.williampatrickwriter.com.

Justin Scace

After achieving an undergraduate degree in psychology from Colby College, Justin Scace worked a variety of jobs including bartender, census taker, and volunteer for a horse carriage-driving program. He graduated with his MFA in creative writing (fiction) from Fairfield University in January of 2011. About a month later he was hired by his current employer, one of the largest independent audiobook companies in the nation. He lives in southeastern Connecticut.

Sarah Z. Sleeper

Sarah Z. Sleeper writes fiction and poetry. In her twenty-year writing career prior to completing her MFA, she freelanced for *Fortune, The Christian Science Monitor, The National Journal* and others. http://www.SarahZSleeper.com.

Barbara Wanamaker

Barbara Wanamaker writes every damn day nestled in her porch office, her dog Riley curled up at her feet, overlooking Stratford, Connecticut. Her non-fiction piece, *Errands*, appears in the inaugural issue of *Spry Literary Journal*.

Michael C. White

Michael White has authored six novels: *Soul Catcher*, a Booksense and Historical Novels Review selection, and a finalist for the Connecticut Book Award, *A Brother's Blood*, a New York Times Book Review Notable Book and a Barnes and Noble Discover Great New Writers nominee; *The Blind Side of the Heart*, *A Dream of Wolves*, and *The Garden of Martyrs*, a Connecticut Book Award finalist. His novel, *Beautiful Assassin*, won the 2011 Connecticut Book Award for Fiction. He was the founding editor of *American Fiction* as well as *Dogwood* and is the director of Fairfield University's MFA Creative Writing Program.

Matthew Winkler

Matthew Winkler's passion for hands-on learning has propelled him twice around the world and through all fifty states. Matt is currently teaching at South Kent School while writing a nonfiction book related to his TED-Ed video, "What Makes a Hero?" Follow Matt at EducationUnusual.com or @EdUnusual.

Baron Wormser

Baron Wormser is the author/co-author of thirteen full-length books and a poetry chapbook. Wormser has received fellowships from the National Endowment for the Arts, Bread Loaf, and the John Simon Guggenheim Memorial Foundation. From 2000 to 2006 he served as poet laureate of the state of Maine. He teaches in the Fairfield University MFA Program and is director of educational outreach for the Frost Place in Franconia, NH. His most recent book is a novel, *Teach Us That Peace*, about which Kirkus Reviews wrote, "Wormser has a miraculous ability to evoke a sense of time and place."

Zac Zander

Zac Zander lives in Connecticut with his dog, Kaki, who is named after the musician, not the pants. He holds an MFA from Fairfield University and is working on a collection of essays.

Heather Zullinger

Heather Zullinger, BA/English Literature & Creative Writing, is a professionally trained instructor in the Barre Fitness method, which she teaches regularly throughout Fairfield County. Prior to this time, she was an advertising manager in the consumer magazine publishing industry.

Foreword

"Where do I turn for writing advice?"

"How do I keep writing while working a job, raising a family, mowing the lawn?"

"I feel so alone now that I've graduated from my MFA."

These are fairly common concerns voiced by many students who've recently completed an MFA program. After several years of being part of a vibrant, supportive community, they are suddenly on their own.

I recall my own post-graduate experience. I attended the University of Denver in the late seventies. For three years, I felt I'd finally found my home, my community, my niche in life. Surrounded by fellow writers—faculty mentors and fellow students—I felt part of a tight-knit family. The people I met there had become my mentors, my friends, my comrades. I could go to them for advice on craft and technique as well as engaging in late-night, heated debates (over wine) concerning the merits of this or that writer. I could share with them when I had writer's block or had received "another" rejection notice, or simply when I wanted to talk about the profound pleasures of getting a scene right. For three years—artistically, the most intense, transformative, and gratifying period of my life—I was surrounded by people who understood and shared my vision of the world. It was a heady and thrilling time. And then, overnight it seemed, I was pushed out of this comfortable nest and forced to go it alone in the world, severing ties and connections and friendships. In some ways it felt as if I'd been on vacation for three years and then had to return to the pedestrian world of work and responsibilities.

In my particular case, when I finished grad school I took a teaching job fifteen hundred miles away in the mountains of North Carolina. It was an hour's drive from the closest city, and I had no fellow writers around me. Moreover, I was soon to become a father, was thrown into teaching a four-course load, became a home-owner, and felt as completely isolated as a writer could feel. Who would read my work? Who could I talk to after my latest magazine rejection? Where could I turn for advice on topics ranging from how to end my novel, find an agent, or juggle the all the aspects of writing, teaching, and changing diapers? What I yearned for was the community of writers I'd joined when I attended grad school.

Every year thousands of students graduate from MFA and Ph.D creative writing programs, leaving that friendly and supportive nest and to make their way, alone, in the world. When writers apply to MFA programs, it's primarily with the intent to learn about craft and to become writers. However, they soon realize that such programs offer them much more than a knowledge of craft; they find they've joined a community that offers them a variety of support systems— psychological, emotional, financial, and logistical. Yet upon a student's completion of a program, most colleges and universities offer woefully little in the way of organized, wide-ranging support for their graduates, beyond some sort of career planning and placement service. At the University of Denver, for instance, it amounted to an hour seminar on how to write a resume or the importance of maintaining eye contact for a job interview. Creative writing programs figure their primary job is to teach creative writing, and while I don't necessarily disagree with that position, schools need to better prepare the student writer for more than writing issues. In the case of our own Fairfield MFA graduates, leaving the program is both a more literal and a more symbolic event than it is at most MFA programs. As a low-residency program, we offer our twice yearly residencies on a stunning island off the Connecticut coast, reached by crossing a causeway. When new students arrive, they feel that they have left the pedestrian world behind them and have crossed over to a magical place where their writing can be inspired, a place that becomes for them their home away from home. For two years, in addition to learning their craft, they form close friendships and bonds that last a lifetime. However, after their graduation night, which is held on the island, they are, in both a real and metaphoric way, forced to leave this sanctuary and go out and make their way as writers. Many of our MFA grads tell us that graduation night is both the highest and lowest points of their writing careers. After all the hard work to finish their degree, they are rewarded by receiving a diploma but also by having to leave their island home and the community that has fostered their growth for the past two years.

Based on the needs of our graduates, we decided to develop a short pamphlet for them, one that made the transition to the real world easier by going over the basics of "life after the MFA." It would include such useful but necessarily broad topics as how to get an agent, where to look for lists of journals and magazines, what to say in a cover letter, and how to get a teaching job. We thought it would be, perhaps, twenty pages. Yet as the student editors and I spoke about the various needs of our graduates, we soon realized that we couldn't possibly cover, in a meaningful and pragmatic way, all those needs in twenty pages. What about health insurance for writers? Or information concerning the legal side of the business of publishing? What about funding for writers? How do I go about applying for grants and fellowships? What are the benefits of attending a writing conference or retreat? How can I network successfully? How do I get a teaching job or one in publishing? How do I "brand" or market myself, or how do I make sense of a contract? And what about all the new technologies or social media affecting not only one's writing but the promotion of that writing, including webpages, blogs, and other "platforms"? How do I develop a Skype writer's group? Should I consider publishing my work as an e-book or even self-publishing? Of course, there were all the issues related to the emotional side of writing: how does a writer juggle "life on the outside" while maintaining the "writer's life" established in the program? Or how can I overcome writer's block or maintain the momentum that I developed in the MFA? How do I develop the sort of community of writers I came to depend during my grad school years?

What started out as a short, no-nonsense pamphlet soon evolved into a comprehensive book of hundreds of pages, one that we hope will serve as an on-going resource for all graduates of creative writing programs. It developed by talking to students and faculty (who themselves had been students facing the same problems), and by discussions among students. In these discussions we found other questions and other needs that post-graduate writers have about the non-MFA world they find themselves in. The writing was done by

Fairfield students, alumni and faculty. Some of the articles in this book are fairly technical (for example, Basic Copyright, by Joe Carvalko) while other works are more personal and emotional (for example, Travis Baker's The Ghost Life). The tone ranges from the serious (Pete Nelson's article about The Creative Imperative) to the light-hearted and humorous (Steve Otfinoski's ultra-short story, True Confessions of an MFA Grad). The book also offers a plethora of online resources and links to follow. And because of the changing nature of the current state of the publishing world (and thus, of the requirements of writing), we've decided to publish this work first as an e-Book so that we can make regular changes and updates to it. We intend this book as a useful guide to those who find themselves, or will shortly find themselves, negotiating the complex, often confusing, many times depressing post-grad world.

I would like to thank the several prime movers of this project, former MFA students in the Fairfield program who had the vision, as well as the pragmatic insight, common sense, and determination to develop and complete this book and offer it as guide to all post-grad writers: Ashley Andersen Zantop, Michael Bayer, Adele Annesi, Erin Corriveau, A.J. O'Connell and Jean Medeiros, as well as the dozens of other students and faculty who contributed articles, essays, poetry, fiction, checklists and resources. Like you the reader, they have had to make their way in the post-grad world where writers have to continue to write, publish, and establish a community.

—Michael C. White, Ph.D.

Letter from the editor

If you've gulped that last swish of coffee and contemplate brewing a second pot over wet grounds while staring into the empty bag for an excuse to escape the squint of your cursor, and you just want someone to tell you what to do next, and next after that, and next after that, and next after that, because you're tired and your head hurts; if the final line of your essay, poem or chapter evades you like a cat runs from a bath, and you've forgotten how to type a period because you can no longer differentiate a run-on sentence from Joycean prose, this book is not for you. Well, actually, it *is*, but you may not think so until you calm down and get some sleep.

There is no single route to success as a writer. There is no app that prompts you start at "current location" and end at "success" with a satellite-guided list of directions in between. There is no treasure map to hold up to the light, no secret instructions revealed in photosensitive ink.

In a time of crisis, a quick browse through the authoritative advice of one successful writer can seem like you've found that secret decoder ring for your treasure map. Plotting a journey of mimicry in the hope of duplicating a shred of borrowed glory and of relieving yourself of the burden to decide what to do next can seem like the right move. If that's what you're looking for, avail yourself of the myriad single-author "how to pen a bestseller and be famous" texts for writers. We're all tempted to in those moments of desperate reaching. Some of these texts even offer a few effective suggestions to help us refocus.

Understand that chances are you will not find meaningful success in a recipe of pure imitation. While learning from other writers is tremendously important, imitating the entirety of another writer's path, even a fabulously successful one you admire, requires constant comparison between your own work and life and that of your exemplar. Baron Wormser, a writer whose work and life *I* admire, once told me "Comparison is insidious." (Perhaps I was over-inclined to agree, after hearing an earnest confessional read by a peer and thinking my own work trifling along side, but since then, his advice has proven itself many times over—if you spend your energy solely on mimicry, you miss the new, the original, the best in yourself and others.) Writers are children, snowflakes, fingerprints or partially mangled chassis in the junkyard—we're all unique, and while we share commonalities with others of our kind, the right combination of strategies for salvation and success is different for each of us.

If you decide to cut your own path, you're already *on* the right path. Twenty years in publishing has taught me just a few absolute truths. One of the most important: There is no correct way to succeed as a writer. The research for this book bears this out chapter after chapter. More than forty contributors share their stories and knowledge of how to find sanity, satisfaction and success as a writer; they are each unique. Consider the ones that resonate with and challenge you. This guide provides the raw ingredients from which you can create your own recipe, your own secret sauce: Advice, inspiration, suggestions and tips from diverse and even conflicting perspectives.

Unlike guides dispensing vague directives—"act great to be great"—and other platitudes, this work is both authentic and practical. It was originally conceived as a simple resource to be created by and distributed to MFA candidates nearing graduation from Fairfield University's creative writing program. Part way through the program, Adele Annesi, editor of chapter 5 of this work, began to wonder how newly graduated MFAs would be prepared to meet all the challenges that face writers trying to find their way and make their voices heard. She approached program director Michael White with the idea of creating a handout to be distributed to each Fairfield University MFA candidate prior to graduation. In this document, students and alumni would provide advice and contacts concerning a variety of issues facing new graduates.

When Michael and Adele brought this idea to the program's newly formed alumni association, I couldn't resist the temptation of investigating if there might be a broader application. A small group of us did in fact research and compile a basic list of writer's resources, which we provided to program graduates. But, this research only served to confirm that there are very few centralized resources for writers that offer practical advice, connections to important services, critical information, inspiration and guidance. These materials are scattered across the writing landscape like bread crumbs through an endless wood. The publisher in me couldn't let go of the idea that if we consolidated all of this material in a single location and made it available to writers everywhere, writers could spend more time writing and less time wandering through the forest in search of bread crumbs.

Thus, "The Guide" editorial board was formed. After more than two years of planning, writing, researching, culling submissions and editing, this work compiles reccomendations, observations and information from nearly four dozen contributors and a team of dedicated editors who all live a writing life. I encourage you to use this collected wealth of hard-learned wisdom to craft your own personal strategy for success. Select and use these tools as sextant and compass. Be both navigator and cartographer. Draw your own map. Photosensitive ink optional.

—Ashley C. Andersen Zantop, MFA

PART ONE: YOUR PROGRAM

Before the Degree and Immediately Thereafter

Map for the Weary Traveler

by Linsey Jayne

ˈréˌsôrs,ˈréˈzôrs,riˈsôrs,riˈzôrs/
an action or strategy that may be adopted in adverse circumstances
"Sometimes anger is the only resource left in a situation like this."

But, of course, it's never a focused anger. It's anger
dispersed in a pot, stirred
with exhaustion, and the last pen you had *and run
through the dryer with your white load
no doubt*, filled to the brim with coffee or one of those
energy drinks your mother
promised was going to be the death of you. It's
desperation, or something like that;
like you're trying to move the hair that's tickling your
cheek from under your glasses,
but it's caught in the hinge of your frames and never
quite goes away. Desperate
pleas as you stare at an empty search box, cursor
blinking, softly chanting lines
half-remembered from some song you need, you need,
you so badly need. *Google, can't you see me? Feel me?
Touch me? Heal me?* Who sang that? Prayers to the
technosphere for godly opportunity. Receipt of angelic
dispassion. Onset realization:

you didn't write the phrase "angelic dispassion," and
you can't determine who did;
can't credit them, and can't find the proper way to cite

the source who wrote the one thing
you need in the two hours remaining before your
critical thesis is due.

Traveler of the vast, algorithmic pools of search results,
here is your beacon.
Writer, slouched in the embrace of that chair with the
poor lumbar support (that you bought
because it looked cushy and affordable but now the
back is tearing away
from the upholstery), you need look no further. In the
pages set before you
find the crushed-leaf path worn down by explorers
who wandered this way once by the glow
of their faltering desktop monitors. Before you, find
cartography. Your chart

of the stars or the highways or the addresses of the
places you can seek help.

Lost boatsman, your mind a canoe on a far-off river:
take heed, use this atlas
and let the resources here guide you, plot the course
to all the sure shores you seek.

Chapter 1

INVEST EARLY

edited by Ashley C. Andersen Zantop

To make the most of your writing career after your degree, start while you're in the degree program. Your writing program and the community associated with it represent rare opportunities for developing your craft and your relationships in the writing world. This chapter explores both creative and practical approaches to making the most of your time in your writing program and the unique bonds and connections you form there.

*L*ife after the MFA begins during the MFA. Or, rather, a *good* writing life after you graduate from your program begins during your program. Writing is one of the most ancient, crowded-lonely arts and trades known to humankind. Build success as a writer by creating the most comfortable, supported, motivated life you can muster as an artist and craftsman. Begin with your degree program and the projects and community associated with it.

The time you spend in a writing program may feel like a period of tremendous stress; you have requirements for reading, writing, workshopping, possibly teaching, writing, more writing, and you have all of your "real world" commitments and obligations to meet. What you may not realize until after graduation is that time spent in your program is also a rare and precious period of focus. You, your faculty and your cohort together generate a nucleus of energy, creativity, commitment and collegiality you may never again experience with the same concentration and intensity. Seize this opportunity. Form bonds that will help sustain you in your life ahead. Forge habits and build skills that will serve your art. Value the work you create.

Bill Patrick explores examples of students' work that live beyond the scope and purpose of program requirements, and he challenges us to seize our unique opportunity to think like artists.

How Can I Use This? The Creative Use of Academic Requirements
by William Patrick

I can't remember now whether Lizzie came up with the idea or I did. But once it was out there on the table in front of us, it seemed so obvious. Lizzie is entering her third semester in the Fairfield MFA in Creative Writing Program, and she needs to design an academic project that will complete a requirement for her degree. Officially, she can pick a suitable literary topic, do the necessary research, and write a substantial critical essay. Or she can find a semester-long opportunity, like teaching writing in a prison or interning at a publishing house, and write a report about that experience. But Lizzie hasn't warmed to either of those two options. What she has is a memoir in prose and poetry, with lots of dialogue, that begins, "Once upon a time, there was me.

I was nobody special, just another little black girl in Harlem, but my parents loved me—best they could." She wants to turn this memoir into something that will fulfill her academic obligation, but I'd like her to find some compelling use for it beyond this third-semester project.

I've been on the faculty of Fairfield's MFA Program in Creative Writing since its second residency, five years ago. Since I work in four genres—poetry, fiction, literary nonfiction, and dramatic writing (stage plays and screenplays)—I often function as the program's utility infielder, taking my position whenever a hybrid genre might satisfy a need. To me, Lizzie's project is screaming out, ONE-PERSON PLAY, and that fits exactly with how she has been envisioning it. All the ingredients are there: I can see that she's smart; she says she likes to act; I've heard her project her prodigious voice way past the cheap seats; and, with her memoir, she's got all the raw material she needs to go from page to stage. This project, if it works out, could easily have legs, and it's easy to see how Lizzie could turn an academic requirement into a dramatic work that might have life after the MFA.

Seems like a slam dunk, right? Keep in mind that Lizzie and I are still at the start of this project, and the collaborative process of mentor and mentee trying to transform one genre into another isn't always so smooth. A couple of years ago, a student named Dennis Quinn came to me and said he wanted to adapt his novel into a radio play as his third-semester academic project. I discouraged him about adapting, but at the beginning Dennis wanted what he thought he wanted. Here's his version of what happened.

Dennis Quinn

"Kill the swan," said Bill Patrick.

At that point in my third semester project, I would rather have killed Bill.

That poor swan had been through hell—smashed with an oar; torn from its young; blown up by a cherry bomb; bounced around at breakneck speed in a pickup truck; and finally forced to endure an improvised, emergency amputation of her wing. That damned swan deserved to live. On top of all of her other challenges, the swan was also the offspring of two sexually deviant angels.

Well, not exactly. I had always intended my third semester project to be an adaptation of my novel into a radio play. The novel contained the aforementioned deviant angels, a demon cursed with the need for love, a Corvette capable of time travel, alternate realities, a magical lake, and a talking dog.

When I sent him my first draft, Bill said, basically, "I don't know *what* this is, but it's *not* a radio play. Something this complex needs the expanse of a novel to keep the reader involved. With a radio play, you've got to hook listeners early and keep them hooked or they'll change the station. It's all about through-line. Scrap the novel adaptation and start the radio play from scratch."

Ugh! Not remotely what I'd planned, and I had no ideas for a new, stand-alone radio play. So Bill and I brainstormed. I'd always resisted collaborative efforts in writing. I thought of it as cheating, but as a result of Bill's mentoring, I've come to enjoy the process of tossing ideas around with other writers, with editors, and even with the guy who services my oil burner. It really doesn't matter where the raw material comes from; it all a goes into that sloppy blender we call the creative process and comes out something uniquely our own. This was one big take-away from that third semester.

Bill's own award-winning radio play had grown out of his experiences with emergency responders, and at one point he asked if I'd done anything similar. I told him I had volunteered for Wildlife in Crisis and had recently rescued a swan with a mangled wing. I'd even been pressed into after-hours service as an operating room assistant for the veterinarian who had amputated the swan's wing.

"There's your radio play," said Bill. "Just fill it with sound and keep the action moving forward."

In the first draft of my radio play, the swan survived.

As the veterinarian who had performed the emergency wingectomy held the sobbing, volunteer wildlife transporter and said, "She was a fighter. We did all we could," weak honks could be heard from the operating room. The honks grew louder, and as they rushed to the room, they saw the swan coming out of the anesthesia and struggling to stand up.

"I saw *that* coming a mile away," said Bill. I don't remember if his exact words were, "This writing is sentimental and predictable," but it was something to that effect. And though I hate to admit it, Bill was right. My writing had deprived my listener the catharsis of gut-aching loss because it was just too uncomfortable for me to travel down that dark road.

Bill taught me that, as writers, we must explore every option—force ourselves to peer into dark corners, take a stick to the hornet's nest, and sometimes even kill the characters we love. I hate sadness—hate it to an almost pathological degree—and killing that swan was a painful lesson for me. However, it also gave me the courage to take my writing and my storytelling to exciting, unexpected levels.

As a result of what I learned from Bill during my third semester, my stories are always full of the sounds that define characters in place and time. And though I take full advantage of the freedom that a novel gives my writing to reflect and unwind at its own pace, I always counter with action and forward movement.

I did take Bill's advice. I did kill the swan. In a last-minute twist, a police sergeant searches the marsh where the swan was attacked and finds her cygnets— weak but alive—and he brings them to the vet's office. In the final scene, the task of nurturing the cygnets back to health hints at a possible romance between the veterinarian and the wildlife rehabilitator. I'm sure when Bill read my ending he muttered, "Hopeless sentimentalist," but he let me keep the scene.

Pushing past his comfort zone forced Dennis to enter a riskier creative space and, because he allowed himself to accept that challenge, he ended up with a more unique radio play than he ever expected to write. Sharon Bloom, a novelist who became one of my mentees in the Fall of 2013, presented a much more academic idea for her third-semester academic project. She was partway through an ambitious novel, *Shadow Boxer*, about a young man who migrated from Mexico to America during the Great Depression. Her central character, Ruben, based firmly on her own father, eventually winds up stationed in London, working as an intelligence officer for the United States Army. Sharon had discovered a huge collection of actual letters that her parents had written during those years and, for a while, she thought she had found a writer's Holy Grail. Be careful what you wish for.

Sharon Bloom

Could there be a greater treasure trove for a budding novelist than finding letters written between the real people her characters are based upon? I felt compelled to use this cache of family letters from WWII in the telling of my story, but how to use them was the issue. Before the discovery of over 1,000 letters hidden in a moldy Iowa basement, I had included fictional letters in a couple of passages within my novel to reveal my protagonist's inner conflict, his loneliness, and his shame. But now I had the real deal—a whole era inadvertently chronicled by my parents as they tried to stay in touch during the war.

I embarked on a twofold journey. Initially, I read all the letters and created a log that not only noted distinctive images from the period but also provided insight into my parents' personalities. I wasn't sure what I was looking for, but I trusted that their voices would show me a way into my characters. Secondly, I read and analyzed five examples of epistolary novels that Bill and I brainstormed, including Updike's *S.*, Bellow's *Herzog*, Walker's *The Color Purple*, Stoker's *Dracula*, and Kostova's *The Historian*, all to determine if there might be a model that could help me find a workable structure for my own.

More than anything, I wanted the fictional character of Ruben in *Shadow Boxer* to reflect the duality, complexity, and inner longing of the real man. And there, spread on the floor around me, were fragments of that very man—puzzle pieces left for me to create a living portrait. How seductive is that for a writer? But I should have paid more attention to the "living" part of that portrait. What was my actual motivation in using letters from my father to shape the character in my novel?

After weeks of chronicling these letters, Ruben's duality became more apparent. Prior to reading the letters, I had only an inkling of his inner thoughts, but the letters reinforced my instincts. He became more ardent in his need for Mabel, his sweet Iowa redhead, and yet what he wrote about were ambassador parties and living in Lady Churchill's flat. I could feel Mabel's lips purse in disapproval as she struggled alone to manage the family lumber company during the harsh winters in northeast Iowa. Ruben's ambition to succeed was always tempered by his need to belong. It all fit perfectly with my character—his need for acceptance and social status. Ruben's major flaw, his aura of discontent, was nipping at his heels even at that stage of his life.

It didn't take long to confront the major challenge in this project. Bill had warned me, but I didn't want to listen: "Those letters are more of an anchor than a lifeline, and they're weighing you down." How could I separate the fictional Ruben from the real story? I had to remember I was not writing memoir or biography, but fiction, and I had to be the one in charge—not the shadows from the past. Ruben swirled in my head almost all the time and, the closer I got to the real Ruben and Mabel, the harder it was to deviate from the facts. But I knew I had to deviate if I was to create a compelling story.

In this age of tweets, e-mails, and hash tags, formal letters seem archaic, but the more I read, the deeper I fell under their spell. I saw how letters could deepen character, and they supplied concrete, cinematic images I could work into scenes: Mabel wringing a chicken's neck; Ruben suffering through boot camp; Mabel in trousers, "manning" the lumberyard; and Ruben, dressed to the nines, hobnobbing with those ambassadors.

I also realized that letters could reveal my characters' secret, inner lives, their values and beliefs, in a way that dialogue or narrative may not capture. They contained a mythological view of an unattainable world. In order to withstand the separation of war, my parents needed to believe they were part of creating something better. But that belief was often shaken by the reality of life: the boredom of a night watch, years of separation, and the horrors of man's inhumanity to man. In their unvarnished voices, all that came through. Trying to duplicate those tones as an omniscient narrator, I could see myself easily wandering into the missteps of authorial intrusion.

As I moved through the research, though, my notion of how to use the letters changed. Initially, I had intended to write the third section of *Shadow Boxer* in a strictly epistolary form, creating fictionalized versions of the correspondence between Mabel and Ruben. However, I was aware that shifting to that exclusive structure two-thirds of the way through the book could appear abrupt and forced. By evaluating how other authors had used the form, I concluded that a hybrid approach, with letters appearing occasionally throughout the narrative, might work better in my novel. That is the approach Saul Bellow uses in *Herzog*. His protagonist has a deep and complicated inner life, similar to my character, Ruben, after all. So my current plan is to employ the letters when Ruben is most alone and needs to bare his soul. I will reveal his inner life in a way that seems more organic and less contrived.

When I started my third-semester academic project, I was sure I could find the answers I needed in my collection of family letters, and I definitely viewed several months of studying epistolary novels as an unwanted detour from the writing of my novel. What I learned, though, was the invaluable lesson of distance: actual documents can offer up countless, specific details, but they can also weigh you down with the day-to-day realities of someone's life. Fiction demands more than life. With the letters as a baseline, I am learning how to create distinctive, fictional characters without trying to re-create the actual people represented in the source material. Now, every day, I'm anxious to get back to the writing of *Shadow Boxer* and apply what I've learned. ⌨

Matt Winkler's academic project seemed less exotic than a one-winged swan but more familiar than the letters of an immigrant spy: he wanted to write about teenagers, and I knew he was more than qualified to do it. Matt taught in China, and in Japan, and at several colleges and high schools in the United States. He even created a special homeschooling curriculum for his struggling son, Logan, which morphed into a 24,000-mile travel and education plan that involved Matt's video chronicle of Logan skateboarding in all fifty states. Just as he had hoped, their epic journey had successfully boosted Logan's academic performance and reignited his interest in learning.

So it wasn't a surprise when Matt explained his plan to work theories from Joseph Campbell's *Hero with a Thousand Faces* into a third-semester academic project that involved teenagers. Matt's critical paper, *Teaching Heroes: Mentoring Teens through the Hero's Journey of Adolescence*, also had an ambitious goal—nothing less than offering readers a new understanding of adolescence. In his overview, he said, "For many adults, daily life is a routine grind, but for teenagers, it is an epic struggle for identity. *Teaching Heroes* will remind readers of the connection between ancient myths, modern storytelling, and the dramatic journey from childhood to adulthood." But I cautioned Matt about his angle of approach. If he couldn't find an unusual way to handle the over-worked subjects of troubled adolescents and Campbell's hero theories, he'd end up with just another dry, sociological essay.

Matt Winkler

During my first and second semesters, I felt like a third semester project would be a distraction from my urgent mission: to complete a manuscript before graduation. However, by the end of my second semester, I was hitting a wall with my manuscript and banging against it for some kind of breakthrough. At that point, the third-semester project offered a welcome change of direction—an alternative path around or through that wall.

I had originally conceived of it as a research paper into one particular aspect of my manuscript. My mentor, Bill Patrick, saw even more potential in my topic. He challenged me to develop this research project into a nonfiction book proposal in its own right. At the end of the third semester, I presented that book proposal to a literary agent who visited Ender's Island. She liked it and asked me to send her my first hundred pages.

I learned that writing book proposals comes more naturally to me than writing books. I'm good at planning and organizing, but I seem to run out of motivation or attention when I don't see a practical context to the artistic work. My third-semester project taught me how to trick myself into being creative to meet a practical need. Framing a larger literary project within the rigid scaffold of a book proposal led me to specific prompts that demanded tight, timely, and persuasive writing. Those bite-sized challenges stimulated my creativity, but they also appealed to my practical side.

My third-semester project also led directly to my graduate presentation topic. My research into Joseph Campbell's theories about the monomyth revealed a profound thread running through my favorite books and movies, certain episodes of my life and, ultimately, through my entire worldview. How had I never heard of it before?

I am continuing to develop that project into a manuscript. It's a work in progress, but I'm finding that the subject has limitless potential. Completing it also gave me the expertise to write a script for a four-minute TED-Ed video (What Makes A Hero), which has bolstered my resume and garnered well over 500,000 views on YouTube. I'm hoping it will eventually lead to my first nonfiction book deal. 🖳

"What are you looking to acquire from your MFA program? What I think you should be seeking while you're there, primarily, is a wild habit of artistic imagination."

In a limited sense, this article is about developing the specific ability to change academic requirements into creative works, or at least about encouraging you to transform what you have to do into an unexpected something that might inspire the writing you actually want to do. But in a broader sense, and not to encourage narcissism, what I'm recommending is that you start thinking as a writer, always, and in new ways—not as an MFA student, or an employee, or a family member, or a significant other. Let other people think in prescribed ways. I'm not saying you should fail to fulfill your obligations or stop caring about the people you love. Live your lives and celebrate them. But let your mind navigate the world differently.

What are you looking to acquire from your MFA program? A degree at the end of it? Of course. Maybe a faculty that offers you all the pragmatic tools of the writer's trade, including the ability to understand the various options that will make your work insightful and professional? Definitely. Colleagues who lend emotional support, provide spiritual solace, and become your consistent network, during and after your time with them in the MFA program? Sure, if you're lucky. What I think you should be seeking while you're there, primarily, is a wild habit of artistic imagination.

When else will you have the freedom to nurture something so radical? That habit is more elusive than the necessary motivation to apply seat of pants to seat of chair, or the important need to read constantly, or the insistent demand to learn the compassion crucial for creating marvelous characters. Those are the typical habits how-to-write authors will trot out again and again, and they're all essential. And they all work. But what I'm talking about is channeling your conscious and unconscious experiences into an imaginative blender, 24/7, with a single-pointed determination to generate hybrid ideas or poems or plays or memoirs or novels. Don't settle for the mediocre or the trendy, or live in a territory that someone else has already staked out. "Make it new," Ezra Pound said over a hundred years ago. That's still the real deal, no matter what Hollywood or the best-seller lists demonstrate. Go try it.

f you are inspired by Bill Patrick's examples of turning course requirements and academic projects into something larger and more imaginative, something that ignites your creativity and maybe even helps you craft a truly unique publishable work, something impractical and new, consider the *practical* advice of Jennifer Emerson. Jennifer discusses new ways to think about the dreaded semester reading list while you're in a creative writing program. You may initially consider this a counterpoint to Bill Patrick's advice to form a "wild habit of artistic imagination." But, if you plan well, instead of treating your reading list as a semester-opening chore, you can craft it with the aim of informing and inspiring incorrigibly creative course work. If you're able to weave the threads of creativity, originality and requirement together, you may produce work that can become a publication or that can directly inform all or part of your creative thesis, or that can become something radically new.

Your reading list and corresponding course requirements shouldn't be considered time spent away from your publishable work. Your reading list is the opportunity to construct a growing reading resume that informs and inspires your best creativity, your wild imagination, your best work, during your program and after.

A Method to the Madness: Reading Lists
by Jennifer Emerson

"Why do I need a reading list and have to do all this other stuff? I just want to write *my* book!"

"I have to read *how* many books this semester? How do I know which ones to choose?"

"Everything will be fine…once I have my degree."

Thoughts like these sometimes surface when in the midst of an intense writing program. They did for me, I admit it. But let me put a question to you that someone (thankfully) asked me: Why wait until graduation to feel like a success? The time to embrace that success is now.

A substantial part of growing as a writer is focusing upon and implementing different methods of organization. Granted, organization means something different to everyone. That is why you must use your time in your program as a form of creative navigation. Like a sailor, you are going to chart the course for where your writing takes you. One of the best ways to get that feeling of balance and accomplishment (not to mention keeping your notes tidy) is by compiling a reading list. Don't panic, it's easier than you think, not to mention worthwhile. Far from just one of the requirements for your course work, your reading list will be of tremendous assistance as you move through an MFA or other writing program, and beyond.

Think of your reading list as a map. There will be a beginning, middle and an end to your time in your writing program, and the list will mark each step as you take your craft to the next level. Depending upon which genre and topic you choose to work with, you may already have a few ideas of what books to start by the time you sit down with your new mentor or faculty member. No doubt they will suggest additions for your list. Be open to this exchange of ideas. Use it as creative fuel.

Remember that the books you read for your craft or other critical essays and course requirements will also take up a certain portion of the list as it accumulates. How do you select good books for your reading list? Ask teachers and colleagues for ideas. I guarantee a few of them will offer up titles and authors for you. Some may be willing to loan you a book. Look on the internet (abebooks.com is a great place to get cheap books), visit bookstores (the independents tend to have more unique finds) and take advantage of interlibrary loan.

At first, the reading list may seem daunting, or perhaps trivial. The list may not even be very long in the beginning, and that's fine. But you will be surprised how quickly a little list can help your writing gain momentum and polish. You may also question why you have to read certain books, as they seemingly have nothing to do with your own writing. Although some may not appear to be at first, each book you read will be of benefit in some way. Allow yourself to venture past your creative comfort zone. Inspiration can be gleaned from the most unlikely of places.

Another bit of advice would be to keep your reading list where you can see it. This may be on the wall, a bookshelf, on your laptop or in the front of your favorite journal. As you finish another book, check it off with a fun colored marker, put a funky sticker next to it—if that appeals to you. Remember, when viewed in a positive context, this list exists to expand your knowledge of both the craft and the business of writing. And by the time you reach your larger academic projects, this list will have grown considerably, and will only add to your sense of accomplishment and knowledge of your chosen genre(s). If you keep it in sight, it will also help to inspire you, to remind you of what you already know, when you get stuck.

Symbolically, your reading list is a declaration that you are open to growth and change. More than just an academic requirement, it is a roadmap of where you have been and where you are going as a writer. Make the most of that journey.

writing program is a combination of both creative and practical pursuits. Your objective for your degree may be to develop mastery in a complex art form, a creative pursuit. But, in order to fill requirements and graduate, you'll face a number of concrete milestones. Here, Adele Annesi provides guidance and a pragmatic approach to early planning that will benefit any candidate navigating the challenges and opportunities of a competitive writing program.

Start Your Journey During the MFA
by Adele Annesi

It's no secret that surviving after an MFA is tough, but survival after starts by doing well during the program. These tips will help you make the most of your program, and will help you create a foundation for what comes after. Listed here in chronological order, this guidance gives special attention to low-residency programs, but it's also appropriate for full residencies.

Before the Program Begins
Faculty: Research all faculty, particularly those with whom you'll be working, and those who will be giving seminars during your residency. Drop a brief note to instructors in advance asking how best to prepare for their workshops and/or panels. Follow up with a thank-you note. Include teaching assistants in this process.

Students: Research and reach out to as many students as you can who are in your workshops, and who will be participating in panels and readings. When they respond, follow up with a thank-you note.

Information Packets: Study all the information you receive. Most programs provide valuable material on the program that is more detailed than you received in your acceptance packet, and in a more targeted way than is available on the website. The information usually falls into two categories:

- **about the program:** Even if you've read the information and fine print before, it's helpful to skim this information again. You may find changes in the program, and more resources than were available in the introductory packet.

- **about the residency and/or semester:** It's essential to review carefully what your program directors provide, as prior information—including faculty, scheduling and course offerings—will inevitably change. Often included in what you receive, and you'll receive several mailings before the program begins, are handouts that accompany faculty lectures. Review these before attending the lectures, to help you prepare for and make the most of whatever you attend.

Contact Information and Links: Consider adding a link to your blog and/or website, and posting on social media regarding the program and its literary journal. Also connect with any social communities your program provides. This will help put faces and personalities with the contact information you receive.

Where to Stay: For low-residency students, consider staying on campus for the first residency, and possibly one other before you graduate. Many programs require or strongly recommend this feature. Staying on-site is usually less expensive, offers more social and networking opportunities, and sometimes is just more fun. For students of other types of programs, staying on campus, or as close as possible, offers the same perks.

Workshops: Workshop assignments and what's required for them are typically issued well in advance of the start of the workshop: Carefully review the information regarding the workshop, and learn as much as possible about the faculty or other leader, and about the students. Send your best work, but where you're unsure of what type of sample to send—a work in progress or a published work you may want feedback on or to repurpose—contact the workshop leader to see which submission will be in your best interest.

At the Start of the Semester or Residency
Arrive Early: It's best to arrive early when you begin an MFA program, particularly the residency. This gives you a feel for your living arrangements, and minimizes the culture shock of reentering college life, especially for those who have been away awhile.

Orientation: When starting out, attend orientation. You'll get to know students and faculty from the start and at a slower pace, and you'll have an opportunity to ease into your new surroundings. Pay particular attention to students and faculty who work in your genre, but be open to others who are not. Most programs offer cross-genre studies, and you never know who you may collaborate with later in the program.

When the Semester/Residency Is Under Way

Lectures and Panels: These are opportunities to maximize your MFA investment. Most programs require students to attend a certain number of faculty lectures and panels, but it's best to attend as many as you can. One often surprising feature is that you can learn almost as much from student lectures. Since many programs require a special third semester project, you can get a sense of what types of projects students have worked on, and what you might like to do when you reach that stage.

Handouts and Resources: Collect and keep the handouts and resources. Many programs have a special repository for information, literary magazines and news. Keep an eye on this location for what you may find helpful, and bring your own items to give away. These can be informational, or they can pertain to projects you're working on. Many students have already published books, articles and short pieces, and many programs allow you to put a few things of your own on display.

Student and Faculty Readings: These readings are typically held during the day and in the evenings. Evening readings often are required, with book signings after. Many students use the readings as opportunities to learn new techniques, and more than a few discretely take notes on what they have heard. After the readings, be sure to touch base with faculty and students, especially those from whom you have learned something, and with whom you may want to eventually work.

Workshops: Once the study portion of the program is under way, and once you have a sense of how your workshop functions, carefully consider the workshop advice you receive—from students *and* faculty. Many student comments or observations are addressed more succinctly by faculty, who are also more likely to provide a prescription for how to improve your work. Yet, students bring one undeniable perspective to the table — that of the audience. It's tempting to dismiss some feedback as unhelpful, but in most cases a particular criticism, especially one that reoccurs, is likely to have merit. These often relate to a lack of clarity in some aspect of the work, which doesn't necessarily mean a major fix. Keep in mind that you can always ask the faculty workshop leader, or your mentor, whether he or she agrees with the assessment. In some instances, faculty, particularly your mentor, may agree to take a quick look at the section you've revised.

Mentors: Among the most important, if not the most important, relationships you'll form while in a Master's program are those with your mentors. Many programs require students to work with more than one faculty mentor during an MFA, and this is especially true for writers working cross-genre. The main aspects of the mentor relationship are the before, during and after.

- **choosing a mentor:** Things to consider when choosing a mentor include good communication, a solid track record (particularly in your genre or one in which you will eventually work), teaching skills, editing skills, market knowledge, literary/artistic ability, and the person's ability to strike a balance between understanding and maintaining the integrity of your writing project and remaining committed to bringing it to the next level.

- **working with a mentor:** Perhaps the best description of the mentor-student relationship is that of an editor and author. During the mentor selection process—which varies in range from zero input from students as to whom they work with to a highly collaborative method—the student is, in essence, doing the hiring. Once the mentor is selected, that phase is over. Afterward, the student benefits most from viewing his or her mentor as an editor at a major publishing house. The writer is free to accept or not accept input, but failing to carefully consider and act on constructive criticism, critique, suggestions and edits usually work against the student. When receiving commented work from your mentor, use the principles that apply to feedback from a literary journal or publisher: The more red marks the better. Don't react emotionally, or right away. Put the mentor's comments aside before responding. Read them at least three times. If concerns persist, and some will, politely request clarification, and pose the request as a question, not as cleverly or not so cleverly disguised retaliation.

- **After the Semester Ends:** Once the semester ends, maintain the view of the mentor relationship as that of an author to an editor. Send a thank-you note, and resolve any outstanding questions or concerns. If your program allows student input into the mentor selection process, ask whether your mentor is willing to recommend the next mentor for your work. He or she is in a position to know you best, sometimes even better that the MFA program director, and if the relationship has been productive, is the best prospect for suggesting how a fruitful relationship can continue. Since some MFA programs allow students and mentors to work together for more than one semester, you may even ask if your mentor would consider being a reader for your final thesis. Also, consider how you may be of help to your mentor. Can you recommend him or her for a writing project that requires the particular skills he or she brought to your working relationship? Considering these relationships as valuable and long-term can help both students and faculty.

Assignments and Reading Lists: Most students, as a matter of course, keep their completed assignments, craft essays and other work, but not always with the idea of repurposing the content. Implementing the suggested faculty corrections and completing the revision process can yield publishable articles, poems, craft and other essays, stories, blog posts, guest posts and submissions to literary journals, magazines and, eventually, even your own workshop. Students who go on to teach will find the reading lists they receive during an MFA program to be invaluable tools to begin a semester without having to start from scratch.

Midstream: Halfway Through the Semester/Residency
Downtime: Many on-site and low-residency programs offer a break in the action midway through. Make use of the opportunity to unplug, relax and rest. When a break from the routine is offered, take it. You'll have a chance to recharge your batteries, and you'll need to do this in order to make your way through the rest of the residency. Make time to meet with family and friends, and with your new friends, too. Comparing notes can help provide information you may have missed and clear up misinformation. The same caveats apply to the Master's

program as to life. Don't neglect the basics of sleep, exercise and nourishment. A healthy approach can optimize what you get from your Master's and help you enjoy it.

Working With Other Students: Consider other students you have an affinity with, and make a special effort to get to know them. These are the students you're most likely to keep in touch with after the program, and with whom you may form critique and support groups that can last the rest of your writing life.

Back in the Saddle: Working Through the Rest of the Residency/Semester

Follow-Up and Feedback: If you've made use of the downtime your program offers, you're in a better position to go the distance and complete the residency or semester. Remember, a Master's program is more marathon than sprint, so pace yourself. As you prepare for the rest of the semester or residency, send thank-you notes to faculty, administrators and students who have helped along the way, particularly those with whom you've had workshops.

More Links and Resources: Once you get to know your specific program and what it offers, you'll have more resources and links to add to your website, blog and other social media. If your program offers a newsletter, add it to your press release list, so that you can keep your peers and contacts in the loop.

Into the Home Stretch: Completing the Program

Writing Retreat and Study Abroad: Once you've had time on campus, you may want to consider a residency or living arrangement that takes you off campus, maybe not at the end of the program but the semester before your last. It can be as close as the next town over, or if your program offers study abroad, it can be another country. Consider this as a mini-vacation or writer's retreat. Freelancers may even be able to deduct a portion of this, or the program as a whole. Staying off the main campus may cost more, but if you're attending the MFA and working at the same time, this may be the only "time off" you have. Consider how to make the most of it.

Checks and Balances: As you come into the home stretch and look toward graduation, make sure you're not missing anything, including courses and payments. These can prevent your graduation, or taint the way you begin life after an MFA. Check with your program director and/or administrator to make sure you've done all that's required. Also take the opportunity to ask what's new or planned in the way of perks for graduating students. You may be surprised to learn that more has been added to help you once you've completed the degree, or you may find a niche to fill with your skill, as a way of keeping in touch with the program as an alum.

After the Program Is Done
Make Suggestions: Now that you've asked what perks are available to you as a graduate of a Master of Fine Arts degree, make use of all that you can. If you have a need that hasn't been filled, consider inventing a way to fill it and sharing that with your fellow grads.

Other Perks: Keep in touch with faculty, students and administrators, and make use of the concepts in this article after graduation as you did before. Look for opportunities to stay involved and active in your MFA community, for example, through the MFA alumni newsletter, the MFA newsletter and student directory. The writing life is often what you make it.

Parting Notes
If all of this sounds a bit businesslike, it is, at least in part. You're paying for the program you attend, and it's wise to get the best return on your investment, as this will help support your creative efforts after the program is done. As a result, it's helpful to keep in mind that active engagement in the program begins at the beginning, intensifies throughout the ensuing weeks and months, and continues long after you receive the degree. A solid underpinning from what you learn during the MFA, and from the community of creative people you meet along the way, will help keep you productive and connected after the courses are done.

Chapter 2

ALUMNI COMMUNITY: FIND YOUR PEOPLE

edited by Ashley C. Andersen Zantop and Erin A. Corriveau

A strong alumni association can be one of the best forms of literary community to turn to for support, critique and even opportunity. If your (former) writing program can't boast of an effective alumni organization at present, don't count yourself unlucky and move on. In this chapter, explore what you can do to help build an association that will strengthen your 'home' community and writing family.

alum·nus

noun

plural **alum·ni**

a previous member, contributor, employee or **inmate**

origin: from *alere* to nourish

fam·i·ly

noun

a group of people united by select convictions or a common association or affiliation : fellowship

*F*amily. Can't live with them. Can't write without them.

When it comes to staying connected to your craft, writers often insist there is no stronger motivator than a *family* of writers. I don't mean your kids or parents should all attend a writing program with you; for some of us, a writing family takes the form of a writing buddy, a yearly workshop or conference. For some of us, it's a regular writer's group. No matter how you engage with them, a dedicated group of writing colleagues can help you hone your craft and keep you honest about your goals and deadlines. If you're still in a program or connected to a program, look around you. Your fellow students and alums are already a community of some kind and a rare resource to turn to for writing kinship, inspiration and motivation. But, you need to do your part to stay connected.

In the following essay, Michael Bayer, co-founder and co-president of the alumni association for Fairfield University's MFA in Creative Writing program, discusses the merits of a strong alumni organization and provides advice on how to build one yourself.

Literary Siblings: Engaging Your Alumni Community for Lifelong Inspiration
by Michael Bayer

As the youngest of my parents' six children, I had mixed feelings about my brothers and sisters for the first twenty years or so of my life. I saw them as competitive, anti-social, condescending, selfish, volatile, funny, inspiring, protective, entertaining, and mean, sometimes all at the same time. Today, however, as a middle-aged man with an appreciation for history, I view each of my relationships with my five siblings as a precious gift. My brothers and sisters shared my upbringing, my values, and my insecurities about growing up in a particular place at a particular time. They also shared the flight away from my family household, the loss of my father, the aging of my mother and the comfort in knowing that someday, maybe even after we've lost spouses and friends, we will hopefully still have each other to share and cherish our collective life experience. After all, they're the only people on earth with whom I have shared the entire arc of my life.

Sibling bonds, however, aren't limited to genetics. Our classmates can serve a similar function in our lives. Take high school, for example. No, we didn't share a family or a household, and nobody forced us to be friends, or even enemies, but our high school classmates stay with us, if not through the arc of our life, then at least since our adolescence. I recently attended my 25th high school reunion, and was shocked by how close I felt to these people, some of whom I'd forgotten ever existed. We glanced at one another with knowing smiles. We had all been all *there*, and *then*. We emerged from adolescence—and became mature adults—together.

So, does the principle of siblinghood also apply to MFA classmates, with our various backgrounds, geographies, and age brackets? For me, the answer is an emphatic yes. In fact, in some ways, an MFA family offers, and demands, greater intimacy than either a biological *or* adolescent family. We've exposed to each other what, for many of us, is the most precious corner of our identity. Like high school, we entered the MFA program as novices and dreamers, and we left as mature writers with direction for our literary futures.

Most writers, but not all, grow up writing in isolation. Our talents may be politely acknowledged by our mothers and an occasional English teacher, but we're often unable to share the passion and power we feel in the written word. We've heard that the writer's life is a lonely one, and we taste that loneliness more fully with each passing year. When we finally enroll in our MFA or other writing program, everything changes. We meet dozens of human beings who *need* writing and literature as much as we do. We don't share genetic material or a zip code with these new classmates. We share a love that, despite its literary force, can't be put easily into words. Some students call it finding our "tribe," but even that term doesn't sound quite right. We're finally able to open up our writer's hearts, share our creative insecurities, and feel less strange and alone in our literary explanations for the world. We throw our frail writer bodies to the workshop wolves. We learn to embrace the sting of critique. We read our work aloud to dozens of strangers. And on graduation day, the emotions are surprisingly palpable, as if we're leaving home for the second time.

Fortunately, we haven't actually lost anything. As with our biological and adolescent brothers and sisters, we can choose to avoid our fellow graduates, but we can never lose them.

Keeping a Family Alive

MFA programs vary widely in their commitment to nurturing an active alumni community. Some slap up a Facebook page and call it a day. Others launch a formal alumni association with active calendars and far-reaching activities. Most fall somewhere in between. The truth is that alumni engagement shouldn't be the responsibility of the program. It's the alumni's role to build their own vibrant community that meets their needs as *former* MFA candidates. The alumni are an extension of the MFA program, but one that must be self-governing and self-motivated.

If you let them, your fellow alumni will keep you inspired. They will keep you motivated. They will keep you *writing*. And isn't that what drew you to an MFA in the first place? So, if you don't want to "drift apart" from your brothers and sisters, the earlier you engage with them, the better.

Informal Alumni Engagement: *Form Your Clan*

Chances are your MFA program has created some form of online community so alums can keep in touch and share ideas and accomplishments. Whatever mass communications and social media tools are available from your program, use them. If you publish an essay, share it. If you plan on attending AWP, send out an open invitation for alumni to meet up at Applebee's or the nearest dive bar. If your local college is hosting a Margaret Atwood reading or a nearby Writers Center is offering seminars in screenwriting, invite your fellow alumni to sign up.

Aside from occasional bursts of social media activity, you'll generally be on your own to keep the MFA fire burning. Your best option is to form your own little writer clan, which will likely comprise some combination of genuine friends you made during the program and classmates whose work and/or work ethic you admired, even if from afar. Choose the classmates with whom you most want to maintain strong relationships, but don't confuse friendships with productive working relationships. If you made good friends during your MFA program, that's wonderful; be sure to stay friends. But if your goal is to engage with alumni to stay inspired and productive as a writer, then those friends may not fit the bill. And that's totally fine. Your clan should comprise those former classmates you most want to collaborate with, and maybe even those you most want to compete with. In short, they should be the people who make you *want* to write.

It's helpful to select members for your clan (and you should certainly see it as a selection process) the same way you choose your First Readers. Would you value their feedback on your work? It's the only question that matters, especially since your clan will inevitably take the form of that most cherished literary social unit: the writers group. Imagine assembling an ongoing workshop of the MFA classmates you would most like to share with and learn from. It's not imaginary. It's one of the essential "offshoots" of any MFA program, and works wonders for keeping alumni inspired and accountable.

For more information and advice on writer's groups and how to form and maintain them, see Chapter 3, edited by Erin Corriveau.

Organized Alumni Engagement: *Form Your Alumni Association*
Like with everything in life, when it comes to maintaining an active community, a little bit of accountability can go a long way. That's why the most vibrant MFA alumni communities are often supported by a formal alumni association. This association may go all the way back to the founding of the program, or it might have been created on a whim by a handful of zealous graduates. (Some associations may receive funding from their university or program, but most don't.) If your program has an alumni association, then you're in luck. Embrace it. Use it. Get involved. As the years go by, and your life zigzags through competing priorities, that alumni association could someday be the only spark for rekindling your writing life.

If your program doesn't have an alumni association, why not start one? Somebody has to do it. This is just another opportunity to create something. Successful founders will be those who believe passionately in the need for lifelong literary community. It also helps if they have management experience somewhere in their past. (Note my use of the pronoun *they*; forming an association is most definitely a team effort.)

> "If your program doesn't have an alumni association, why not start one? Get your new alumni association off the ground in as little as 30 days"

It may sound like a daunting task, and it certainly does require a tremendous commitment, but the process can actually be fairly simple. Following the five steps below can get your new alumni association off the ground in as little as 30 days.

1. Define a mission.

Why exactly are you creating the association? How will alumni participate and benefit? What other communities will benefit? These may be obvious questions, but the answers are less so. Every MFA program is different, so every alumni community is different. It's essential that before you do anything else, you and your co-founder(s) have a candid discussion about the primary purpose of the association. Reach out to other alumni—or conduct a survey online—to ask what information and opportunities they would most value. When you have all of your ideas in one place, write a formal mission statement and make sure every co-founder agrees with every word. This statement will guide the association's actions and decisions for years to come. Here's an example:

> *The Fairfield University MFA Alumni Association (FUMAA) provides lifelong community, opportunity and inspiration for graduates of the Fairfield MFA program, and encourages maximum creative output and achievement for all alumni. Founded and operated exclusively by program alumni, FUMAA advocates for Fairfield MFA graduates by providing information and opportunities related to craft, careers, publishing, and teaching, while preserving the sense of community so essential to the success and motivation of writers.*

2. Write a strategic plan.

You're a writer, so this should be easy. Using the mission statement as your lens, draft a strategic plan that documents the needs, objectives, strategies, and programs of the association. This is your chance to think through all the details: what benefits you hope to achieve, what programs you want to provide, and what resources you need in order to provide them. Recruit the help of an alumnus with experience in business planning if possible. Prioritize the most essential programs—types of events, publications, and social activities. Estimate the time commitment required to execute programs. List the tools you'll use to communicate with association members. Decide if you'll need revenue—in the form of donations or member dues—to pay for basic functions.

3 Form a committee of officers.

With your strategic plan in place, it's time to begin your recruitment effort. To execute the plan, you will need a small group of volunteers willing to take responsibility for certain programs and initiatives to realize your mission. Unless you've attracted the support of a major benefactor, you won't have financial compensation to offer, so you'll need to appeal to your volunteers' sense of commitment to the community. Don't strong-arm anyone to participate; only enthusiastic volunteers will be successful in their roles.

Your volunteers become your management team, and should be given responsibility for implementing a very specific aspect of the strategic plan. Accordingly, they should have titles which represent their focus, including:

- President or Co-President. Typically a co-founder, the president maintains overall responsibility for all of the association's functions. He or she (or they) serve(s) as the public voice of the association, recruits and appoints volunteers, makes final decisions related to strategy, and liaises with MFA program administration.

- Director of Communications. He or she is responsible for maintaining ongoing communication across the alumni population, maintaining alumni contact information, supervising the association's social media platforms, and creating any required marketing or educational content.

- Director of Events. He or she is responsible for managing the calendar and coordination of events sponsored by the association, such as readings, residencies, educational forums, and social gatherings, as well as coordinating any alumni activities at popular industry conferences like AWP.

- Director of Publications. He or she is responsible for content and distribution of any publications that are part of your strategic plan, which may include a regular newsletter, a literary journal or website.

- Treasurer. He or she is responsible for managing any budgets and financial accounts related to the association's activities, including both expenses (venues, services, materials) and income (dues, donations).

4. Launch.

Once you have your plan finalized and your officers in place, it's time to announce the association to the community. You should have your communications platform (mailing list, Facebook, LinkedIn) in place at this point, so you can send the initial announcement through those channels. Consider formatting this as a letter from the president stating the mission, benefits and programs of the new association. Announce the officers, and include a supportive quote from the MFA program director if appropriate. Be specific about what alumni need to *do*. For example, do they need to formally become a member? Pay dues? Join a dedicated group on LinkedIn? Provide their preferred email address to the director of communications? If you make it easy for alumni to participate, they will.

5. Maintain Momentum.

While the launch may seem like the culmination of all your hard work, it's actually just the beginning. Maintaining the energy and relevance of the association requires a long-term commitment. As you implement the programs from your strategic plan, be sure you have a steady drumbeat of activity throughout the year; you need to seize a variety of opportunities to engage alumni in a variety of ways. Here are a few examples of ongoing activities that can help maintain a vibrant association:

- Quarterly meetings where association directors and volunteers review activities on the horizon, challenges of execution, new ideas, etc.

- Social media news and communications based on a pre-established editorial calendar; your director of communications should plan outreach in advance based on association events, industry events, literary milestones, alumni achievements, etc.

- Association-sponsored workshops or residencies, facilitated by existing program faculty if appropriate, where alumni can re-create the MFA workshop experience in condensed form, e.g., over a long weekend

- Group publishing initiatives, such as an alumni-directed online literary journal, an essay collection, an alumni poetry chapbook;

- Regular check-in meetings with program administration, such as a conference call every six months to discuss opportunities for synergy with currently enrolled students and program events.

Your alumni community is a permanent part of your life now. You all shared a transformation, an adolescence of sorts, and nothing can take that collective experience away. Like all relationships, however, you will get back only as much as you give. Whether you've just graduated or are looking back thirty years, whether you're a prolific novelist or haven't written a word since grad school, reaching out to your MFA brothers and sisters can bring you right back. Right back to that thrilling moment of transformation when you finally, once and for all, became a writer for life.

Michael Bayer's essay provides us with clear, actionable steps for building and launching an alumni association. If you or a small group dedicate energy to an alumni initiative, you can be ready to launch in short order. As you work toward your goal, be mindful of Bayer's caution about maintaining momentum. Organizing and launching an effective alumni association can feel like *the* major effort and the ultimate goal. But, the goal is to be, to maintain, a vibrant writing community, not just launch one.

Graduates of writing programs with ineffective alumni communities often cite continuity, or the lack thereof, as a reason for their failure to engage with their fellow program alums. They may not know or remember who their alumni association's officers are, what the established mission is, or what, if any, initiatives are underway. Some organizations launch with high aspirations, but fail to maintain any consistent messaging or communication venues for their community.

Take this challenge into consideration as you define and establish key elements of your organization, such as ideal terms of service, succession planning and scope of roles. It's important that alumni association officers and directors have the time and opportunity to establish a relationship with program leadership and to launch initiatives and events. Directors and officers should do their best to ensure they're committed to their role for at least a year if not longer. But, that means the scope and effort associated with any given role need to be manageable and interesting for each person involved.

Recruit your key team members based on interests and other talents—Michael Bayer is a master at sizing up a complicated scenario or opportunity and breaking it down into manageable component parts, as he clearly demonstrates in his essay. If you have someone like him in or associated with your program, recruit him to help you build your alumni organization. Natural talent in this area will be a tremendous asset to you and the larger community. Do the same for other critical roles or positions your organization might need: If you have someone who is an excellent and prolific communicator or social media maven, consider her for a director of communications role. Do you have someone in your program who likes to perform or organize productions? Why not put him in charge of creating a virtual or in-person alumni talent showcase?

Finally, consider what happens when someone does need to step down. Define a process of appointing or electing new leadership, so the program and its valuable initiatives you've created don't fizzle out when officers, directors or team members inevitably want or need to change their focus or move on to other challenges. Celebrate their service and ensure your organization continues as the vibrant community you've helped build.

PART TWO: YOUR LIFE

After the Degree and the Rest of Your Writing Career

She is Asked, Do You Write According to a Set Schedule?

by Baron Wormser

Up at dawn to greet the sun's mute
Joy-shriek, bowing inwardly to this
Distant steadfast prince while beginning
To mull a stanza or two concerning

Her human rigmarole and others—
Dear bullying father, damp-hearted mother,
Marriage to a toff who also rises early,
Brews middling coffee, then sits pulling at

His chin as though to encourage thinking.
One chatty cloud can blot the clearest sky!
She neither sighs nor despises her slow craft.
Learning takes time. She will put it right

One of these indomitable mornings
While amid headlines and broadcast fret
A trickle of pure insight will rise|
Into her words, as if ordained, then set.

Chapter *3*

STAY CONNECTED TO
YOUR PEOPLE

edited by Erin A. Corriveau

Even the most successful authors needed community and support at one point or another in their careers. Many of them attribute their success not only to their dedication to their work but also to the community of writers that help them be their best. Learn about the variety of ways you can continue to give and receive critical feedback even after graduating from your writing program.

MFA Community

by Linsey Jayne

And when I say "community," I mean it
in the almost biological sense. The
sense of symbiosis. The proud wholeness that
comes when the arms and the core work together to
perform a pull-up, and despite your dead weight
legs, the brain exudes serotonin for
the self in its entirety. I mean it
in the sense that each word carries equal heft
in a poem; each poem that heft in a chapbook,
each kiss its equal sand in love. I mean it
like each slice of bacon in the BLT.
Like the weight of each oar in the whaleboat. Like
each whaleboat against the sea. Like molecules
of water in a glass. Like each erupting
supernova in the galaxy of stars;
like the fading light of dying stars; like dawn:
black, then each rise of the brilliant, blinding sun.

*P*ursuing your MFA allows you to spend time mastering your writing craft, but it also enables you to connect with intelligent, passionate, like-minded individuals. After spending hours alone with your manuscript, it is easy to feel alone as writers. This is why we must foster and nurture the relationships we formed in our programs, or even reach out and make new connections. There are many ways to do this; in this chapter, Cisco Covino, Michael Bayer, A.J. O'Connell, Chris Belden, Phil Lemos, Adele Annesi and Linsey Jayne each present different perspectives on writing groups, workshops, and other ways to build relationships and stay connected to a community.

Isle of Write, Or How to Reach Out to Others For Writing Stuff
by Cisco Covino

Every writer must be an island. Isolation is, after all, key to the writing process and unavoidable. Without it, we don't exist as writers. Solitude is the office where we must labor if we ever want to bring our sentences and ideas to life. It requires an almost-mad commitment, to words, to being alone, and to the belief that when we once again greet the world, we'll have a butterfly-like manuscript to show for it, or at least an incredible new high score in Tetris.

Often, however, this self-mandated solitude can become a balancing act between being alone and loneliness, writing and hermitage, and, on the other side of these things, being a healthy, active member of society but not writing a damn thing. This is the game we play. And it's up to each individual to establish his routine and his limits.

Attending an MFA program can be a nice, near-absurd event, like a wonderland for like-minded people who are interested in word counts, the best approach to metaphor, the role of fiction in memoir, another glass of wine, etc. Suddenly writing is more about solidarity than solitude. You're still an island, but one amid a cluster, an archipelago, and there are even maybe a network of bridges running from one island to another, or at least some little pangas for inter-island travel.

This is perhaps the greatest resource that an MFA can offer: a community. If we look at writing as an equation, and isolation is the constant, then community can be the variable that will lead us to the summation of all our work. It's value might lie in writing workshops, a place to bounce ideas off of one another, a chance to see what others are writing and an ability to learn from it, or, at the very least, it'll beef up your Facebook feed, which is like digital gold when you're ready to read just about anything as a form of procrastination. It's important to not only revel in this during your time at school but to also find people that you can keep in touch with when all is said and done, because eventually every writer must go home.

And now that butterfly-of-a-manuscript suddenly seems more like a caterpillar, or a moth at best. You're not sure if one section makes sense. You wonder if the island metaphor is getting out of hand—or not getting out of hand enough. You're beginning to doubt that future-tense second person might the best choice after all...

It's not uncommon to find writing more difficult at first once the MFA has concluded. For one thing, you're smarter now, which is terrible because suddenly everything you write looks like shit. Maybe you miss the structure of residency or classes or you simply miss camaraderie of fellow writers-in-arms, but even if your MFA community is out of reach, there are other options.

One of the greatest resources we have—okay, or the worst, if you're Jonathan Franzen—is the Internet. Sure, it might be our greatest nemesis when we're trying to reach our word count for the day and then Buzzfeed goes and posts a new article composed entirely of kittens playing in the snow, but beyond all of the adorable cats, there are actually a wealth of resources available on-line.

If you're looking for insights into writing, you're in luck, because insights are in no short supply. In fact, there is a greater number of blogs out there focused on how to be a successful author than there are successful authors. The best part is that if you dislike any of the advice, there's always another list out there that is preaching the exact opposite.

Much more important, however, are the online communities that have been built around common interests, and they're only a Google search and an amusing user name away. There are too many to list, but it's important to realize that if you're looking for something in particular, then there's probably an online community based around it. Reddit alone has groups for comedy writing, fantasy writing, literary writing, and poetry. It also has plenty of forums to discuss just about every aspect of the writing process, from writer's block to self-publishing to best way to utilize commas.

In addition to your MFA community and the Internet, there is one more important resource not to be squandered: the non-writers, the normals, your close friends and family. This final group is sure to be a bit divisive since some of you surely come from very writerly family, with parents that met at their own writing retreat and instead of lullabies you got Alighierian cantos at bedtime; but regardless of whether you come from a family of bohemians or dentists, it's important to realize that non-writers can offer some of the most basic and useful interpretations of your writing: is it fun? Interesting? Readable? Sometimes the best readers are people that don't care to write a lick of it.

Of course, it's important to remember that most people's lives are not revolving around your literary brainchild. So no matter how awesome of an experience you think reading your work is, don't think that anybody owes it to you, unless you're repaying the favor by getting their client's dental records in order. Or at least get them a beer.

There's no shortage of resources for writers out there, as long as you're willing to put yourself out there, which is, after all, the most important part. Besides being an island, which, while the exact opposite pretty much, is also, probably, the most important part. So while you might take advantage of everything that your MFA community, the Internet, and your non-writing acquaintances might have to offer, don't forget to get back to your island—although, you are the island—whatever, fuck the island.

Archipela-go get writing.

So now that we know that there is certain to be life (and community) after the MFA, how will you know what options you've got? What direction you should go? Who you are as a Master of Fine Arts? In this next essay, Phil Lemos breaks down some of the options available to freshly graduated writers, and what they can do to ensure that they keep in touch once they have that degree in-hand.

Community and Support
by Phil Lemos

There comes a time—usually after you've sent off your magnum opus to your thesis readers and have woken from a long, post-thesis nap—when it hits you.

You've fulfilled the MFA program requirements. You're about to graduate. For the rest of the world, this means one thing: "Congratulations, MFA graduate. Playtime is over. Now go work on those invoices/pay stubs/miscellaneous boring projects." Your loved ones will expect you to rip off that "Writer" badge you've been allowed to wear over the past couple of years, go back to your cubicle and resurface in "The Real World."

You're probably stressed out about how the hell you're going to put that MFA to use, and how to continue to convince the important people in your life that this two-year journey was worthwhile. That's not even factoring in student loans. To complicate matters, you have other thoughts on your mind that have nothing to do with money. You think about the fellow MFAers who have become your true friends and trusted confidants. No more campus or residency to return to every semester. The folks who run the program love to talk about class reunions or "Alumni Day," but you only see a handful of graduates come back and it's for an hour or to and then they disappear—or it's the graduates you didn't like. Will the professors still talk to you? Who will you be able to turn to if you need help? And what about those friendships you made? How many of your high school or college friends do you really still talk to? Probably not many. You wonder if you'll ever speak to any of your MFA friends again.

Fear not. You won't lose touch with your cohort or classmates. For those of you graduating from low residency programs, this doesn't apply if you spent your residencies banging on everyone's doors at 4 a.m. in an ill-advised quest for an 18oz Bud Light, or telling fellow workshoppers that their short stories made you want to gouge your eyes out with a hot branding iron. (But you weren't That Guy, right?) There are many ways to maintain a community and a support network after you walk the graduation procession. Some of them are the logical progression of a writer's life. Others are more outside the box. Most are pretty straightforward and can be done with a targeted effort.

I'll attempt to tackle some of them here.

Writing groups:
You got an MFA to become the next Michael Chabon/Mary Karr/ Charles Simic/Diablo Cody, so this only makes sense. Getting together with a handful of your writing friends on a monthly basis can deepen your connections and emulate the workshop environment in the post-MFA world. They help so much that I'm now in four of them. Several of my MFA colleagues have started writers groups in order to force themselves to continue writing. One of my groups formed naturally among folks with whom I frequently found myself in the same workshops, and they generously invited me to join. They all live in the New York City area, so I have three hours of driving to do. But the feedback I get is invaluable. And whenever I have a different reason to be in or around New York, I let them know, and I get invited to dinner, or to watch the Patriots-Jets game. We bond as we talk about the writer's life. Not only has it helped my writing, but it's also reinforced the friendship we all have. That's an added bonus. In the MFA program you're stuck with whomever the program assigns to be in your workshop. In the post-MFA writers' group, you don't have to include That Guy.

This got me thinking. There's no law that says I can only be in one writer's group —at least not yet. During my time in my program there were also, including myself, four people from Massachusetts in the same MFA program. So I reached out to my fellow Bay Staters. Thus the Fairfield MFA/Massholes Writer's Group was born.

Those are two of my groups. You're probably wondering about the other two. Well, just because you've earned your MFA from one school doesn't mean you can't take classes elsewhere. Many local colleges offer writing classes through their extension school or adult education program. I mean, you're in student loan hell for life now. How much further will an extra class set you back? If you work for a college or university, this is a golden opportunity. Harvard Extension School classes often cost between $2,000 and $3,000, but Harvard offers those classes to its employees for $40. OK, fine, the $40 is nonrefundable. But remember, you're a serious writer. You don't take writing classes to drop out of them.

I bring this up because my other two writers' groups consist of recent grads from other MFA programs that took fiction-writing classes with me at Harvard Extension. There's a lot of anecdotal evidence that a ridiculously high percentage of students stop writing after receiving their MFA, and we wanted to buck that trend. We made a conscious effort, and it's been mutually beneficial for all of us. I receive excellent feedback from everyone in all the groups. But everyone has their own writing and editing style, and while I'm fortunate to have such a committed group from my own program ready to assist, I also like to have a set of eyes from outside the program look at my work. Not everyone in the Harvard groups has an MFA, and sometimes it's good to get a different perspective, one that has been uninfluenced by the faculty I've worked with over the past three years.

Four writer's groups. I know, I know, how do I make the time for all these meetings? I won't beat around the bush – being single and childless helps immensely. It's easier to clear my schedule to make time for all things writing when there are no mouths to feed or significant-other events on the calendar. Making the time to submit 15-20 pages of fiction, read and critique the same from a handful of others, and meet once a month is no exception. If you're not blessed with those luxuries, a word of caution: divorce is expensive, and it's illegal to sell your kids. Maybe you should start with one writer's group and see how it goes.

Also, keep in mind that you have to determine if that group is a good fit for you. You may have to attend a group a couple of times to get a good feel for how the members operate. (A good group would likewise want to test you out to see if you're a fit anyway.) You probably don't want to be in a group with a caustic bully, who is mad at the world because he or she "can't understand why so-and-so is published but not me," because the bitterness will seep into his or her critiques. Likewise, you don't want to be in a group in which one of the members expects the others in the group to hoist him (or her) on their shoulder, carry him around the room and tell him how great his writing is. We're in this to improve as a writer, not to lavish each other with compliments. It's supposed to be a writer's group, not a second date.

If your writer's group is going well, you may find yourself with an opportunity to join more groups. One thing that's worked for me is that each group got finagled in such a way that all four meet on different nights of the week—I have my Tuesday group, my Friday group, my Saturday group and my Sunday group. Things happen in life, and it's impossible to make every single meeting in perpetuity. Your group mates will forgive an occasional excused absence. But don't forget about Skype if you're tied up elsewhere (someone in one of my groups got a new job and moved out to the Midwest, so we Skype her into the meeting now). Besides, if you're serious writer, you'll be able to make the commitment most of the time. So if you find yourself in a position to dictate when the meetings are held, jump at it.

Not everybody likes to share their early drafts with the world, however. If writer's groups aren't for you, or if you're looking for another forum to keep your writing muscles fit, you could try your hand at blogging.

Blogging:
If you've ever thought about writing a blog, and haven't done so already, earning your MFA is a great excuse to start. Blogging has been helpful to me. It's a great way to tell the important people in your life, "Oh, by the way, I'm still a writer, working on that novel/memoir/chapbook/screenplay." I started blogging about a year-and-a-half ago and now I have nearly 100 "followers" on the blog's site (and many more who don't comment publicly, though frequently mention a post or two when they see me). It's not even difficult to start. Blogger,

Wordpress and Tumblr are all easy to set up, and will walk you through the process until you're ready. And they're all free. You don't have to work in IT or have Trump as your last name to be a blogger.

Blogging accomplishes several things. One, it reminds your family "that MFA thing" you were pursuing wasn't just a hiatus from reality. You're still serious about trying to keep yourself in the writer's realm, and they should take it seriously, too. Two, it's a great opportunity to freewrite. Sometimes it's good to ignore spell check and basic grammar and just write. Often one of these blogs, while far from grammatically correct, has inspired an idea for my fiction (though you can always go back and spellcheck a blog before publishing it). Third, blogging is good for accountability. I try to blog every day, and most of the time I succeed, even if it's just two or three sentences about something weird that happened to me that day. If I talk about my writing, others will ask me about it too, and it becomes harder to put my writing down and give up on it. The last blog I ever want to write is one that says, "I'm admitting failure and I've thrown my novel in the trash."

Now that my blog is established, I haven't been able to let it die a peaceful death anyway. In the months after I graduated I found myself switching jobs and looking for new jobs a lot, and I did have to take a step back from blogging as regularly as I'd like. It was tough, because I found that I enjoyed blogging. The benefit of all my blogging is that, whenever I go a couple of days without it, people do welfare checks on me. I don't want people to dialing 911 because I didn't blog today, but there's no better way to get your mojo back than when you have a fan base waiting for you to deliver your next blog.

The blogosphere is one way writing builds community. But not everyone has time to blog every day, unless they're microblogging. That's where other social media, such as Facebook and Twitter, come in.

Social networking:
An obvious way to stay connected with your writing community is by following or friending them. People also love to post good essays and stories on social media sites. So it should be second nature to link any short stories, essays or poems on your Facebook Wall, Twitter and any

other social media you use upon publication. (You can also plug your blog by posting links on them.)

Now, while useful, using social media to promote yourself can be tricky. Some folks, even writer types, are fairly introverted and not interested in catching up with people on "this social media thing." We all have that option. Is Facebook narcissistic? A little. But this is another way to make sure your non-writer friends know that, "Oh, by the way, I'm still a writer." Plus, at least there's a purpose to this. It's more productive than posting a status update in which you announce which aisle you're in at Stop & Shop, with agonizing detail about how you look, what you're wearing and who you're with.

And social media can also open up other networking opportunities. Instead of posting as your Facebook status, "I'm drinking tea with [insert friend here] at [insert coffee shop here]," why not instead post, "I'm going to be in Fairfield County tomorrow. Any of my writer friends down there want to get together?" It's a perfect opportunity to set up more writing plans for yourself. I've set up writing challenges with some of my buddies through private writing groups. I've applied for writing jobs or submitted stories to literary journals because a friend posted a link on Facebook.

While Facebook is more of a community of friends (or at least acquaintances), you never know who's going to be in the Twittersphere. I try to tweet five times a day—I tweet a link out to my followers, and then a handful of random comments, some writing-related, others not. Sometimes I retweet something that somebody else tweeted. And it helps you build community. Because Twitter doesn't require you to accept someone as a friend, you'll wake up one morning and find that you have three or four new people following you on Twitter. And you have no say in the matter, since unlike Facebook you don't have the option of accepting or declining their request. Most of the time I'll reciprocate and follow the person back. Some Twitter followers are simply going to tweet their 10 steps to getting you more followers—relentlessly, upwards 100 times and hour—and it's perfectly reasonable to conclude all that noise isn't worth having on your Twitter feed and unfollow them. But you're all about building community, right? Keep the tweets going and it won't be long before you have hundreds or even thousands of followers.

Outside activities:
There are many outside-the-box activities to keep the writing fires stoked. Once I wrote a piece of fiction that was set in a restaurant in Harvard Square that I'd never been to before. Obviously that scene wasn't ringing true. So I grabbed a few friends and we met at the restaurant one night. I got some quality time in with friends and picked up the necessary setting my scene needed. Having writer's block? Get in touch with some friends and schedule a designated dinner night at a place that has wifi (or just take pen and paper with you). One of my friends holds writer's retreats at her house a couple of times a year. We get together in the morning, shoot the breeze for a bit, and then by noontime we commandeer quiet enclaves in her house and start writing. By early evening, we're exhausted from all the writing. But we're ready to cook out on the grill and celebrate the progress we made on our respective projects. We've kept the fire burning inside of ourselves and continued a friendship.

There you have it. You use your imagination every day when you write. All you have to do is implement that same creative flow into your personal life. Now you have no excuses to maintain and build upon community after you receive the MFA.

So we've learned that writing workshops—both in-person and online—can be great tools post-graduation to keep the creative juices flowing and foster a relationship with fellow writers. But how do you go about finding a workshop, and what type of workshop would best you're your needs? A.J. O'Connell discusses different options and opportunities you may encounter in this next essay.

The Necessity of Writers' Groups After the MFA

by A.J. O'Connell

There is nothing like a forgotten writing group deadline to make you write more in one night than you have in a week.

It was January—winter break for academia—and I had some time off from teaching. Winter break was the time I'd planned to use for revisions to my novel, but the work just wasn't happening. I had been stuck on my novel, a nearly-300 page document, for almost a month. I'd sit and stare at it, unable to make the changes. I'd get distracted. I'd check email. I'd check my social networks. I'd wash some dishes. Then I'd go back to my desk and stare at my novel some more.

One day, I was going through this listless cycle and when I checked my email and got a jolt. There, in my inbox, was an email from a fellow writer, a member of one of my writers' groups. Our next meeting was less than a week away and she was sending us a reminder, along with her several-page, polished submission.

The sight of her email triggered an adrenaline rush; within five hours, Chapter 26—the piece that had been giving me such trouble for a week—was revised. It wasn't perfect, but that was fine. It was done. Work was expected of me, and so I performed.

It's how I work best. Deadlines, expectations and the understanding that I'm not working in a vacuum are my best motivators. For two years I got those things from my MFA program. Now that I'm a graduate, I need to get that motivation elsewhere, so I've joined and formed writers' groups.

There's no doubt that my MFA program made me a better writer. By the second semester, I was making progress. I was reading good books and writing about 500 words a day. I turned in monthly packets to a faculty mentor, and submitted workshop samples for the residencies every six months. I was knocking out short stories, and producing chapter after chapter for two novels.

I chalked all this up to my work with the faculty. When I joined my MFA program, I was ecstatic about meeting the professors, a team of published writers, some of whom had won awards or been poets laureate. To say I was star-struck would be an understatement, but during my orientation, the director of the program warned us not to focus all our attention on the faculty. He stood up and pointed into the assembled class. "The most meaningful contacts you will make here are not us, they are your fellow students."

"We formed a group of six. It's been a year, and I don't know what I would do without them."

Whatever, I thought at the time, but about halfway through my third semester, I felt a mounting anxiety; graduation wasn't far off, and I began to wonder what would happen to my writing once I removed my mortarboard and hood. My mentors would be gone. There would be no more residencies. No one would be waiting for my work at the end of the month. I had written in isolation before, and it hadn't done much for me. Fueled by panic, I approached a few other members of my writing program during my penultimate residency. These were people whose writing I admired, and whose comments I most agreed with in workshop. We formed a group of six. It's been a year, and I don't know what I would do without them.

It's not my first; I have been a member of four writers' groups. At the moment I belong to three. Two—including the group that I mentioned above—contain other members of my MFA community. One group has no affiliation with the MFA program at all. All three groups work differently, have different guidelines and meet at different times.

There is no set model for creating a writer's group—the members have to do what works for them—but here are four formats that have worked for me.

1. **The large, open-to-everyone group.** My first writers' group, which I joined well before I'd even heard the term "MFA," no longer meets at all. The group, which advertised its meetings in the newspaper that employed me, met at a commercial bookstore. It was a large group—sometimes as large as 20 people—which met every other week. Sharing work wasn't mandatory. Members—if they wished to share—brought up to five pages of any kind of writing, and read those pages aloud during meetings. Sometimes printed pages were passed out so that the group could read along and make notes. Critique was mostly verbal and delivered on the spot.

2. **The online group.** After a few years, three friends and I left that group to form our own smaller group. In the beginning we met weekly at a local bar, but then everyone moved. Now we all live in separate states. We try to meet once a year for a retreat, but most of our interaction is now online. We have an online message board, which we use to post the work we want critiqued by the entire group. This past year, we participated in National Novel Writing Month as a team. Sometimes we do group activities in person; we've hosted writers' retreats and small private conferences, and we've had professional headshots taken. Mostly, we work individually with one another, emailing stories and chapters back and forth. It's a loose model, and after a decade of working together we have no set rules, but it works for us.

3. **The eclectic group.** I belong to a group that contains myself, two other MFAers and a fourth author. We are a group of mixed genres—two fiction writers and two non-fiction writers—and we meet once a month, come hell or high water. Because we are a group of mixed genre writers, I've found that we are a bit more willing to

experiment with the sort of work we give each other. Often a non-fiction writer will submit fiction, or a prose writer will submit poems. There is a willingness in this group to submit unfinished pieces or notes for consideration and discussion, which is an attitude I've never experienced before in writers' group. We also read each other's full first drafts, and hold special dinner meetings to discuss the longer work. Because of these elements, the group meetings take on the air of a writers' salon; there is a lot of discussion about the craft of writing. Ideas and writing suggestions are tossed back and forth, and everyone is enriched by the literary discussion and experimentation. Also, we meet in an old library, which adds to the salon feeling.

4. **The single-genre group.** The fourth group is the group I mentioned at the beginning of this essay. There are six of us, all fiction writers who know each other from our workshops at the MFA residencies. Four of these writers were in my workshops during my first residency, so we know each others' work well. We meet once a month, taking turns hosting, and email our submissions to the rest of the group about a week before we meet. This group is easily the most intense writers' group I belong to; because there are six of us, our meetings take the better part of a day. We tend to spend about an hour discussing each piece. This year, we decided to do more than simply submit writing samples; now we set writing goals for ourselves and share the goals with the group. Some of the goals are monthly goals; others are yearly goals. We've also incorporated a book club element into our writing group; every few months we read and discuss a piece of fiction. In many ways, this fourth group has been exactly what I've needed; it's taken the place of the MFA program in my life.

So, how does one find a writing group?

First you have to know what your needs are. If you're not looking for an MFA replacement, as I was, you might want to join a local group. Open writing groups are often hosted at libraries, community centers, and in bookstores. You can find them listed online, in newspapers, or on bulletin boards. If you don't find a group, don't despair—you can easily create a group by talking to your local library or community center and asking permission to host your own group there. You can also create online groups by connecting with groups of writers on blogs or via social networking.

Since you're reading a Post-MFA Writer's Survival Guide, however, I suggest that you start with the MFA program itself. Cherry-pick from among your fellow MFA students and graduates. After two years of classes, workshops and seminars you know whose work you most respect. You know whose comments on your work most resonated with you in workshop. Think of who would be in your dream workshop, and then invite those students to join you.

Also consider the students who have been reading your work for the longest period of time. If you've been in the same workshop with another student for two years, that student has lived with your characters, and they've watched the work develop. They may be your best allies as you continue to work on the piece post-MFA.

For more information and ideas about forming effective, lasting writer's groups, see Michael Bayer's feature, A Workshop for the Rest of Your Life, at the end of this chapter.

*S*uccessful participation in writing groups enables you to lead your own writing groups, either for practical teaching experience or as a way to supplement your income. Running the group can be beneficial in many ways, as you not only learn from the participants, but you might be changing someone's life in the meantime.

Workshop Options
by Chris Belden

On graduation from an MFA program, you may start jonesing for a workshop—regular meetings with fellow writers who will take your work seriously, and who will expect the same from you. Most writers benefit from a deadline, and a workshop will provide that, too. It's also nice to just sit around with likeminded folks and talk writing.

Many choices are available for those who want to continue the workshop experience. The most obvious is to remain in touch with your favorite MFA grads and organize a regular get-together. You can meet at a designated place—a library, café or restaurant, or at someone's home—or vary the venue. Email your work to the group a week or so ahead of time, and you know the rest.

If you don't live near your old schoolmates, you can look for an established workshop in your area. Check the local library—libraries often run workshops, some by genre, and local writers may advertise on the library's bulletin board. Large cities have a plethora of choices, from long-established for-profit workshops (such as Gotham Writing Workshop and The Writers Studio in New York) to more informal groups that don't cost anything to attend.

Another option is to start your own workshop. Put up flyers at the library and bookstores, and wait for the phone to ring. It probably will—there's no shortage of writers out there.

You can also start up a workshop as a volunteer. Senior centers and other community organizations are sometimes looking for people to run classes. This can be an amazing experience for new teachers. Other possible venues are after-school and continuing education programs, shelters, and even prisons and detention centers. I've facilitated a weekly writing workshop in a maximum-security prison for more than three years, and it has been one of the most rewarding experiences of my life. Most writers would agree that tapping into our creativity can be a life changer. Imagine a prison inmate, an "at risk" youth, or a lonely senior citizen suddenly finding a new, constructive way to communicate their ideas. It's no exaggeration to say that, by running a workshop in an alternative setting, you could change someone's life.

If you're so inclined, you can even turn the workshop experience into a moneymaking proposition. Here's one way to do it: Ask your local library if you can hold a free, one-time workshop for a few hours on a Sunday afternoon. Have people register ahead of time, and ask them to show up with short pieces. When everyone arrives, follow the game plan of your favorite MFA faculty member. You might plan a brief exercise, then have people share their work, and, of course, guide the discussion. After the workshop, ask whether anyone is interested in joining a new workshop you will be running for a fee (it's best to charge an overall fee for a certain number of sessions, e.g., $400 for eight or ten sessions). If you need ideas, consult the many books out there that provide writing exercises and breakdowns of the elements of creative writing (e.g., Janet Burroway's *Writing Fiction*, Sherry Ellis's *Now Write!*, and Brenda Miller & Suzanne Paola's *Write It Slant*). Make sure going in that you have a set number of workshop participants in mind (eight is a good maximum), and which genres you'd be willing to cover (a fiction writer may not be comfortable with poetry, for instance, and vice versa). Of course, now that you're the leader, you'll lose the advantages of being a workshop member, but you'll learn a ton by putting your energies toward guiding others to be better writers. You'll also gain great teaching experience and make a few bucks while you're at it.

*I*f group work doesn't fit your needs, or if you've outgrown your current workshop, you might consider finding a like-minded friend to help you move through your literary career. Individual relationships like these can be an opportunity to discuss ways to enhance each other's careers, not necessarily only by sharing your writing, but for sharing fellowship opportunities, contests, jobs, and conference materials. Other beneficial relationships include finding another writer who is familiar with your work, so that you can share drafts of your writing with someone who understands your work and it's context, while still allowing a separate set of unbiased eyes on your work.

The Power of Two: The Advantage of the Writing Buddy
by Adele Annesi

Writing workshops have their place and typically last two years, on average. After that, writers migrate to different workshops or move off to write individually. Yet, serious writers who are dedicated to the art and craft of writing and to growing as writers still need the close connection only a one-on-one meeting of creative minds can provide. Here are some reasons to seek and cultivate a writing relationship with that trusted someone whom you can regularly meet.

Meeting with one other person who gets you and your work makes targeted follow-up easier and more streamlined: When two writers meet outside of—or instead of—a group, it's easier for each to recall what the other needs in the way of feedback and resources and to send that information along when it becomes available. In a real-life example, one writer needed a textile design expert and the other had recently met someone in that field. While talking with the textile designer, the writing buddy mentioned having a friend who was working on a book that included the field of textile design. The mention and personal referral were worth a lot, in this case, benefitting the writer with a valuable resource and the designer with a mention in the book.

An intimate atmosphere paves the way for better and clearer communication: Writing groups are great for stimulating the senses and producing ideas, but they're not always best for vetting those ideas. There usually are lots of comments, often conflicting, to sort through. Time for clarification often is limited, and conversations frequently get sidetracked. When two writers sit down to talk, however, it's easier to pause the conversation to clear up an ambiguity, and to pursue what-if scenarios. As noted by novelist Chitra Banerjee Divakaruni in a recent Writer's Digest article, this is essential the writing process and to flesh out ideas that arise.

Fewer are better when it comes to realistic and manageable accountability: It's imperative for writers to set goals, but it's also important for those goals to be realistic and quantifiable. These criteria are easier to manage when you're working with one person who can hold you accountable for promises you make but may not be able to keep, and for taking a risk in committing to a goal that may be out of your comfort zone but would expand the boundaries of your work.

Targeted networking is a time saver in a one-on-one setting: In an age of social networking, the in-person meet isn't required. But when two writers are meeting anyway, their ability to share specific contact information is streamlined, especially if they plan to bring at least one resource to the next meet. This step can easily become part of a one-on-one that's writing based, especially if it's the last item on the list. If each writer commits to finding at least one resource for the other, the search process alone is likely to yield new venues and names. Consider the headhunter whose role it is to match one person with the right job opening—a task that's lots easier to do when you know who and what you're dealing with.

Meeting with one trusted buddy provides a safe setting in which to discuss topics and writing challenges: Sometimes writers choose some tough topics to write about and face challenges that are difficult to address. For proprietary and a host of other reasons, the writer may not feel comfortable divulging the subject of a work-in-progress to more than one trusted colleague. If this becomes mutual, the bond of trust can become even stronger. Writers also may find themselves facing a particularly nettlesome rejection or revision, and even though support is helpful, it probably won't help the situation to broadcast it.

Workshops will always have a place in the world of writing and social is the new norm. But after the workshop ends—and at some point it will—writers who want to keep writing will need the support and understanding only another writer can provide.

If all this sounds a bit like dating, that's because cultivating a rapport with a writing buddy who has your best interest at heart is a form of relationship building—and essential in this often disconnected age. There's more than one way to maintain writing camaraderie, and your sanity. The power of two can be stronger than crowdsourcing.

*s Adele mentions, there are many ways writing peers can help you. In fact, you can interact with a few different writing peers to meet varying needs. Some fellow writers will be most helpful with resources, such as finding fellowships or job opportunities. Others are best as a careful set of eyes to share writing ideas with or edit your already-written manuscripts. And occasionally, when all goes right in the world, you might be lucky enough to find a peer who can play all of these roles for you—a friend, a confidant, a job-searcher, a manuscript-reader, or even a co-writer. If you're lucky enough to find that person, treat them well, and return the favor.

Literary Mind Link
by Linsey Jayne

Writing Buddy

/ˈrítiNG/ /ˈbedé/

Noun

1. A close friend with whom you share writing for critique.

2. One who pushes you to write alongside them; one with whom you share craft expertise and embrace the writing experience.

Literary Mind Link

/ˈlite,reré/ /mínd/ /liNGk/

Noun

1. A person whose lifestyle and thought processes complement one's own in such a way as to be fluid between the two parties, allowing them to share in projects, challenges, and successes.

As a student in a low-residency MFA program, the critical thesis (affectionately nicknamed the "third semester project") was the first sincerely daunting task I encountered. After all, devoting an entire semester compiling a thesis you are completely passionate about, for evaluation by your mentors and program directors, well, that's just not an easy feat. "Here, world," you say, meekly handing over 75 pages of interviews, research, reading, and unique observation on disambiguation between prose poetry and flash fiction. "Here is my literary soul. Take this and judge my merit!" And then, of course, the waiting.

While the critical thesis might be the first daunting task you encounter as a writer (or perhaps it's not, each experience differs), it will certainly not be the last. After this and your creative thesis, your readings and the lectures you teach, you still have a world of public readings, writer's block, submissions, rejections, presentations, classes, and workshops to follow. The writer's life is not for the faint of heart. In my experience, the one common road to success that each of these outlets necessitates a literary mind link. Someone who is enough like you to understand your current position; different enough to provide an outside perspective and challenge you to pursue options you wouldn't have thought were viable.

Changing in a Dark Room

Sharing writing with a close friend, or community of contemporaries, is without question one of the crucial elements to successful writing (and to not losing your mind along the way). Or, at least, it has been for me. As a poet burgeoning into the performance and publication world, there have been plenty of weeks in succession where I have been writing without any input or idea as to how the world was perceiving my work - which I have found to be the most dangerous practice, and most detrimental to any potential writing career. The dangers of writing alone can manifest in a number of ways.

When you write alone, you are changing in a dark room without a mirror, or a second opinion. You face the very dangerous prospect of walking outside with eyeliner smeared on your cheeks, a pair of unmatched shoes, or (for those truly like me), without the moment of self-reflection that allows you to say "Hey, maybe these lime green tights aren't the best to wear at a funeral." With no one to ask the critical questions that challenge your work, or help you reflect upon your work, you not only deny the work some wildly inspired new directions, but you stifle its chance to turn on the lights and be revealed.

Facing the world unchecked is a big undertaking, as you yourself likely know, if you've ever asked a best friend or significant other for her/his opinion on *anything*.

A writing buddy or writing community can be the friend or partner to check you editorially—to help you identify and evaluate the decisions available to you with regard to your work. The literary mind link, however, will push you to new plateaus, just by virtue of serving a vastly different function, as evidenced by their definitions above.

Having a literary mind link has helped me experiment; turn my third semester project into an anthology/essay hybrid. Between the two of us, we have pushed ourselves to submit to countless literary journals, develop work that is entirely three-dimensional. Perhaps my favorite benefit of the mind link, however: it has pushed us to succeed in other endeavor—co-founding a literary journal that embraces our shared passion for the economy of words.

With a literary mind link, writer's block has become an easily overcome obstacle. Together, we are able to work through places where our writing is stuck within one story; we can take on the fear of being unoriginal with prompts and mutually set deadlines. For example, if my mind link knows I've been having a bad few weeks with little writing to show, she'll propose a prompt and a deadline to which we'll both adhere. Knowing that I owe something to her makes me feel more driven to complete it, and before I know it, I've got some halfway decent writing to boast. (*And* if it's not my strongest writing, I have someone I can trust to help me change that, without judging me or making me feel incapable. It's truly magic.)

If you can find someone with whom you feel comfortable communicating; with whom you're willing to show even the stupidest piece of writing you've composed because you know they will help you make it better? You're golden. (I mean, let's be honest—even this essay was the product of consultation with my mind link.) No matter what, my advice is to keep on writing, keep on sharing, and keep your mind open to all the new connections you've made along the way. In doing so, there's no way you will fail.

*M*ost writers crave, indeed need, feedback of some kind before they feel ready to send their work into the world. Some seek the more intimate relationships, like the ones described by Adele Annesi and Linsey Jayne in this chapter. Some prefer forging writing bonds with larger groups. If you crave the range of feedback and discussion you experienced during your writing program workshops and you decide a regular writing group is a good fit for you, Michael Bayer's article below gives you practical advice and some easy steps to follow to run your own successful writing group. Some workshop veterans warn that writing groups only last two or three years before participants naturally migrate to other interests and associations, but Bayer posits that a properly run writing group can last longer than any single individual's participation. Bayer is the successful driver behind both regular writer's groups and alumni community events and he shares some of his wisdom for effectively managing a group of writers with a variety of interests and needs here.

A Workshop for the Rest of Your Life
by Michael Bayer

During the MFA program, we waited with nervous excitement for the day that our work was up for critique. We expected one extreme or the other: universal acclaim or universal condemnation. We rarely expected a middle-of-the-road response, but that's almost always what we got. We couldn't help feeling at least a little disappointed that the consumption and discussion of our work didn't generate the same exhilaration that we felt when we produced it. Still, the workshop, with its shared passion and silent bond, was the most natural place on earth for us to be.

For many of us, our first MFA workshop was an almost mystical experience, where our new instructor and classmates were the first strangers *ever* to read our work, or at least the first to read it and talk about it. We had let them in—to our strange writer's mind and solitary writer's heart—because they understood our struggle, the wrestling of our vision to the page. We felt part of a tradition that went back to the Bloomsbury Group, the Inklings, and the Algonquin Round Table. When we graduated, we knew the trust, intimacy and fragility of the workshop was what we'd miss the most.

Fortunately, if we so desire, we can be part of a workshop that goes on for the rest of our lives. A workshop that continues in perpetuity. It's called a writers group, and it's the most natural social offshoot of an MFA program.

Like an MFA workshop, a writers group provides a built-in audience for your work, a forum for honest critique, and, most importantly, a deadline. Unlike an MFA workshop, it involves a long-term commitment, comprises only hand-selected members, and often creates a social circle even more open and honest than your own family. To me, a writer without a writing group is like a painter without a studio. Every artist needs a sacred place. (And with Skype and similar technologies, that *place* is no longer restrained by geography.) It's no wonder that writing groups are so common among MFA graduates.

Membership in a writers group, however, is a very different undertaking than *management* of a writers group; too many writers groups are short-lived because they fail to understand this. Members become distracted by other priorities in life. Expectations are abandoned. A passion becomes a chore. Participation wanes. And nobody is in charge, so it dies. (It's almost always a slow death.) In this sense, the breakup of a writers group must be viewed like the breakup of a marriage: maybe it's nobody's fault, but it's still a *failed* marriage.

Like any human relationship, a writers group is healthy and successful only when it meets the needs of those involved. And here lies the challenge. Every writer needs something different. And most writers can't—or won't—articulate what they need from the group anyway.

Let's imagine a writers group called the Muses' Fuses. One member (let's call her Lola) lacks discipline and so relies on the group's monthly deadlines to keep her accountable and productive. Jack, another member, struggles with self-confidence and needs critical feedback delivered in a supportive way from people he trusts. Jill is in the thick of a 1,000-page novel and needs the same readers following along chapter after chapter, while Eddy isn't ambitious in his writing career, but loves being *around* writers and talking about their work. Do these four writers have very different needs? Yes. Are these needs incompatible? Absolutely not.

When you join a writing group, you're entering into a covenant with three, four, or five fellow writers. This covenant rests on a single pledge among the group: to help every member achieve their writing goals. It's that simple. A successful writers group doesn't require that every member is on chapter ten of a crime novel, or shopping a poetry chapbook, or needs a good ass-kicking. In fact, different goals, projects and attitudes make a group more interesting and more valuable.

> "Different goals, projects and attitudes make a group more interesting and more valuable."

While member goals can be vastly different, the rules of engagement for the group must be absolutely consistent. A good writers group deserves good governance. It's not magical; it must be managed. To prevent a slow death, group members must understand how fragile their special place is, and must take proactive measures to keep it meaningful. I recommend the following five practices as a starting point:

1. **Appoint a leader.** No organization can run itself, so hold a vote to elect a group leader. Write down the "job description" and make sure the group leader is willing and capable of the job.

Only choose someone who is assertive and comfortable with "cracking the whip." Like any elected official, the group leader can also be voted out of office by a majority whenever they're not cutting it. Consider an annual (re)election.

2. **Codify rules.** All members must agree on a list of rules, or policies, which demand compliance for the sake of the group's long-term health. These rules need to be written down, circulated and re-visited at least annually. They should cover areas like submission deadlines, submission length and format, absenteeism, responsiveness, and succession (see #5).

3. **Document goals.** Once a year, use the first 30 minutes of a regularly scheduled meeting to conduct a "summit" during which each member is required to discuss their personal writing goals for the next 12 months. These goals are documented, combined and shared across the group, with members asked to report on their progress regularly. Some members may want to be kept accountable through a bit of "tough love," and the group should be willing to oblige.

4. **Limit membership.** The proper balance of intimacy and diversity is essential. Five is the ideal number of members. Six is feasible, but not ideal. More than six is not recommended.

5. **Welcome succession and reinvention.** Change is natural. In a writers group, members come and members go. Eddy gets a big promotion at work and has little time for writing. Lola misses three meetings in a row without explanation. Jack's been invited to join a group exclusively for science fiction writers. Whatever the reasons, members should leave—or, occasionally, be asked to leave—as soon as their level of engagement noticeably wanes. A writing group dies not when members leave, but when they don't leave fast enough. This is why succession planning is an important aspect of group management: make sure you have one or more qualified candidates waiting in the wings at all times. Embrace the notion that someday the group may still exist, but without any of its current members.

It's not easy to leave a writers group, to abandon that special place of art, inspiration and friendship. You'll try to stay loyal at all costs. You'll fear that leaving the group represents leaving your writing life. You'll feel guilty. You'll waver. But the moment the group has become an *obligation*, it's absolutely time to leave. Like everything else in life, you only get back what you put in. Are you giving the other members what they need from you? Have you broken the covenant? Assess your level of engagement by answering the following questions with brutal honesty:

1. Do I feel excited for the next group meeting?

2. Have I attended at least four of the past five meetings?

3. Do I submit new work more often than revised work?

4. Does the group inspire me to set aside time for writing?

5. Do I usually submit my work by the agreed deadline?

If you answer no to any of these questions, it could be time to reconsider your participation. Your circumstances, priorities, and needs have probably changed, and that's absolutely fine. It's only *not* fine if you pretend they haven't. You owe it to the group's members to let them know if you've become even slightly less engaged, for any reason. It doesn't mean you have to leave forever, but perhaps it's time to take a break.

It would be nice if writers groups could run themselves, fueled by nothing but members' collective good intentions. But that's a fantasy. Like a business, a writers group must be managed if it is to remain strong. Like a relationship, it must be nurtured if it is to remain the fragile, magical place that it is. When writers' lives are at stake, the risks and rewards are too important to leave it up to fate.

Chapter 4

STAY CONNECTED TO YOUR INDUSTRY

edited by Michael Bayer

Many creative writers see themselves primarily as artists. But whether your goal is to create art, sell entertainment, or somewhere in between, every writer is part of an "industry," they like it or not. This chapter explores a few of the ways you can make the most out of your participation in an ever-growing literary industry.

*Y*ou may not know it, but as a writer, you're part of an industry. Your work, whether or not it's been published, is the content that fuels a marketplace of ideas and literature. Whether your long-term goal is to publish books, teach writing, or submit occasionally to literary journals, you are participating in the industry of writing. As such, it's to your advantage to nurture an ongoing connection to the community that keeps this industry going.

While the writing and publishing industries overlap considerably, the writing industry also intersects with parts of the academic, corporate, and non-profit sectors. Wherever creative writing connects with work or commerce.

Like all industries, the writing industry has its own institutions that help participants find information, monitor trends and best practices, and support each other. These include trade publications, membership associations, conferences and training venues. Writers who take advantage of these tools will not only feel more informed and more connected to their peers, but will have greater access to opportunities.

This chapter offers advice for writers who want to understand their optimal role within the industry and take advantage of the conferences, forums and publications that exist to help them improve their craft and secure opportunities for work and publication. Don't miss the helpful lists of conferences, residencies, membership organizations, and publications throughout the chapter.

*W*riters and artists are often reluctant to see themselves—and their work—as part of an industry. We idealize our writing as a magical process that requires nothing more than creative inspiration, and the idea of industry is anathema to artistry. The starving artist trope has remained stubbornly resilient. Ashley Andersen Zantop discusses how successful writers understand that they are part of a larger community, and take advantage of everything that means.

Welcome to Your Industry
by Ashley C. Andersen Zantop

art·ist
noun

: a person who creates art

: a person who is very good at something

trades·man
noun

: a person who works in a job that requires special skill or training

: someone who sells goods

Most MFA and other creative writing degree programs teach candidates how to become better writers. MFA programs in particular focus on honing the elements of your craft, building skill as a literary writer and artist. This makes perfect sense; candidates seek degrees to develop mastery in their field. Writers often hope and expect such mastery reflected by a degree will help them earn money as a writer, if not as an expert on creative writing.

Now that you've graduated from your program, you might be an artist or on your way to becoming one. But, what many degree programs don't prepare you for is the business of writing. If you sell your writing, you're also a tradesman. If you're a tradesman in the writing industry, not only do you need to know how to write what your customers, patrons and readers find valuable (other chapters will tell you more about that), you need to understand how to participate in the commerce related to it.

Don't worry. I do not suggest that you top off your expensive MFA with an MBA. I do suggest you take a moment to consider: If you plan to earn a living even in small part from your writing, you are part of an industry based on the buying and selling of writing, writing services, coaching and skills. To be effective in this industry, to develop into a prosperous tradesman as well as a talented artist, you need to understand it.

Many writers know or at least suspect this, and as candidates draw closer and closer to graduation day, real fear sets in for some of us. We sense we are not equipped or educated in the ways of our new industry, but we're not sure what to do about it. This, in part, fuels the "agent fantasy." A writer dreams she finishes her manuscript, finds an agent who adores it (the first one she sends it to), let's her agent negotiate an enormous book (and movie) deal and she never has to sell anything ever again if she doesn't want to. That probably sounds good to any writer, but especially a writer who has no idea how to navigate the industry. Fear of the unknown, of how to sell work and get paid, often drives us to want to abdicate the whole enterprise. We want an agent to handle it all for us. Most of the time, this just isn't how it works. Most writers handle all of their own transactions in the industry. Even those with agents don't always use their agents for everything. They may be represented by an agent for one project or one type of writing, but not for anything else. Not knowing the industry norms and standards is a good way to get taken advantage of.

Leaving aside the transactional aspects of selling your work, think about your customer. Who is your customer? Is your customer your audience, your readership? Only if you are selling your work directly to your readers. Perhaps you have a subscription blog for which readers pay you a monthly fee to read your posts (you would be in a very small minority). Major publications like *The New York Times* struggled to get readers to pay for online content for years. Perhaps you've self-published eBooks using an eBook retailer's self-publishing tools and readers are swarming to buy your titles and know just where to find them? If none of the above applies to you, the customer for your work is not your reader. Your customer is likely a publication or organization willing to pay you for your work and then put forth some effort to market, promote, distribute and sell it, or use it for internal purposes. Big or small. Online or in print or both. (For more on various publishing options, see chapter 10, edited by A.J. O'Connell.)

One important aspect of success in any industry is to know your customer. Understand what your customer wants and needs. Understand your customer's challenges. All of those things might be opportunities for you. If you learn enough about your customer, you may find ways to practice your art while creating valuable work your customers and readers want.

If you're serious about building a life in this industry, you need to commit yourself to a life of learning. Pop culture, world events and technology not only affect what readers want and will read, but also how the industry conducts business. You'll need to build an understanding of how the industry works and then continually maintain it. How do you do this? There are as many ways as there are writers, but they can be distilled into two fairly clear categories:

Start. Continue.

Just start somewhere. When you have a piece or pieces ready to submit, do it. You'll make mistakes, but keep at it. When you have a piece accepted by an agent or publication, you'll likely overlook something in a contract you'll regret later, or make any number of other mistakes. Learn from your mistakes and don't make them again. Placing small bets, submitting small pieces, is a safe way to learn the process without risking too much. Submit articles, essays, poetry, short stories, flash fiction wherever you can, just for the experience of the whole process. From writing query letters to filling out online submission forms. The more you do it, the better you'll get at it.

Pay Attention.

Take the time to invest in understanding your industry. Attend writer's conferences and trade shows. Talk to other writers about their experiences. Speak to publishers' respresentatives at trade shows and booksellers in bookstores. Find out what they are excited about, what they are worried about. The value to you in attending industry tradeshows is to learn about and better understand your customer and your audience. The value in attending writer's conferences and retreats is to learn about, hone and better understand your craft and your community. Both provide important professional development and further understanding of your industry, but you should know the difference so you can make the best choices about what combination of events is right for you and your writing career each year. See the article "Hello, My Name is _____" by Michael Bayer and my summary of "Conferences and Trade Shows" in this chapter for more information.

Another easy opportunity to learn about your industry is the range of industry publications available. Subscribe to them. These are print and online journals that focus on the business of writing and publishing. They can be as specific as the Science Fiction Writers of America bulletin (http://sfwa-news.com/Default. aspx?pageId=1462864), or as general as Book Business (http://www. bookbusinessmag.com). Numerous daily email publications are free if you provide your contact information. Pick a few that are interesting to you or would be to your readership and/or target customers. Many of these publications not only publicize information about the type and size of publishing deals being made on a daily basis, but they also offer stories and features on new publishers, distributors and self-publishing services, content trends, challenges and economic factors facing the industry. You don't need to read every story in every industry mag, but you should skim enough to be able to articulate the biggest challenges and opportunities in the segment of the industry you care the most about. For more information on these types of publications and associations, see the listing at the end of this chapter.

You did not become an artist or an expert in your field overnight. You won't become an expert in the industry overnight, or maybe even ever. But, you don't need to be an expert, you just need to be proficient.

Learn from your mistakes, forgive yourself when you make them and move on. Pay attention. Be curious about the business that values the art you create and the trade that sustains you.

See Michael Bayer's article on writer's conferences in this chapter to learn more about the specific benefits of attending writer's conferences and residencies.

*M*any writers are terrified by the thought of attending a conference. Can't we just sit at our desks and write? For those of us who feel that way, conferences sound like a lot of work, a lot of socialization. On the contrary, conferences can be attended in a way that solves your personal problems and answers your personal questions, and nothing more. Whether or not the prospect of conferences, conventions or parties gives you the willies, read on to learn about all the ways you can benefit from engaging in targeted industry conferences and other forms of professional development.

Hello, My Name is _____

by Michael Bayer

Writers tend to be introverts. When many of us must attend a party, we count down the minutes until we can make a graceful early exit. We do everything we can to keep our weekends free of social obligations, unless they involve other writers. Spending a month—or a summer—in a cabin in the woods is our idea of paradise.

That's why for many writers the Internet has been a lifesaving medium. Now we can socialize without really socializing. We can network without really networking. We can promote ourselves and our work through a few keystrokes on our couch rather than hosting a book launch party or giving a public reading. We convince ourselves—and our readers, contacts—that our screen personality is our center of gravity, our authentic self. Let's call it screen-washing. The computer screen is our mask, and the literary community is our masquerade ball. We can be as outgoing as we like without the vulnerability that comes with real human contact. Our avatars are more eager to socialize than we are.

No doubt the Internet has revolutionized many aspects of personal marketing and networking, those dreaded skills our MFA faculty told us were indispensable to literary success ("no writer has ever been discovered without leaving his bedroom") and seemed to come naturally to one, or maybe two, of our extroverted classmates who we all secretly hoped or assumed were poor writers, as it would be seriously unkind for God to have given them two talents instead of just one. But, while one's digital avatar can certainly augment and enhance communications with the literary community and the reading public, it most certainly cannot *replace* in-person human contact.

If you have a new book coming out soon, and 85% of the items on your marketing checklist can be handled from your porch, then you probably need to rethink your strategy. If you're a young writer awaiting your first "big break" in a literary journal, and you've never met an editor in person in your entire life, you should consider suspending your email account for 30 days and leaving the house. Just because you have your blog, your Twitter account, your GoodReads author page, and two eBooks available on Amazon, that doesn't mean you can—or should—sit back and let your avatar do all the work. You're a human being, and until artificial intelligence takes a giant leap forward, those who will buy and/or appreciate your creative work are also human beings. As every successful political candidate knows, when you're trying to build a reputation, nothing beats person to person.

> **"Writers' conferences and residencies. . . they're ideal networking venues [even] for an introverted writer."**

That's where writers' conferences and residencies come in. They're ideal networking venues for an introverted writer because (a) they're highly structured and don't leave you on your own to meet people, (b) they're filled with nothing but writers and/or lovers of writing, and (c) they're extremely efficient as they consolidate twelve months of reluctant networking into a few manageable days or hours.

Like it or not, as a writer, even a not-yet-published one, you are part of an industry. Scientists attend scientific conferences. Educators attend education conferences. And writers attend writers' conferences.

What do you have to lose by attending a conference? A few days of your life, and several hundred (sometimes thousands) of dollars, which should not be taken lightly. What do you have to gain? Quite a bit. Let's boil it down to three key benefits.

Networking

While many writers have felt like oddballs since childhood given our insatiable appetite for writing and reading, writers' conferences offer an alternate universe. The only oddball at a writers' conference is the non-writer who wanders in to the convention hall by accident. For everyone else, this is your tribe. You're in the presence of hundreds of people who share your passions and your goals, *and* your insecurities about both. Every attendee potentially has something to offer you. Maybe he's an editor of a journal you admire. Maybe she's an agent on the lookout for new talent. Or maybe they're both novice writers looking for support and friendship from like-minded peers. This is the beautiful irony of a writers' conference. Human beings who would generally prefer to keep their distance are forced to acknowledge that they need each other.

If you let your hair down even an inch, you will find networking at a conference a piece of cake. You can simply harken back to your MFA program and walk up to that interesting stranger and ask, "What's your genre?" You can ask if he's going to the Margaret Atwood keynote speech tonight, or if she has an agent, or if he knows anyone at the *Paris Review,* or if she knows anyone looking for sci-fi novellas. There's something about one writer approaching another that levels the playing field. As the author Patricia Highsmith once said, "Writers and artists belong to no class." We belong to each other.

So, print business cards ("writer" is your job title) and bring them. Bring a few hard copies of your latest poem or your first chapter. Bring a list of ten people, real or hypothetical (a quirky agent who loves lesbian horror, the poetry editor for *Guernica*), whom you would love to meet at the conference, and challenge yourself to find them. Most importantly, ask yourself who, at this stage of your writing career, has the most to offer you, and vice versa. For example, your novel is done and you need an agent. You're a poet feeling isolated and need to meet other poets in your area. You're an adjunct composition instructor looking for department chairs who might need full-time creative writing professors in the fall. Or you're feeling stuck halfway through your memoir and need an editorial eye from someone who understands what it's like to grow up as the only minority in a white town. Guess what? Chances are, these people will be attending the conference, so make it your business to find them. Don't meet people just for the hell of it. Find and meet the people with whom you're most likely to develop a mutually useful relationship.

Learning

Another important benefit of conference attendance is simply staying apprised of trends, techniques and innovations in writing and publishing. If you have your MFA, you may suspect that while natural writing talent cannot be learned, helpful concepts of craft, discipline, and marketing *can* be. Think of a conference as a mini-MFA program: three days packed with knowledge and self-improvement.

Most conferences feature seminars and panel discussions, usually on a wide variety of topics, and usually promoted to conference attendees well in advance. Create your detailed conference schedule before you arrive. Think of it like selecting your courses for the spring semester back in college. Depending on the conference, you may have access to seminars on fictional world-building, writing from a child's point of view, feminist poetry, the secrets of suspense, how to create a literary journal, how to balance writing and parenthood, best practices in voice dictation, surviving the adjunct life, Muslim poets, television writing, stream of consciousness, or the epistolary form. Passionate and accomplished experts on each of these topics will be waiting to engage you in public discourse. Each panel is like a visit to the writer's town square.

Bring a list of questions to your conference of choice, specifying what you'd like to learn from attendees, seminars, panel discussions, and other sources of insight. What's the market for literary zombie fiction? How can I write sex more convincingly? How do I go about starting a non-profit writing center? How can I balance my passion for writing with the demands of my day job? How can I simplify the revision process? Should I use first person point of view for this story? How can I build a following as a sonneteer? Which universities are hiring full-time creative writing faculty? Whatever your questions, and we *all* have questions, choose the conference that will give you the best answers, and arrive with a determination to find answers for every one of them.

Inspiration

The least tangible, but perhaps most valuable, benefit of attending writers' conferences is simply the inspiration you'll feel from comingling with writers who are just as passionate as you are about the literary arts. Look around and notice the hard-won accomplishments of your peers. Go up to them and congratulate them on their most recent publication, their new teaching gig, or that award they just won. Writers need each other. And that goes for both unknown beginners and bestselling authors. We live in a culture where art is rarely rewarded, but in the presence of a thousand other writers, it's amazing how important literature suddenly becomes. Soak it in!

Remember that unspoken blend of camaraderie and healthy competition you felt during your MFA program? Writers' conferences exist to recreate that. So, when you sign up for a conference, make the most of it. Arrive a day early. Register for as many workshops as possible. Apply for a manuscript consultation. Eat lunch with strangers. Troll the book fair. Attend the cocktail parties. Regardless of the content, there's something magical about being surrounded by a community of writers, those desperate souls who see time on Earth as a precious gift worth documenting in language.

It's important to carefully select which conference you attend, and the best sources for conference information are *Poets & Writers* and the AWP/*Writers' Chronicle*. Keep in mind that some conferences are designed exclusively for teachers of writing, while others are designed exclusively for the commerce of book publishing; the majority fall somewhere in between, blending art and commerce in endless configurations. Some, like Bread Loaf, offer a limited number of spots, resulting in a highly competitive application process, while others are open to anyone and everyone. Most entail some combination of writing workshops, lectures, panel discussions, manuscript consultations, book fairs, and/or social functions, but every conference's focus is different, so review the program details carefully. Often conference organizers bring in one or more big "names" to provide a keynote address or some kind of headline event, but don't let that Joyce Carol Oates lecture tempt you into attending an event that isn't right for you. Conferences are part marketplace, part writers' colony, part academy, and part cocktail party, so know what you want and research thoroughly before registering.

Keep in mind that not all conferences will be valuable. If you're a novelist, avoid poetry-biased venues. If you're a horror writer, make sure that commercial fiction is represented on the agenda somewhere. Some tend to attract mostly novice writers without serious commitment to their craft, while others attract only serious literary authors who know little about commercial realities. Know what you want, and research where to find it.

Following is a list of some established conferences in the United States. Turn to the end of this chapter for an annotated list of some additional important writers' conferences or writer-friendly conferences in the US and around the world, as well as a listing of industry trade shows.

Aloha Writers Retreat/Conference, Kapalua, Maui, HI, www.alohawritersconference.com;

Antioch Writers Workshop, Miami Valley, OH, www.antiochwritersworkshop.com

Aspen Summer Words Writing Retreat & Literary Festival, Aspen, CO, www.aspenwriters.org

Bear River Writers' Conference, Petoskey, MI, www.lsa.umich.edu/bearriver

Bread Loaf Writers' Conference, Middlebury, VT, www.middlebury.edu/blwc

Cape Cod Writers' Center Annual Conference, Hyannis, MA, www.capecodwriterscenter.org

Grub Street Muse and the Marketplace Conference, Boston, MA, www.grubstreet.org

Juniper Summer Writing Institute, Amherst, MA,
www.umass.edu/juniperinstitute

Key West Literary Seminars, Key West, FL, www.kwls.org

Napa Valley Writers' Conference, St. Helena, CA,
www.napawritersconference.org

San Francisco Writers' Conference, San Francisco, CA, www.sfwriters.org

Santa Barbara Writers' Conference, Santa Monica, CA, www.sbwriters.com

Sewanee Writers' Conference, Sewanee, TN, www.sewaneewriters.org

Squaw Valley Writers' Conference, Nevada City, CA,
www.squawvalleywriters.org

Wesleyan Writers' Conference, Middletown, CT, www.wesleyan.edu/writers

A Word on Writers' Residencies and Colonies

While a much more private experience than conferences, writers' colonies, retreats and residencies offer longer-term immersion in a small, close-knit community of writers and artists for the purpose of maximizing creative output. Residencies provide some of the same networking and learning benefits as conferences, but their primary value is in the creative inspiration offered via a highly personalized experience in a pastoral setting. Most residencies are also highly competitive, requiring a rigorous application process for a small number of spots in the program, so you'll need to bring your A game if you want to participate.

Following is a list of some of the more established writers' residencies in the United States:

Atlantic Center for the Arts, New Smyrna Beach, FL,
www.atlanticcenterforthearts.org

Dorland Mountain Arts Colony, Temecula, CA, www.dorlandartscolony.org

Fine Arts Work Center, Provincetown, MA, www.fawc.org

MacDowell Colony, Peterborough, NH, www.macdowellcolony.org

Millay Colony for the Arts, Austerlitz, NY, www.millaycolony.org

Norman Mailer Writers Colony, Provincetown, MA, www.nmcolony.org

Starry Night Retreat, Truth or Consequences, NM, www.starrynightretreat.com

The Studios of Key West, Key West, FL, www.tskw.org

Woodstock Byrdcliffe Guild, Woodstock, NY, www.woodstockguild.org

Vermont Studio Center, Johnson, VT, www.vermontstudiocenter.org

Virginia Center for the Creative Arts, Amherst, VA, www.vcca.com

Yaddo, Saratoga Springs, NY, www.yaddo.org

In our oppressively digital world, the experience of attending writers' conferences and residencies is a refreshingly human one. These venues not only invite writers to shed their avatars for a few days, but also to rekindle that primal flame that fueled their earliest passion for writing in the first place. That passion is decidedly human, as is everything worth writing about. So, if you're looking to rediscover yourself—and your potential—as a writer, take a break from the computer screen and dive head first into that imperfect, chaotic, miraculous bliss that is a gathering of writers.

WP is the big kahuna of writers' conferences. This annual gathering is the largest and most diverse in its curriculum, and it can be overwhelming to a novice attendee. Erin A. Corriveau provides a helpful preview and practical advice for the first-timer.

The AWP Experience for First-Timers
by Erin A. Corriveau

You've decided to attend AWP.

What do you want to gain from the experience?

The Association of Writers and Writing Programs (AWP) Annual Conference and Bookfair was founded to celebrate writing and unite writing programs, students and graduates with publishers, editors and the greater literary community. AWP was formed in 1967, and since then, their conference has grown to an annual attendance of over 12,000 attendees and 650 exhibitors as of Boston's 2013 conference. Since you've recently graduated from an MFA or other writing program and are looking for ways to either grow or strengthen your network, AWP would be an excellent place to start.

Each AWP attendee probably has several different reasons for wanting to attend the conference. Some want to further their literary careers by meeting editors and agents. Some want to promote and sell their new books which were published by a small press. Others want to promote their journals by meeting writers who are looking to submit. The first time I attended, I was a recent MFA graduate; however, I was also a recent literary journal founder and editor, a candidate for faculty positions, and a writer of literary nonfiction.

It is important to determine what your goals are, why you are attending the conference. At my first AWP conference, my primary goal was to meet future submitters to my literary journal and to gain new colleagues who were in situations similar to my own. Whatever your goals are for attending, remember that it's impossible to achieve all of them at once. This isn't to say, though, that you can't advocate for and network for different things, because you can and should.

There are quite a few ways you can address your various roles in the conference. If you work for a literary journal, you might want to consider attending a social media panel. You might learn something in the panel that can help your work in the journal, but also further your own career as a writer. If you tend to write in one genre, take a step into a panel for a genre outside of your norm. It might ignite creativity. Join some of the group activities, like the TweetUp or the AWP Scavenger Hunt. Broaden your horizons, and look for opportunities to grow professionally.

It's important and encouraged to discuss your various literary roles with other attendees. If you're an editor conversing with another editor about your respective publications, you might want to mention what you are working on as a writer as well. Your fellow editor might be able to point you in the direction of one of her colleagues who is looking for something similar. While some could justifiably argue otherwise, networking is one of the most important reasons to attend AWP. Take the time to get to know writers, journals, and/or publishers that you've been reading, or have formed an online relationship with. When I attended the conference, I sat down with Submittable to tell them how their product had greatly enhanced my journal, while also sharing some of my ideas of things I'd like to see in the software. I was also able to meet some journals I've admired for a while in the book fair just by stopping by to say I loved their design, or a certain essay or poem they had published.

Panels: Planning ahead, and what to do when your plans fall through

Attending AWP for the first time is similar to visiting Disneyworld for the first time. There is so much anticipation and planning—and no matter how stringent the schedule you create, you will inevitably be unable to see everything you came for. Like the advice I was given before the first trip I took to Disney as a young adult, the advice I was given from all veteran AWP attendees was "pace yourself." In both cases, I promised them (and myself) that I would. Vowed it, even. And as quickly as I vowed, I broke my vows. For AWP, I created a detailed listing (panel name, presenters, time, room number, one-sentence summary) for each day of the conference. A writing colleague and I even teamed up and planned to tackle separate presentations so that we could share the notes from the panels we each missed.

There are panels in various disciplines, such as craft, pedagogy, genre-specific or even readings by authors. Only you can know what panel will suit your needs, but it is wise to consider your needs beforehand. Some would argue the best course of action is to simply attend a mixed group—a few readings, a few craft panels, and some on pedagogy. At the Boston AWP conference, I found it best to attend panels that seemed to be informative. I wanted takeaways; a set of tangible suggestions that I could put into practice in my own career.

Remember that whatever type of panel you choose to attend will be filled with like-minded individuals. People who attend readings are either interested in the author reading or the subject matter. I have friends who have read on a panel about military service. They connected with poets and essayists who had either served in the military or had deep connections to the military. If you attend a panel on starting up a literary journal, you will absolutely find people who have either recently started their own journals or who are considering it. Such panels are where you can meet mentors or, in some cases, mentees.

Some advice: Arrive at the panels early. Not only will they fill up, but you'll want to talk to the attendees around you. At a panel on finding funding this year, I exchanged email addresses with a fellow writer who had different experiences than I did looking for funding. Now we can share resources with each other. After another panel on the future of flash nonfiction, I entered into a conversation with writers who had no clue where to submit their work, so I passed out my journal's business cards.

Some panels will be intimate, with small audiences sitting close to presenters. Others will be full to the brim, with attendees standing or sitting on the floor. You might be the fastest of all speed walkers, but still not make it to the room in time to get a seat. Like me, you may even end up one of the first people locked out of a panel, despite arriving ten minutes early. Dinty Moore was also one of those lucky people—and he was set to speak on the panel. He, along with the rest of us, was forced to wait outside of the room until space cleared in the room and he was allowed in. The rest of us were forced to find a new panel to attend. This is where serendipity kicks in. I decided to enter the panel starting across the hall. The panel I stumbled into ended up being one my greatest finds.

The Book Fair is to AWP as Magic Kingdom is to Walt Disney World

You have to go to the book fair. There is no way of avoiding it. But beware; it is colossal and overwhelming. There are people everywhere. When I first stepped foot into the book fair, I wanted to step out of it just as quickly. It was sensory overload. Unfortunately, that never changes. The book fair is not a place to be shy. It is incredibly easy to be intimidated; you may be afraid to introduce yourself, but don't give in to your fears. Force yourself to be outgoing; introduce yourself and spark conversations.

Planning for the book fair can be just as important (if not more important) than planning your panel schedule. Before you get on the plane, or the train, or the automobile to whatever city will host AWP next, make a list of the journals or presses you'd love to meet. The schedules and exhibitor spaces are listed online. Mark down where you can find your favorite journals. This list doesn't (and shouldn't) be very long, as you will inevitably encounter other booths or journals you hadn't heard of before or realized you were interested in. Where you stop will depend on your goals. Some people might want to meet and thank editors who they've worked with. Other attendees might want to pitch ideas to publishers and journals. Some simply want to donate to the journals they read. After you've made your list, visit those places. Shake hands, make friends. And then, after taking a bit of a break from the book fair, go back in. Start on one side and slowly make your way down each aisle, stopping at booths you find interesting. This was probably my favorite part of the conference. I met so many kind, creative, interesting individuals that I wouldn't have had access to if I'd only attended panels and visited booths I had planned on.

Thankfully for us all, the conference does an excellent job of organizing the book fair—even if you failed to plan your list ahead of time. At any time, you can locate the name of the journal or publisher you'd like to meet, and its booth number will be listed in the conference catalog, an enormous volume you'll receive at the registration booth on your first day. There are signs everywhere, and the majority of booths are easy to find. If your journal or press has opted to rent space in the book fair, then invest in marketing materials. A huge sign or something else to make you stand out from the crowd is worth every cent. As I mentioned previously, my senses were overworked, and the booths that captured my attention were the ones that clearly set themselves apart, yet didn't overtake their own space.

Prominent journals, presses, foundations, and other such organizations rent space in the book fair. Even appointments for job interviews take place there. In some instances, colleges and universities will schedule interviews for faculty positions to take place at the book fair over the duration of the conference. This is something you'll want to prepare for quite early. Most colleges and universities open positions between the late spring to early fall, so will begin the screening process in the fall. Prepare your resume, ask for references and apply for positions the year before you attend AWP. Request an interview, or an appointment to meet face to face, with the colleges in which you're interested. If you weren't offered an interview prior to the conference, don't give up. Prepare a professional resume or curriculum vitae along with a personalized cover letter specific to each school you have interest in and also a statement of teaching philosophy. Then make sure to stop by the booths of your prospective employers. Ask to speak to the program director, and if they aren't at the booth, come back when they will be there. Hand deliver your professional package and let them know you are interested in a position at their school. Make yourself memorable, and don't be afraid to ask for a formal interview with them.

Networking aside, the book fair is an incredible place to purchase books. You'll most often buy them directly from the press, thereby putting more money in the press's hands (versus the deep pockets of big retailers). Finally, another very popular reason people love the book fair is the swag. Oh, the swag. Some booths give out free copies of their journal, while others have tiny knick knacks like pens or stickers. Some are more adventurous and give away temporary tattoos or packets of tea. Others allow you to play games for the chance to win a prize. So don't forget to bring a big enough bag (or backpack) to hold all your goodies.

Notes from a first-time attendee

I registered online as soon as registration opened, and after seeing the line on the morning of the first day (which lasted until quite late into the afternoon) grow through the ballroom and out into the lobby, I'm grateful that I did. Save yourself grief and time that you could have spent in panels or at the book fair, and register before the conference begins.

Not only should you register before the event, but you should also plan your travels early. Consider climate and traveling time. Book a hotel room early if you are coming from far away and need to do so; many panel presenters were delayed at the Boston AWP because of the snow storms and missed their presentations. Some attendees missed a day of events because their flights were delayed. Because of my close proximity to the conference, I didn't book a room. However, the awful weather forced me to find housing the first day. I was lucky to crash on a friend's couch, as the conference hotel was sold out for the event. Book your rooms early for the best rate and a guaranteed place to stay.

Don't forget to experience life outside of the conference. The beautiful thing about the AWP conference is that it's held in a different location every year. There's always something new to see and experience. Be a tourist in the city you're visiting. Let the sights and smells and people influence your writing. Take everything in. Or, if you want to focus your trip solely on literature, and have no interest in sightseeing, consider attending some of the many off-site, AWP-sponsored or affiliated literary events.

Be inspired. You will be surrounded by creative people doing incredible things. Soak it up.

Follow Up

The conference is over, and you're unloading a heavy backpack (and maybe a few extra bags) worth of business cards, flyers, pens, knick-knacks, books and journals you've picked up at the book fair or panels. You'll wonder what to do with everything you have, and briefly consider throwing the majority in the trash. Do not do that. I repeat, do not trash the items you've brought home from AWP. Organize, and reach out to the people you connected with. If people gave you their business cards, head over to their websites and leave a comment. Send a quick email to presses whose tables you visited just saying that you were happy to meet with them and would like to keep in touch. Send follow up emails and phone calls to people you met with directly, whether program directors or editors who voiced interest in your work. You are your best advocate; don't risk waiting for others to reach out to you. Follow up with them.

*W*riters seeking information and inspiration from their peers don't have to look very far; indeed, the number of organizations and publications serving writers is extraordinary. Do yourself a favor and don't involve yourself in everything that seems relevant. Too much can be unwieldy and expensive. Choose just a few subscriptions and memberships, and later on re-evaluate to make sure you are receiving value for your investment.

Associations, Memberships and Subscriptions for Writers

by Ashley C. Andersen Zantop and Michael Bayer

Selecting the right industry organizations to belong to and the right publications to subscribe to can be challenging given the myriad available, but making these connections is important. Writing and publishing organizations and publications that reflect your writing interests and values can help you stay connected to the larger community and help you understand the trends in your industry. The stronger your understanding of your industry, other like-minded writers and your customers, the better you'll be able to navigate the challenges and opportunities of your piece of the writer's marketplace. In some cases you may be able to derive other worthwhile benefits like access to group or discounted health insurance rates, legal advice, contract evaluation services and discounted conference registration fees. The following is a non-exhaustive list of these types of groups and publications, but this list doesn't do justice to the variety you'll find when you embark on your own search.

National/International Organizations

Association of Writers and Writing Programs (AWP), www.awpwriter.org

The Author's Guild, www.authorsguild.org

The Crime Writer's Association, www.thecwa.co.uk

Christian Writer's Guild, www.christianwritersguild.com

International Thriller Writers (ITW), www.thrillerwriters.org

The International Women's Writing Guild (IWWG), www.iwwg.org

Jewish Writer's Association, www.jscribe.com

Modern Language Association, www.mla.org

Muslim Writers Society, www.oneummah.net

Mystery Writers of America, www.myterywriters.org

National Writers Union, www.nwu.org

National Writers Association, www.nationalwriters.com

National Sportscasters and Sportswriters Association, www.nssafame.com

National Association of Memoir Writers, www.namw.org

Pen American Center, www.pen.org

Poetry Society of America, www.poetrysociety.org

Poetry Foundation, www.poetryfoundation.org

Romance Writers of America. www.rwa.org

Science Fiction and Fantasy Writers of America, www.sfwa.org

Society of Children's Book Writers and Illustrators, www.scbwi.org

Regional Organizations

Connecticut Sports Writers Alliance, www.ctsportswriters.org

Florida Writers Association, www.floridawriters.net

Georgia Writers Association, www.georgiawriters.org

League of Vermont Writers, www.leagueofvermontwriters.org

Michigan Writers, www.michwriters.org

New York State Outdoor Writers Association, www.nysowa.org

Southern California Writers Association, www.ocwriter.com

Washington Poets Association, www.washingtonpoets.org

Writers League of Texas, www.writersleague.org

Publications

The New Yorker, www.newyorker.com

The New York Times, www.nytimes.com

Poets & Writers, www.pw.org

Publisher's Marketplace, www.publishersmarketplace.com

Publisher's Weekly, www.publishersweekly.com

Shelf Awareness, www.shelf-awareness.com

The Writer, www.writermag.com

Writer's Digest, www.writersdigest.com

Conferences and Trade Shows
by Ashley C. Andersen Zantop

Conferences and trade shows are immersive venues for learning about the writing and publishing industries, connecting with other writers and publishers and continuing your professional development. While often held simultaneously and sponsored by the same organizations, it's important to understand that conferences and trade shows are not the same thing.

Conferences are generally designed and executed around the principle of professional development: creating educational opportunities for participants around a topic or range of topics. The conference organizer makes money by charging you a fee for an interesting menu of programming. If they're good at what they do, you're happy or at least willing to pay for it. As Michael Bayer describes in his article on the subject, writers' conferences are wonderful places to continue your learning and development as a writer, understand new trends, build new skills and make connections with other writers.

Trade shows and trade associations are more often organized around the principle of commerce—faciliating it and developing it—for the industry in question. Trade show organizers make money by charging exhibitors (usually vendors of some type) to display their goods and services to conference attendees, who are usually customers or key industry contacts for those exhibitors. While trade shows may not be created with the sole purpose of driving professional development and further learning in a field—although this surely helps facilitate commerce indirectly—publishing industry trade shows are terrific venues for learning more about your potential customers and your readership. If you want your work to succeed with publishers who sell to libraries, for example, what better place to learn about how that segment of the industry works than at the annual American Library Association trade show? Exhibitors are usually publishers or other service providers who sell to libraries, and attendees are usually librarians from around the United States. As a writer, that's a rare opportunity to interact with both your customer and your audience all in one place. Unlike a writer's conference, any programming provided during the trade show will likely be focused on issues facing that piece of the industry—libraries directly, in this case, rather than writers of books for libraries. Undoubtedly topics of interest will overlap; for instance, how should publishers and authors be compensated for eBooks circulated in a library's collection? If that's your primary source of compensation as a writer, you'll be just as interested in that answer as your publisher who sells eBooks to libraries.

More and more, trade associations are organizing joint conferences and trade shows to attract as many industry participants as possible—consistent high attendance rates help differentiate inconsequential trade events from the influential hubs of commerce some have become. There are dozens to hundreds of possibly applicable conferences and trade shows in the United States alone each year, so your time and budget will likely demand that you choose amongst them carefully. Start by selecting the best or most applicable to your current goals or those you can attend locally to save time and expense. The following is an incomplete list of major conferences, trade shows and trade associations and resources for locating such events. Good luck and enjoy the exploration.

CONFERENCES

AWP Annual Conference & Bookfair; http://www.awpwriter.org/conference/

Association of Writers and Writing Program's annual conference and bookfair event, which includes seminars, panels and keynote speakers for writers, writing programs and the writing community. This also includes a book fair and trade show event for small presses, literary journals and other publications.

Digital Book World (DBW);
http://www.digitalbookworld.com/conferences/
Digital Book World, StoryWorld and Digital Book World
Discoverability and Marketing conferences address the digital
publishing industry trends in publishing, narrative, user experience,
buying habits and discoverability. The annual Digital Book World
event in Manhattan each January includes a small trade show for
exhibitors, but this event is predominantly a series of presentations,
panels and discussions for publishers, authors and booksellers.

NewPages.Com;
http://www.newpages.com/writing-conferences
A listing of writing conferences, workshops, retreats, centers,
residencies, book and literary festivals in the United States
by region.

ShawGuides; www.shawguides.com
An online resource that allows you to search for conferences and
workshops in and outside of North America by month, region
and genre (Autobiography/Memoir, Business/Technical, Children's,
Fiction, Horror, Humor, Journalism, Marketing, Mystery, Nature,
Non-fiction, Playwriting, Poetry, Publishing, Religion, Romance,
ScienceFiction/Fantasy, Screenwriting, Travel, Young Adult)

ThrillerFest; www.thrillerfest.com
An annual conference, awards and celebration of thriller writers
and thriller writing. This is an example of several genre-specific
conferences and events now held annually or bi-annually around
the world. If you identify with a particular genre of writing, do an
online search for conferences or associations in your genre.

Writers Conference & Centers (WC&C);
www.writersconf.org
An online resource that allows you to search for regional,
national and international writers' conferences, centers, festivals,
residencies and retreats. Search by region and/or genre (fiction,
creative nonfiction, poetry, children's literature, playwriting and
screenwriting), including scholarship-funded opportunities.

Wikipedia;
http://en.wikipedia.org/wiki/List_of_writers%27_conferences
A list of domestic and international writers' conferences in English.

TRADE SHOWS AND ASSOCIATIONS

American Library Association (ALA);
http://www.ala.org/conferenceevents/
The ALA hosts roundtables, conferences, tradeshows, forums and
other educational events attended by American public and school
librarians, publishers, distributors and authors. At the tradeshows,
publishers and distributors provide the bulk of the tradeshow
exhibits and often host author signings and Advance Reading Copy
(ARC) giveaways.

American Booksellers Association;
http://www.bookweb.org/resources/regionals.html
A listing of regional independent bookseller associations with links
to their regional book fairs and trade shows.

Association of Canadian Publishers (ACP);
http://publishers.ca/links/bookfairs-a-tradeshows.html
The Association of Canadian Publishers is similar to the
Independent Book Publishers Association noted below, so the
content of this site is directed primarily at publishers, but they
provide a terrific listing of Canadian, American and, in particular,
international book fairs and tradeshows on this site. Handy for
publishers and writers alike.

Bologna Children's Book Fair;
http://www.bookfair.bolognafiere.it/en/info/
If you're interested in children's literature, this might be the most
charming book fair, industry tradeshow or conference you can
attend. The events include a tradeshow, educational programming,
an agent's center, an illustrator's exhibition and the Tools of
Change conference, all dedicated to children's publishing and
media. Bologna, Italy, is a university town loaded with cultural
events and destinations, beautiful historic architecture and

delicious food. Worth a trip at least once, if you can afford it (or get a publisher to afford it for you).

Book Expo America (BEA); www.bookexpoamerica.com
An international (but more heavily focused on North America) publishing industry tradeshow and conference including discussions, panels, blogworld and new media expo. Publishers and distributors provide the bulk of the tradeshow exhibits and often host author signings and Advance Reading Copy (ARC) giveaways.

Frankfurt International Book Fair;
http://www.buchmesse.de/en/fbf/
One of the largest international book fairs/tradeshows in the world, attracting publishers, literary agents, distributors, and booksellers from all over the world. Publishers and distributors provide the bulk of the tradeshow exhibits and often host author signings and Advance Reading Copy (ARC) giveaways.

Independent Book Publishers Association;
http://www.ibpa-online.org/
The content of this site is directed primarily at independent publishers, rather than authors specifically, but there is useful information about the industry to be found here. Scroll down the homepage for a listing of upcoming events including regional book fairs, tradeshows and conferences.

Chapter 5

WRITE

edited by Adele Annesi

All writers write, right?
What happens when you don't? Adele Annesi explores a variety
of strategies, tools and attitudes to keep you writing, even when life
threatens to usurp your opportunity to create.

*O*ne reason writers fail to keep writing and achieve their goals isn't just that the demands of life interfere with writing. It's that we let those demands have the final say in whether or not we write. Yet, one reality writers don't actively call to memory, and that MFA programs may not emphasize enough, is that in the same way that eating builds appetite (so say the French), writing rekindles the desire to write. To help MFA grads keep writing, accomplish their publication goals and enjoy the benefits of this hard-earned degree, this chapter covers ways to write as much as possible as often as possible.

Any life-changing event can permanently disrupt and derail even the most diligent writer. Having a child is one example. Yet, this writer, author, professor, Ph.D., poet—oh, yes, and mom—found a way to work through her life-changing event, and to flourish as a result. Let her lessons guide you, too.

Life Happens: How to Keep Writing Anyway
by Suzanne Matson

When I was expecting my first child, a colleague from my university had this advice for getting writing done after the baby came: "Don't do anything when the baby is asleep that you can do when he is awake." In other words, don't do laundry, take a shower, cook, shop, or exercise when he is asleep. You can do all that when he is awake, even if he isn't always happy that he doesn't have your undivided attention. What you can't do when he is awake—and so must save until his head hits the pillow—is read and write.

I credit this advice with saving my writing life throughout early parenthood. I followed it religiously, and wrote my first novel, *The Hunger Moon*, during my firstborn's naptime. New mothers sometimes look at me cross-eyed when I tell them this, and it's true that all my boys were exceptional nappers. So some luck was involved. But it's also true that I regarded any and all naps as my literary space. I didn't go running into their rooms at the first little noise they made in their cribs when they were waking up, and found that they would often fall back asleep for an extra ten or twenty minutes. They were very good nappers, yes, but it's also possible that holding fast to every minute of my writing time helped turn them into the power nappers they became.

The boot camp of new parenthood taught me how precious writing time is, and how it must be ruthlessly grabbed and guarded whenever possible, even if the available chunk is an hour, rather than a day. What can you get done in an hour? Plenty, if you use it. A paragraph or a page, both are progress. I'm the first to admit how difficult it is to get your head into writing after being caught up in bills or laundry or dishes or yard work—not to mention whatever else you do from nine to five that brings home a paycheck.

I still struggle with this, but I've learned some tricks. I start by giving myself the small and manageable assignment of reading what I've written the day before. Even a sleep-deprived or distracted writer can open a file and fasten her eyes on a block of text. Getting an "in" to the writing is sometimes the most valuable move of all. It's the rare writer who can read an unrevised paragraph of work and not want to start tinkering, making small changes and improvements to the language. By the time you reach the end of yesterday's passage, you'll be writing, especially if you've done the smart thing the day before, and left off in the middle of a scene or sentence that you know how you want to finish.

Poems, I grant, usually have to be birthed in whole first drafts. But, in poetry, a quick spill is often the best kind of lyric draft, which makes the "read and tinker" assignment all the more valuable, since, in my experience, many, many revisions are what make a finished poem.

With or without kids, the business of daily life will always try to get its tentacles around your writing time. If it's not family life or a day job, it will be distractions like the false imperative of social media—tending your blog, updating your Facebook and LinkedIn sites, tweeting. All that stuff will play a role in getting the word out about your work, but only if you've got finished, published work to tweet about.

No matter how slender the increments of your writing time, use them. Say no to anything else you can decently say no to—the bake sale, the committee assignment, the editing favor for a friend (say instead, "Let's trade pages when I've got my story done"). Then, when you've put in your hour, or morning, or however much time you've been lucky enough to carve out, go play with your kids or hang with your partner. They're the ones who help you keep it all in perspective when a story or a batch of poems or an essay comes back with a "no, thank you," or when your grant or fellowship application goes unfunded. They're the ones who celebrate madly with you when the good news comes. So go ahead, say yes to all of it—the day job (and who, after all, can say no to that?), the family stuff (there's a lot you can get done in a car while waiting for lacrosse practice to end) and, yes, the writing life. Don't wait for the clean house, the perfect silence, the round hour. Seize what's possible; make peace with the fragmentary; love the unruly energy that comes from the stolen moment.

*I*f you tell yourself you'll wait until you find the right time—and place—to write, you could be waiting forever. Enter the writer's residency. There's something about getting out of your routine, usual head space and tyranny of urgency that can jump-start your work in a way that nothing else can. If you think residencies are out of your price range or too far out of your way, think again. Put aside these false notions and others that make residencies seem expensive and exclusionary. Instead, let your writer's imagination be wooed away to just the right place, and one you can afford, with this enticing exploration by writer, author and professor Karen Osborn, who encourages writers to take more than a stolen moment, but an extended retreat.

The Writer's Retreat
by Karen Osborn

I arrive at the Virginia Center for the Creative Arts (VCCA) in Amherst, Virginia, in late May after dark, dropped off by a couple who used to work at the VCCA and now run a cab service between the residency and the airport and train station. They show me the cubbyhole where my keys have been left and walk me down the dark, silent hallways. My room, a bit larger than a monk's cell, contains little furniture except a neatly made up bed, a dresser, and a night table. There's a shared bathroom next to it.

So begins my three-week writing residency. The VCCA grants fellowships to artists, writers, and composers. Each fellow is given a private bedroom and a separate, private studio located in a refurbished barn a fifteen-minute walk from the residency. Participants eat breakfast and dinner in the residency dining room, and lunch is delivered to the studio. The food is always delicious and plentiful. I wake just after sunrise, sometimes spending an hour or so in my studio writing before breakfast. The dining room is large enough for one to sit alone in privacy, and posted signs state that some fellows may wish to not speak at meals. This gives me permission to maintain the silence I need to descend into the world of my work. I sit in a corner with a bowl of oatmeal or a plate of eggs. Sometimes, I read over what I've written the day before. Then, I gather up my things and trek out to my barn where I'll spend the day in my studio.

The path to the studio cuts through grassy fields bordered by maple trees and rhododendron. The Blue Ridge Mountains hug the edge of the woods, and a glance in any direction reveals their gentle curves. It's greener here than in New England, where I'm from, and as I walk I feel the full burst of early summer. Roses bloom along the path, and horses gather by a fence where I will go to write. The morning is warm, the sky overhead clear blue. In the distance, a hawk dips toward earth.

My workspace has a large wooden desk, a bookshelf, a quilted bed, a rocking chair, and, most importantly, a picture window that overlooks the landscape. On the nights when I work late, I will sleep here. All around me, in similar rooms, other artists and writers are at work. In the silence, I feel their efforts, like the early hum of summer. In this first week, I hunger for this space, the limitless time, the lack of constraints. I don't have to be anywhere, do anything but write. My cell phone is off, and my automated email response will notify people that I'm away. This first week there is only my writing, and I can't get enough of it.

I arrive early at my studio each morning and begin writing. Lunch is served in an open space in the barn. Some residents break from their work to sit at the picnic tables where they can watch the horses. Others, like me, carry a plate back to their studios. I write at my desk all morning and afternoon. While I sit at a table with others at dinner, I usually return to my studio afterward. I move back and forth between writing a new short story and a novel. Outside my window horses run through the pasture or stand at the fence—sleek, dark brown, lovely.

As I slowly settle into a routine, I observe that I'm pushing, and I realize that in my hunger for my work, I'm exhausting myself so that at the end of the first week I'm tired, too spent at times to be effective. It takes a few days to relax this stance, soften my routine. Some artists hold open studios and a couple of the writers give readings. After dinner, rather than return to my work, I walk with a poet or an essayist. We tell stories and jokes, and talk about how language unwinds for us. We discover the herd of cattle that shares the pasture with the long drive that leads out to the road. One night I meet another novelist who is a game player, and we establish a ritual of spending an hour at word games. This demand on my brain turns off my normal thinking, and when I return to my work everything is changed. I see a new direction for the action or a side of a character that didn't exist before. The rhythms of my sentences have an added dimension. Each day in the silence of the mornings and afternoons, my written voice grows stronger.

During my three weeks at the VCCA, I seldom leave—once for a group trip to the Sweet Brier library, once to see a new Woody Allen film, and once to go to the Sonic drive-in for milkshakes. After the first week, as my desire to do nothing but work subsides, I fall into a routine of work (I still write eight to ten hours each day) and pleasure. I gaze at paintings and sculptures in-progress and attend impromptu concerts. I hear other writers read poetry and fiction. All of this feeds my writing and nourishes my spirit. Yet, the true gift of the residency is silence and the permission afforded by fellow residents to descend fully into the work. We are all here to participate in this descending, and our collective absorption with creative work produces not only a sense of permission, but also an energy that is palpable, exciting.

Writing retreats, sometimes referred to as writing residencies, are offered in locations all over the country. Many of these retreats cost nothing for the writer, and while the VCCA, like some, requests a modest contribution to offset escalating expenses, they don't turn anyone down who can't afford to contribute. The main part of the application involves a sample of written work. Winter, fall, and spring are less competitive than summer months, so summer applicants who are turned down can find it worthwhile to resubmit for a different season. The residency lengths vary based on the program, and often are decided by the writer. One writer friend of mine is enjoying a month-long residency in Spain. He applied to at least a dozen places and was turned down by most, but the residency in Spain was one of several that accepted him. Treat your submission for a residency as you would the submission of your work for publication. Apply to several places and be persistent. The space and silence in which to find and develop your voice await you.

—◆—

$\mathcal{W}$riting is like getting healthy. We all make promises, tell ourselves it will be good for us if we exercise more, eat healthier. But what about telling ourselves not only that we'll enjoy the results, we'll enjoy the process. More than professional benefits to making the time to write, there are personal benefits, too—ones you won't get any other way. The key is to call to mind the joy of writing, and then just do it.

Afternoon Delight: A Cup of Tea and a Writing Fix
by Rebecca Dimyan

Our days begin as they do each and every morning: The sun rises, we rise, routines unfurl in perfunctory breaths. We fall easily into the comfortable curves of the morning, letting ourselves become focused on the many things that must get done—the work, the household chores, the errands. And it becomes too easy to forget that we are writers, and writers must write. If we look for the time to sit and pull out our notebooks or laptops, to try and find those invaluable moments among the countless important things that cram the space of our days, we will not find it. Instead, we must make the time, set aside a short hour, or even half hour, to allow ourselves to indulge in our love of the written word.

A few days a week, in the late afternoon, I stop at my favorite local coffeehouse. After devoting my morning to work-related phone calls and deadlines, a sink filled with last night's dishes, and, finally, a grocery store run, I find myself needing to recharge and refocus for the rest of the busy day. Like many people, I purchase a hot, caffeinated beverage. But my afternoon boost is not yet complete; I find a seat by the window overlooking the main thoroughfare. I set up my laptop on the chipped wooden table and recline in the stiff-backed, velour-cushioned seat. I observe the people coming and going, their casual interactions with the amiable baristas, the speeding cars. And for thirty, forty, or maybe even sixty uninterrupted minutes, I write.

Words pour onto the blank white space of the computer screen: "I did not know I was lost until I came upon an old man on a dirt road." The one sentence I had been struggling to write for weeks was finally completed in perfect Times New Roman twelve point font. The beginning of the piece I had been working on for the last few months began to take shape in those few words, words that came to me only because I had taken the time to sit at a chipped table in a busy coffee shop window and let my mind wander unrepressed by the burdens of the day.

On a different afternoon, I sit at the same table watching the interaction between the construction workers outside. Something about the way one man laughs casually as if he is chatting with a friend in a bar, not a co-worker in the midst of a hard day's work, inspires three new pages of my novel. On that particular afternoon at the coffee shop, I only spent thirty minutes writing, but for that brief period of time, I could simply be a writer. Not a busy adult with obligations and a litany of things that really must get done. I am the person who decided to pursue my love of writing by getting an MFA, and I am remembering to use it.

During this all too short afternoon break, I am fueling my body with caffeine, but I am recharging my mind by allowing my creative energy to flow unfettered, channeling it into the words I love so much and the process of stringing them into sentences and pages. Having a specific place where I go to participate in this twice- or thrice-weekly ritual adds comfort and excitement to the tradition. Each time I walk into the tiny shop, the smell of freshly brewed coffee greeting me as warmly as the smiles on the employees' faces, I feel as though I am coming to my safe place, the place that has become synonymous with writing time. I know when I leave I will have the sense of satisfaction and accomplishment that comes from having written something that day. I will also experience the mental acuity that is the direct result of getting my creative thoughts out of my head and onto paper, making room for other thoughts that need attention. At the end of the day, I take solace in the familiarity of the routine and inspiration from the observations I make while sitting at my table by the window.

"Who will teach me to write? asks Annie Dillard, and who will keep me writing? Although it may be the page that will teach the writer to write, as this next essay observes, it is the writer who keeps on writing."

To Learn to Write and Keep Writing
by Bonnie Cook

When I was close to finishing my MFA, panic gripped me. Without the camaraderie of workshops and the support of mentors, without the readings and seminars, the sharing over dinner or a drink, how would I carry on? I worried that I wouldn't continue writing without imposed deadlines, and I didn't have anyone to read my work, calm my fears and give me feedback. Graduating felt akin to being dropped on a deserted isle.

By myself, how would I do all the experts said I needed to do (finish my book, get an agent, build a platform, launch an online presence, market myself, submit work, find a publisher—or self-publish—and market the book) to be successful?

After the inevitable post-graduation letdown, I asked myself: Why had I undertaken an MFA in the first place? What was *my* standard of success?

People enroll in MFAs and other writing programs for myriad reasons: to improve their writing, make academic and writerly connections, further their career and employability, and learn how to live the writing life, which usually means getting published and earning a living from writing.

Most students in my MFA program were talented twenty-somethings on fire to make a life in the writing world, but when I entered the program, I had rounded sixty and already had a Master of Arts and a career in teaching. I entered the program to keep a promise to myself to write a book before I died—to release the burden placed on me by a seventh grade teacher who expected me to write the Great American Novel. I also enrolled to keep from going under when the floodwaters of life were rising and I wasn't sure I could swim. What I sought had more to do with self-improvement than livelihood. (In my more illusory moments, I admit imagining myself on Oprah, brilliantly discussing my bestselling memoir.)

There were others like me in the program, older students who wanted more: to fulfill a neglected dream to write a book, record the story of their families' lives, improve their skills enough to change or start a new career, or support and expand their writing skills simply because they loved to write. Like me, many were there to transform life wounds into more, something called art, to "transform anger into steaming red tulips," as Natalie Goldberg said.

Some say writing isn't therapy, yet it's often therapeutic. Through writing, wounds are healed, revelations revealed. Sometimes the writer doesn't know the work will be transformative, but, then, there it is. Some of us went to the MFA to consciously do that work; others discovered it en route. Drowning in the dissolution of a marriage, I found the MFA a lifeboat. The glut of memoirs dealing with the traumas of life shows I am not alone.

In the writing life, there is room for all of us: those who will publish and become widely famous; those who will teach and modestly, heroically, nurture the talent in others; those record-keepers who write one book, one memoir, one diary, the treasure of which might one day enlighten future generations. Others continue to put their poems in drawers. It doesn't matter.

H. D. Thoreau said, "The youth gets together his materials to build a bridge to the moon, or perchance a palace or a temple on the earth, and at length the middle-aged man concludes to build a wood-shed with them." And what a shed Thoreau built!

Writing assumes an audience, but writing is also for the author, because in the act of creating, something happens; something is transformed. Writing helps break part of the old self away to make room for the new. It uncovers and opens, and that sacred art, that act of creation, is in itself holy, worthy, even if the work it produces never reaches the bestseller list. In seeking to understand, we become more wholly ourselves.

Annie Dillard says, "I write because I am trying to come alive, and I write out of hurt and how to make hurt okay; how to make myself strong and come home ... We shall always want waking."

So, what to do after completing an MFA? First, ask yourself again why you write? Then honor yourself and your dream, and if your dream is to become really good and get published, to become a writer who supports himself or herself, who becomes, why not say it, rich and famous, go for it with gusto, and make of this writing life the best you can dream.

If your goal is not to sit on Oprah's stage, don't be intimidated by the rush of the world. Be who you are. Walk the path least trod. Honor yourself and your work. Don't worry overmuch about what the world screams at you. Not all genuine acts of love and art need to be in the marketplace. The writing required to earn an MFA is valuable in itself, and can be a lesson in how to live life holding onto dreams, driving that car in the dark and leaning into the light, even if you never publish a thing.

I may never write the Great American Novel, but that's okay; that work is better left to those on fire. I learned that I don't come easily to the long writing hours and isolation of most writers' lives. Does that make me not a writer? Does it consign me to the detestable rank of dilettante? Perhaps, but that, too, is okay.

What I seek is more inward. All the frenzy of platform building on Facebook, Twitter and blogs is disquieting. Instead, I want to get quiet, listen deeply, peel away the layers of self-delusion and expectation, and live and write as honestly and skillfully as I can. The rest, I trust, will take care of itself. With age comes the luxury of balance: a little meditation, reading, exercise, a manageable amount of teaching, a modest amount of writing, along with more travel and time with friends. When I yearn for a workshop, I sign up for a conference or retreat. When I missed feedback, I started a writers' group.

When the inevitable doubts about writing arise after "the program" is done, remember to return to your reasons and dreams, to listen first to *your* self, your life. Though your path may be similar to others, it is not the same as that of any other—it is your path.

Surely, MFA'ers, now that we are more practiced, more adept, will be better able to walk our own writing path. So use the tools in this book to further your experience and expression of writing, but don't forget why *you* are writing. And remember, there is no such thing as a deserted isle. We may walk our own paths in our own way, but we are always in the company of those who put words to paper.

In workshop, we laughed from delight and amusement, revelation and sometimes frustration. At times, we despaired, found ourselves in tears. How would we ever do this? How would we get through, finish? We struggled to be brave despite doubt and occasional self-loathing, engendered by the evil-twin voice that whispered *not good enough, never good enough*. Sometimes we thought our honest workshop mates might be evil twins personified. Why couldn't they get how hard we'd worked? How good the writing really was? After our tirades and the mentor pep talks (and perhaps more wine), on we'd go—rethinking, revising and re-envisioning, reworking, rewriting, readjusting. Like life. Pressing on, pressing against the odds, holding onto dreams, driving in the dark, leaning into the light.

Just as there's no best way to diet and exercise that works for everyone all the time, there's no single-best way that will always keep writers writing. What works for the working mom may not work for the aesthete, the artist or the technocrat. But when you find yourself flagging, change your approach. Be intentional, creative, deliberate, dedicated and knowledgeable, but above all keep writing and use these techniques to achieve your goal. Having a variety of tools in your writing tool belt is a strategy that works for the same reason we subscribe to writing magazines, attend conferences, go on retreats that regularly remind us of what we already know—we need to keep writing, and writing builds the appetite for more.

Technically Speaking—and Writing; Software and Other Writing Aids, Tricks and Tools
by Adele Annesi

As writers wrest their time through stolen moments, grand-theft retreats and the deliberate delight of an afternoon coffee break, there's still that in-between time in the car, on the train or on a power walk. If there's always room for Jell-O, there's always an opportunity to write, and probably and app for it, too.

Advanced English and Thesaurus Dictionary from Mobile Systems helps writers increase their vocabulary, create word categories and lists, save last-visited words for reference, and learn more about language.

Daedalus Touch text editor from The Soulmen has none of the usual file lists, folders, or documents, but uses paper stacks and sheets. It offers always-on global search, a responsive editor for texts that can reach 20,000 words and more, and full iCloud sync and backup.

Documents 2 from SavySoda lets users take documents anywhere via Wi-Fi, Google, or Email. You can view and edit lots of document types on the fly.

Dragon Dictation from Nuance Communications is a voice recognition application that uses Dragon NaturallySpeaking to allow users to dictate content and instantly see texts and email.

Evernote from Evernote helps writers create and edit text notes and task lists; save, sync and share files; organize notes by notebooks and tags; and more.

iA Writer from Information Architects allows writers to create content without the usual distractions of word-processing programs.

My Daily Journal from JI Software lets writers create daily journals and keep them secure. It supports dictation, categorization, Twitter integration and sharing, and search by date.

My Writing Desk from Wombat Apps enables writers to create their work distraction-free via an enhanced keyboard, and features full text search, document sort, spellcheck, export and more.

Pages word processor from Apple enables writers to create, edit, and view documents from any location. Documents can be edited, customized and formatted, and images can be added.

Writer's Studio from miSoft lets users create e-books, presentations, story books with narration, and event books with sound that they can save and share.

Most apps are optimized for the iPhone 5, and work with the iPhone, iPod touch, and iPad.

Chapter *6*

CONVICTION, COMMITMENT AND FORGIVENESS

edited by Erin A. Corriveau

All writers struggle to create at one time or another. In this chapter, explore both practical and inspirational ways to ensure you remain committed to your craft and your life. Look at proven methods to manage conflicting priorities and set goals. Learn to what and whom successful writers turn for motivation and creativity.

Ode to the Cursor

by Zac Zander

The cursor on the computer screen is a heartbeat; something that I desperately want to kill by finishing a sentence or even finishing a word. But, still, it blinks its vertical eye hoping to be pushed farther down the page face. And does it really ever die? Am I just hoping that at some point I will be able to look at the scattered letters and words and phrases and see finality while the cursor still blinks?

It's been a month since I have written anything, and I believe that this cursor will live forever, wishing to be put to sleep. Maybe I should sleep. I wake up in the middle of the night with stretches of imagination and genius waiting to be transferred to some paper or screen, but it is my dreariness that fools me into thinking that, "I'll remember this tomorrow."

The next morning, I force myself into the chair at the desk, and the cursor meets me right where I had left it. The cursor is not a heartbeat anymore but a reminder; I must not be a punching bag, and this cursor must not be the fist. It blinks to remind me that there is so much more to write. It blinks to remind me that I will always write. It blinks to remind me that it's always there, waiting to accept the phrases I mold. It's blinks to remind.

*'ll be the first to admit that when I graduated, I stopped writing. It felt as if I were on vacation. No deadlines—or at least fewer deadlines—hanging over my shoulder. I had time to pursue other hobbies. Things were great, until suddenly, all my newfound free time became consumed with other activities and deadlines and responsibilities. My writing output waned, and I badgered myself for it. So what's a writer to do? In this chapter, Zac Zander, Pete Nelson, Jean M. Medeiros, Matthew Winkler, A.J. O'Connell, Rachel Basch and Baron Wormser offer some solutions to the challenges of how to commit yourself to your craft, and how to forgive yourself when some things slide.

It's easy to get bogged down when you think of an entire novel or anthology that needs writing, but you need to recommit and believe in (and be kind to) yourself and your talents. Pete Nelson offers some compelling arguments for embracing your creativity.

The Creative Imperative
by Pete Nelson

As a teacher, my job is to help students venture, without trepidation or hesitation, into the darker more confusing parts of themselves, to discover what's there. For all the work we do together on craft, part of the teacher's job is to be a kind of guru, because living life as a writer is a spiritual journey, or it had better be, because that's the difference between a writer and a stenographer. Ministers and priests and gurus describe the experience of being "called." They believe God has spoken to them, telling them what to do with their lives. To them, there is no arguing with God. The writer is also *called* by an inner voice that tells him, or her, what to do, and there's no arguing with it.

In Rilke's *Letters to a Young Poet*, Rilke advises, **"Write because you must."** I read that, when I was a student at the Iowa Writers' Workshop, and thought, "Who, me? Seriously? Write because I *must*? I don't *have* to do this. I could do something else."

After you write for a while, you start to see what Rilke meant.

You write for the same reason ancient peoples felt compelled to make paintings on the walls of caves—to make a record, an accounting. I often say in workshops: "Look around. There are ten of us in this room. According to the actuarial tables, the odds are, one of us, in the next ten years, is going to die. Hit by a bus, shot by a stray bullet, cancer, whatever. So ask yourself, which one of us is going to be dead in ten years?

Then ask, "If it's me, what am I going to write?"

And you may not have ten years—for all of us, the clock is ticking—what will you do with the time you have? What are you going to write?

"Write because you must…"

Because you've learned something someone else needs to know.

Mortality provides a perspective young writers lack, simply because they are young. Writing with an awareness of your own mortality, you realize that what you write is what you leave behind, and what you leave behind had better be something important, even if it's only important to you. If you don't want it to be important, why bother? There really are other things you could be doing. Then you're writing because you *want* to, not because you *have* to. Writing because you like the idea of being a writer, of being famous, going on book tours, working at home, is not a good enough reason to write. That's vanity, and works of vanity have no shelf life.

Write because it's impossible not to. The writing instructor's job is to help the student see that the way to express that "narrative imperative" is to make a book only he or she can write. The way to do that is to tap into your soul and drill down as deeply as you can go, until all the joy and all the pain and fear and love and hate you've ever felt starts to flow onto the page the way paint flows onto a canvas, because after the paint dries, after you're gone, there's a museum somewhere where people are going to see what you did.

"Write because you must…"

Because you don't know what else to do with the things you know.

Rilke was saying, "Write because you have no other way." We leave other things behind, in the lives we've altered or affected, the friends we've made, maybe a business we started or a house we built, and writers can do all those things too, but what writers know is that the book we leave behind is where we put our best selves, our memories and ideas and fanciful thoughts. We write books because we don't really have a choice —we have nowhere else to put the things we have to say.

"Write because you must..."

Because it's painful to keep it in.

Write because being a writer is like being permanently pregnant. There is something inside you that has to come out, ideas combining and taking shape, growing, beyond your control, and you can't get it out, or even find out what it is, until you write it. The process is more biological than cerebral. I learned at Iowa is that my best work doesn't come from what I read or analyze. My best work came from playfulness and whim, and from fear, and from being crazy in love, and from having my heart broken.

To cite one example, my girlfriend and I were in a drug store, complaining about how much birth control products cost, and I said, as a joke, "Why don't I have my sperm frozen for later and then just get a vasectomy?"

CLICK!

I thought, what would happen? I wrote a story, to find out. There was no other way to know. In the first paragraph, a guy dies in a plane crash, and after the funeral, his girlfriend learns there's a surprise waiting for her at the local fertility clinic—he made sperm deposits, in her name. She learns at the clinic that they can store sperm for ten years. In other words, her fiancé is dead, but not completely, and she can't grieve or move on until he is. What's a poor girl to do? But I didn't think that up with my analytical logical left brain. I was madly in love and scared out of my mind. I was also quitting smoking, so there were a lot of images in the story of internal aching, derived from nicotine withdrawal. I killed the main character because he was me, the part of me that was risking everything, and I wanted out. The girl in the story eventually has the guy's baby, so he gets all the benefits of a relationship, a kid, a wife who can't stop loving him, and none of the responsibilities. One reader compared the story to Odysseus, where it takes the hero twenty years to get home from the war, while Penelope waits patiently. I didn't sit down and ask myself, "How can I write a story that echoes The Odyssey?" I was just goofing around, but I was open to the available subconscious.

"Write because you must…"

Because you're hearing voices that insist on speaking..

This is NOT to say all writing is confession, or thinly veiled memoir. The "you" you put in the book is not the *you* you. It's not the whole you. It's the you that exists at the time you write the book, a partial fractional you, one glimpse. It's the part that wants to speak. Calling on the emotional/intuitive/non-linear side of the brain forces the writer to address and express things that are difficult to face or admit, so you tap into your soul and drill deep, but it's still not you. It's a meme, an avatar, a fiction and an imagined world in which you might be temporarily possible.

> "When you write a book, you're not just inventing a character, a plot or a scene. You're also inventing an author."

When you write a book, you're not just inventing a character, a plot or a scene. You're also inventing an author. You're inviting one part of yourself to step forward and start typing on the keyboard, while the other parts of you step back and watch. The author doesn't ask, "Who am I?" The author asks, "What does this book need to make it the best book it can be?" Your obligation, as an author, is to the book. You must give it what it needs, because it's more important than you are— it's bigger than you. It's what you leave behind as a permanent record, in libraries for a thousand years. It's like that sperm in a sperm bank, cryogenically frozen.

"Write because you must..."

Because it feels good, and you're addicted to the feeling.

Because the feeling defeats death, but then it wears off, and you need another fix. Mortality might slow down a bit, even disappear for a day or two after you finish writing a book, but then you remember it's still approaching, drawing closer. You had ten years to live. Now you only have nine. What's next? But lucky for you, you're one year smarter.

If you learn how to locate and identify, then honor and follow all your passions, the bright shiny white ones and the gloomy dark ones too, you start to see things when you're not looking for them. Ideas meet other ideas inside your head, screaming, "Write me down!" The CLICK! occurs more and more frequently. What used to feel like work turns into joy, and then your only problem is that there aren't enough hours in the day. You stop comparing yourself to other writers, and seek only to make each book a personal best, mindful that we may not all be equally talented, or equally intelligent, or equally experienced, but our souls are equal, because they are infinite, and we all have equal access to our souls.

"Write because you must..."

The teacher's job is to get the student to the point where he or she realizes, you write because you must. Because if you don't, you'll explode.

We've established how important it is to continue writing; to believe in yourself and your abilities. But on those darker days, when sitting down to write feels impossible, how do you gather the motivation to stare that blinking cursor on the page down and start from scratch (or even worse—edit out details unnecessary details that you've already written)? Jean M. Medeiros offers some practical suggestions on how to begin again.

Maintain Creativity, or Why I Went to Workshop the Morning After Graduation
—*Jean M. Medeiros*

Graduation night was mid-July hot, record-breaking temperatures flirting with 100 degrees and not even the breeze blowing off of Fisher's Island Sound providing relief. But we didn't need relief. We had leapt over two years of hurdles to reach this moment.

The next morning, I packed my bookbag, took advantage of the hotel's continental breakfast and told my family to enjoy Mystic and I'd join them after workshop. "You're going to workshop? What are they going to do, take away your degree if you don't show up?" We laughed, but there was a serious subtext too, and I might have asked those same questions if the situation was reversed. Why not lounge by the pool, or troll the gift shops? Still, going to workshop was never a question for me. I wasn't alone. When I drove back to "The Island," as it's affectionately known, there was the usual pre-9:00 a.m. scene: faculty and students chugging coffee and water while chatting on the way to class. The scene included my fellow graduates and we talked not so much of the ceremony and the celebration and the achievement of the night before, but the stories being workshopped that day. It was an MFA residency morning like any other.

Then it hits home when you get home, that your writing life has changed. The monthly deadlines are replaced by new obstacles. You won't share the MFA experience again in exactly the same way, in that bubble of ideas and inspiration. But after receiving your degree there are ways to maintain, and even enhance, your creativity.

Really, I'll Write Tomorrow

For the past two years, you've spent parts of mornings, nights, lunch hours and weekends, writing your monthly page allotment and craft essays. Post-MFA, it's tempting to kick back, go out for dinner, go out with your friends, or just stay home and stretch out on the couch and watch American Idol, CSI, baseball, or the guilty pleasure television program of your choice. You deserve the downtime, you'll write later. Nights become days and then weeks. Later never comes.

You've already carved out pockets of time to devote to writing, why not keep the same schedule? Not to say you don't have wiggle room now to be spontaneous and catch a movie at the last minute, or go to bed early because the kids fell asleep and the house is quiet. But you've developed a writing routine and it's easier to keep than recreate. Remember thinking you'd never have the time to do all that homework required to get your MFA? You did it then and you can do it now, it's just a different kind of homework. You create your own assignments.

Your Muse is Just Not That Into You

You plead, you call, you write, or more likely, you try to write, and nothing comes. You stare at the blank computer screen and the blinking cursor mocks you. You tap your pen on the journal debating if the lines running across are bluish-green or greenish-blue, stuff you never worried about when there were words on the page. Face the facts, the muse is not coming; not for tea, not for a visit, not to fill you with ideas to crack the New York Times Best Sellers' list. Put your fingers on the keys and the pen to paper and write anyway.

The muse has ignored you before during the MFA program, laughing in the face of packet deadlines. When your pages were due the next week, or the next day, and you swore you had nothing left. Maybe you just swore. Still, you wrote and submitted your pages on time. Maybe not the best words you've ever written, but most times, surprisingly, they were pretty good. If they're not now, we all have to revise anyway.

> **"Write through your lack of inspiration. Maybe you'll inspire yourself."**

Take heart, the muse is fickle with most writers. Even Flannery O'Connor admitted, "If I waited on inspiration, I'd still be waiting." This blank page is no different than the one that taunted you as a student. Write through your lack of inspiration. Maybe you'll inspire yourself.

When Are You Due?

We survived two years of deadlines: monthly pages of creative writing and craft essays; workshop submissions and critiques; research and writing a critical thesis; and finally, a creative thesis. Post-MFA, the deadlines disappear, the pressure is finally off.

That's good, right? Well, yes and no. Few of us will miss the cycle of late nights and lack of sleep to mail off a packet followed by intravenous coffee that promises a little energy to push through the day. But unless self-discipline is your strong suit (or you can easily adhere to the aforementioned schedule keeping and muse-ignoring suggestions), the occasional deadline can boost your productivity and creativity.

Joining, or starting, a writing workshop will keep deadlines in your writing life. Whether online, or on-the-ground, workshops can serve as mini-residencies. You'll know how many pages to produce and when, and can depend on getting, as well as giving, feedback. Check with your MFA Alumni Association, fellow grads, other cohorts, or local writing groups to find the right fit with your goals and personality.

If you want to take a break from workshops, be accountable to one person. This can be a writer you exchange pages with, or even a non-writer, just someone you can trust to ask, "How many pages did you write last week?" It's amazing how much accountability can create productivity.

For more information and ideas about writing groups, workshops and writing buddies, see Chapter 2.

So, what if you are writing regularly, but you don't know what your characters are going to do next, or how to wake up your memoir that's putting you to sleep? There are other ways to jumpstart your creativity.

Say Cheese

Pick up a camera and shoot landscapes, or seascapes, or candids on the sly. A photo lens makes you see the world with a different focus. If photography isn't your thing, grab a paintbrush and throw a splash of color on canvas or the walls of that spare room. Whisk a sugary meringue into mountain peaks. Changing your artistic expression can lead to new ideas for your own writing.

Location, Location, Location

My usual place to write is nestled into the curve of my sofa, laptop fired up and warmed by the glow of a floor lamp. You may swear that your best ideas come at a rolltop desk, or the kitchen table. Sometimes though, the same old place gets you the same old ideas. Take your laptop to a coffee shop and eavesdrop on a conversation; you might find a snippet of new dialogue. Go old-school and trade technology for a pad and pen and take them to the beach; describe how the sun feels on your skin. Vary where you write and gain a new perspective.

To Sleep Perchance to Dream

Some of the freshest and most imaginative writing happens during workshop exercises, when a faculty member sets up a basic plot and you have 15 minutes to tell the story. There is no time to overthink the characters, to agonize in choosing just the right verb, just freeform storytelling. The results are often creative pieces of flash fiction.

You can try this Post-MFA by setting up your own exercise prompts. Remember your dream, or nightmare? Turn it into a scene. Look at a photo, or listen to a piece of music and write how you feel.

Read a newspaper and show that "Law and Order" and its spinoffs aren't the only ones who can create stories "ripped from the headlines." Play with children and let their adventures with Barbie and Spiderman spin you into a different world.

Stuck for ideas? Go online. Google boasts millions of websites with writing prompts, some more well-known than others. Check out *Poets and Writers* (http://www.pw.org/writing-prompts-exercises), Writers *Digest* (http://www.writersdigest.com/prompts), Creative Writing Prompts, voted as "101 Best Websites for Writers" (http://creativewritingprompts.com) for ideas in all genres.

Feel like sharing? Try out Plinky (http://www.plinky.com.), which not only provides daily prompts, but lets you post your response on social media. You can read responses from other writers, too. It's almost like being back in workshop.

That's What Friends Are For

You're writing often, in different places, trying weekly prompts and even found a monthly workshop, but your words feel flat. Tell a reader.

It can be your local librarian, or a buddy who pours through the classics, or downloads the latest bestsellers. Ask someone to read your short story, or scene from your memoir. Don't say you're having problems with the characters, or narration, just say thank you and wait for the gut reaction. The reader may tell you that the dialogue you loved sounds fake. Maybe the secondary character is more interesting than the hero. Maybe the reader asks you for more pages, because it's just that good. Whatever the reaction, you could learn something new about your work and your writing.

If you're still searching for more, tell another writer. Bounce your ideas or problems off a sympathetic ear, of someone who has been there. You may get some fresh ideas, a different perspective, or at the very least, you'll feel better. Just don't forget to return the favor.

Read Any Good Books Lately?

Chances are you wanted to be a writer because you love to read. Post-MFA, there are no reading lists, no craft essays, no critical thesis bibliography-in-progress looming over your head. Now, you're free to read whatever you want, a murder mystery, a trashy memoir, *War and Peace*. You learn from good and not-so-good writing. So pick up a book, Nook, or Kindle. Reading probably sparked your creativity in the first place.

So, the morning after graduation, go to your workshop. We're writers; it's what we do. The work doesn't end with the MFA, the creativity doesn't have to end either.

*W*riting more often usually fuels a more efficient output. Jean pointed us in a few directions on how to kickstart, and keep in touch with, our writing. Next, Matthew Winkler will give us a few other options on what to do to stay motivated while you wait for your big literary break.

Writing Reality for Breadwinners
—*Matthew Winkler*

Before you began your MFA studies, you probably wrestled with the decision to spend over $30,000 on yourself, to enroll in a graduate program with no promise of financial reward. You have kids, a spouse, debts, and a retirement account. With thirty grand, you could have zeroed out some old loans, padded your 401k, updated your kitchen, or bought two Hondas. Instead, you chose to advance your own education, and you succeeded. Congratulations! Now What?

If you're holding out for a mythical, tenure-track college teaching position, the laws of supply and demand are discouraging. According to the *Poets and Writers* website [1] your alma mater is one of nearly two hundred MFA programs in creative writing, nationwide (131 full-time, 49 low-res (low residency). Plus 32 doctoral programs). If each one produces roughly twenty graduates per year, then around 4240 terminal degree-toting job seekers are hitting the bricks right beside you. By contrast, only about one hundred tenure-track creative writing positions open up per year. Bummer. [2] If you're interested in teaching a section of Freshman Composition, you can easily find adjunct opportunities, but don't expect to earn a living wage. For more exploration of life as an adjunct and other teaching opportunities, see chapters 8 and 9, edited by Michael Bayer and Ashley Andersen Zantop.

Another obvious career path involves writing for newspapers, magazines, and websites. Of course, many daily papers have recently folded, and the surviving newsrooms are 30% smaller than they were in 2000 [3]. A side effect of this contraction: lots of seasoned staff writers now swim in the vast pool of freelancers, all competing to place stories and articles in the surviving paid outlets. If you dive into the deep end with them, you should hope to secure one placement per hundred queries—seriously. And remuneration varies.

You've spent two years honing your craft, planning this career change, and now you simply want to ply your trade. There are other avenues you can take post-graduation, as evident in chapter 8. Universal to all of these, however, is the old, disillusioned rock star adage, "the music business is 1% music and 99% business." If you want to earn a steady paycheck, your inner muse will be writing speeches for your inner CEO.

Ultimately, you may end up on the same career path that most of those 4240 new MFA grads per year wind up on: Exactly the same one they were on before they got their degrees. To be blunt, you may never get paid to write. The reality for breadwinners is that your writing may not ever win bread.

So what? Consider this succinct writing philosophy, which has earned its owner forty years of awards: "Write. Revise. If possible, publish." [4] Focus on those three priorities. (Note that Ursula LeGuin doesn't mention paychecks.) If you can sell your work, great. If not, be your own patron. Award yourself time to pursue art for its own sake. As long as your breadwinning responsibilities are met, let yourself off the hook for literary profiteering, but keep yourself on the hook for literary productivity.

> "Let yourself off the hook for literary profiteering, but keep yourself on the hook for literary productivity."

Subscribe to the Writer's Almanac (daily podcast or email) and fuel up on the stories of those who have been in your shoes. The advertising copywriter: his secret novels, written one-handed in the desk drawer of his anonymous cubicle. The schoolteacher: her rushed manuscripts, tumbling out during summer vacations. The injured reporter: her epic Civil War story painstakingly researched while her ankle healed. The line worker at Chevrolet Gear and Axle: his poetry, a mental escape from hateful, exploitative manual work. These are your brothers and sisters in arms. Don't let them down.

How can you stay disciplined? The earlier chapters on community offer good suggestions, but one viable formula is to find two like-minded, trustworthy writers and commit to mandatory weekly meetings. Because you must present something every three weeks (no skipping or swapping weeks), there is always urgency to keep producing. And in the intervening two weeks, you must read closely and make insightful comments. Everyone stays sharp, on task, and engaged. This model is articulated by Claire P. Curtis, who writes, "While writing group does not give me more hours in the day, or make my kids' lunches, or grade my students' exams, it has given me a weekly time set aside to discuss ideas, and a cohort to whom I am accountable." [5] With a weekly deadline always looming, your daily writing vow grows teeth.

Of course, your breadwinning, writing, and sundry other obligations all compete for your time and attention. Bestselling author Dick Francis invokes the image of a juggler, skillfully keeping many balls aloft at once. The fallible juggler may occasionally drop a ball, but Francis assures us that all the balls are made of rubber and can be recovered on the rebound—all but one, which is made of glass. And that ball is your family.

So, keep carving out those precious hours to write, revise, query, and submit. Set deadlines, meet them, and proceed directly to your next project. Continuously exercise your hard-won mastery of the fine arts, and your biography may yet grace some future *Writer's Almanac* podcast. Until then, hug your kids, kiss your spouse, and don't quit your day job.

[1] [http://www.pw.org/content/mfa_programs]

[2] [http://www.awpwriter.org/careers/flood01.htm]

[3] [http://stateofthemedia.org/].

[4] http://www.ursulakleguin.com/FAQ.html#Philosophy

[5] http://chronicle.com/article/The-Rules-of-Writing-Group/126880/

*H*aving a plan and setting goals can be very helpful as a writer coming out of a MFA program. If you're an organization-fiend like I am, you're going to want to put your goals and ideas down on paper (or shout them from rooftops). There are many ways to do this, and A.J. O'Connell will share with us a few things that have worked for her.

Setting Goals the Easy Way
—A.J. O'Connell

To do list:

1) Publish novel of staggering genius.

2) Win Booker, Pulitzer and Nobel prizes.

3) Make millions of dollars.

4) Be remembered forever as the best writer to ever live.

Does all that sound doable? Hey, I'm an optimist—sure it does. But is it a manageable list of goals? I don't think so.

If your goal is to become a household name by publishing the best novel written in our lifetimes, that's wonderful, but a goal that big could be a little intimidating. In fact, it might seem a little like staring up at a monolith made of rock, with no way to scale it from where you're standing. But with a lot of little goals, you can build yourself a set of stairs to the top of that monolith. It will take time, it won't be easy and you might not even make it all the way to the top, but you will make progress, and that's better than standing on the ground, staring up at a huge, seemingly unattainable objective. Remember: the more manageable the goal, the easier it will be for you to achieve.

There are different degrees of goal setting. For me, goal-setting is most effective when I break goals down by time period. For example, I use daily, weekly, and yearly goals to mark my progress with various tasks.

The yearly goals are the big ones. At the beginning of each year, instead of making resolutions, I make a list of goals. A lot of the time, these are goals I'm not even sure I can accomplish. "Rewrite my novel" and "send novel to agents" are on this list. For more immediate, manageable targets, I break the yearly goals down into smaller weekly goals. "Rewrite a chapter" is on this list. Daily goals are much smaller. I have a notebook in which I write my daily goals in the morning. These goals range from "write 500 words" to "contact bookstore about reading" to "make the bed," although if I'm having a bad day, I will occasionally add "eat lunch," just so I have something to cross off the list.

This is what works for me. You may not choose to break your goals down by time. You might be more comfortable breaking them down by project, taking a big goal ("write my memoir") and breaking down the big task into lots of small ones ("outline" "brainstorm" "write 500 words of the first chapter") to make it manageable. Do what works for you.

Sometimes, however, goals aren't enough. Sometimes you need the extra kick of accountability. What does this mean? For me, it means that other people know I'm working on a project, and more importantly, that other people know when I'm slacking off. If I set a goal and don't achieve it? No big deal. If I fail to achieve a goal and people are watching? Well, that's different. For example, I post my yearly goals to my blog, and try to post my progress on those goals regularly. That way, I know that even if no one is reading my posts, I've at least put both my goals and my progress online for the world to read.

If a public approach is not your style, consider working with another writer. You can send your goals to each other and check in with your progress after a set period of time. I do this with another writer for weekly goals. It's private, it's personal, and it helps to keep me honest. You can also do this with a non-writer. If a friend or your significant other doesn't mind being your goalkeeper, you can give him or her a list of what you hope to achieve in week and check in at the end of the week.

An important part of having a list of manageable goals is just that: the goals are manageable. If you have a bad week—we all do—and don't achieve a small goal, it's no big deal. A list of small goals is forgiving in a way that one large goal can't be.

It's important to remember, however, that when it comes to motivation, everybody is different. Maybe one big goal is all you need. Or maybe you need pages and pages of tiny goals to keep you on track. There is no one right way to set goals for yourself. Experiment and see what works for you. Eventually you will hit on a system that will help you scale the monolith and achieve literary fame and fortune.

*L*ike A.J., Barbara Wanamaker has developed her own systems for managing her writing time. One specific system that has worked for Barbara, both as a graduate student and even more so after finishing her MFA studies, might work for you as well.

W.E.D.D.
—Barbara Wanamaker

Graduation night has grown late. At home, you revel in the memory of your gown sweeping below your feet and the feeling of the hood you are now entitled to wear bouncing off your back as you stepped forward to receive your MFA. You remove the gown, the hood; twirl the tassel around your finger, watching the little charm decrying the year, sparkle in the lamplight. You see the faces of all the friends you have made, remembering the good times you have shared together these past two years. And then you think, "Now what?"

Now what? The desk is still there waiting; the computer, the pads and the pens. So what is different? The difference is everything is now up to you. There are no mentors, faculty to challenge you, give you prompts, assignments. There are no more workshops to write for, to read for; you are the writer. So, what do you do?

All writers know writing can be lonely and writers must be disciplined. These are two areas the MFA prepares students well for. You now have a group of writers to turn to, align with; a group who knows you and your work very well, who will be honest in their critique, be supportive to your efforts. You can go to your "writing space," whether at home in the kitchen or in an office, in bed, at the local library or Starbucks and your cohort is there with you. Still, what is the next step?

The next step is honing your discipline. Writing is a job as well as an art. Any job broken down is a succession of goals and accomplishments. In an office, employees have certain tasks to complete daily, weekly, monthly and sometimes, yearly. Doing a manual job, the goals are more time driven. A worker may only have an hour or two to complete a small task that works toward the greater whole. So how does this affect a writer?

A literary writer, as opposed to a journalist, must create his own goals, his own time frame; become disciplined, as all artists must. Some writers are prolific and have several projects going simultaneously while others work better when constrained. These writers choose to start and complete one project at a time. The idea is to set goals; short-term goals as well as long-term goals. These goals should not be carved in granite, but have ebb and flow that will not stunt the creative process. Perhaps, in a day, writing so many pages for a novelist or so many lines for a poet works. On other days, getting ideas down, maybe creating an outline is a better goal to achieve.

Another way to establish discipline and create goals is to research and pursue opportunities to expose your work. Knowing there are publications to submit to with deadlines looming, gives you the impetus to finish a submission, provides the drive to reach the goal. If you are fortunate enough to have an agent or a publisher waiting to read a manuscript, this creates another type of deadline, a different kind of goal to work towards.

In any case, these plans do two things: they keep the writing process moving ahead and they put your work out there for possible publication. Having a plan also helps frame out your day, creating a time for work and a time for a personal life allowing that some days, life might be put on hold to make a deadline.

Receiving an MFA puts a label on you. Not only are there additional letters after your name, but you are now proclaimed to the world officially as a "writer." Sometimes, it's hard for that concept to become part of who you are. You ARE a writer. What a powerful statement, what an auspicious group of influential human beings you have joined. You are a writer and you must work at writing just as anyone works at anything that's worthwhile. Your words are important; they convey ideas that have been formed by you. The ideas may be shared by others, but only your words can communicate your feelings. Your words are unique to you alone and you have the talent and the ability to craft them into a final work worthy to share with the world.

Finally, this should become your mantra, your golden rule: "write every damn day." W.E.D.D. You are "wedd" to your craft, your art.

Writing is as much a part of you as breath and blood, skin and bone. To succeed, words must appear each day. You must decide if these words will have life on their own in the future or be merely stepping stones to a piece worthy of submitting. You are the beginning and the end, the ultimate source of power for your work. It will live and die as you see fit. Your MFA will provide or lie dormant; this is up to you, the writer. Grasp the most important objective: Keep writing.

W.E.D.D.

ut what if writing every day doesn't work for you? Or, maybe you do write every day, but you feel only a very light pulse from your muse—what do you do then? Brooke Adams Law suggests lightening the mood and allowing creativity the freedom to play.

From an Artist to Her Self
—Brooke Adams Law

You don't have to be ashamed of being a creative person.

Sure, it's a little weird that you spend an hour every morning, plus a few over the weekend, working on a novel. It's a little strange that you've spent thousands of dollars on an MFA program hanging out with a bunch of other crazy writers. Sure, your acquaintances raise their eyebrows until they disappear when you tell them about your Masters program. "Really," they say. "And what are you going to do with that? Get a job?" There's usually a sneer tacked on to the end.

I know that's part of the reason why you push yourself to write more, to write better. You love to write, but you also want to prove yourself.

I get that. But I'm tired.

In *Bird by Bird*, Anne Lamott shares her ideas about writer's block: it's a misnomer. When we can't write, it's not because we're blocked, she says, but because we're empty. "And writing is about filling up, filling up when you are empty, letting images and ideas and smells run down like water…" I need to be filled up if I'm going to keep producing. The work doesn't fuel itself all the time. Your artist (that is to say, me) needs a boost!

Take me to a museum. Leave your family at home, they get bored too easily. I want to look at the art. I want to go to the playground and swing on the swings. I want to go to the great bookstore in Southampton, I don't care that it takes so long to get there. I want to go to the library and sit in the reading room and read for as long as I want. I want to go to Dunkin Donuts and get a mint hot chocolate and a cruller. I want to take the train New York City and go ice-skating in Rockefeller Center.

In *Walking on Water*, Madeleine L'Engle quotes *The Politics of Creativity*: "'...at the age of five, 90 percent of the population measures 'high creativity.' By the age of seven, the figure has dropped to 10 percent. And the percentage of adults with high creativity is only two percent!'" In short, the world doesn't want to cultivate your creativity. Instead it does everything it can to cut down creativity—yours and others'. So you're going to have to find a way to cultivate it yourself. Part of that involves remembering what it was like to be a child who measured high creativity.

I want you to let me have fun instead of working all the time. Can we play, instead of always working on The Novel? Can we do something exciting instead of trying to eke out three more pages when I'm totally burned out? Can we skip the plain coffee (because it's cheaper and has fewer calories) and splurge on a pumpkin spice latte? Can we go out for a glass of wine instead of watching TV again, or doing more work? Can we stop worrying about the future and enjoy the present? Because that's where creative work gets done. In the present. Here. Now.

The present is where the creating happens. The present is where we can play and have fun and *make* things. Can we make a collage? Play a word association game? Draw a picture? Take piano lessons? And *then* work on the novel?

I want you to work with me instead of against me. I'll work hard for you if you play hard with me.

Let me *paint* once in a while. Let me write in color. Let me handwrite in funny block letters or cursive. Let me imagine. Let me touch things with my hands: Play-Doh, sand, felt. Let me walk down to the bay and smell the salt water and oil from the boats and hear the gulls cry and feel the wind in my hair—without a deadline, please. Without you looking at the clock on your phone and saying, five more minutes.

And then once we've played, we can get to work. Promise.

As a writer, I am naturally two halves of one whole: the creative spirit and the grammar-loving scholar. I've had to learn how to help these two parts of me 'play nice' in order to pursue my best work. In my first MFA fiction workshop, my professor Eugenia Kim said, "We are here to create for ourselves a life in which writing is central."

> "We are here to create for ourselves a life in which writing is central."
> —Eugenia Kim

That sums up my goal perfectly. It's not only to finish my first book. It's to create a life in which the process of writing is central.

Anne Lamott has said of writing, "The Gulf Stream will flow through a straw, provided the straw is aligned with the Gulf Stream and not at cross purposes with it."

How do I as a writer align myself to the "Gulf Stream" of creativity? How do I balance the need of both my inner artist and my outward, deadline-driven self?

During a MFA program, we have constant feedback from our professors and classmates and workshop groups. Creative minds surround us. For a time this may distract us from the reality that writing is a solitary activity. So what do we do when we graduate and suddenly find ourselves at our desks—alone?

Here are a few ideas.

Process over Product

Our society reveres the *product* of creativity but denigrates the *process* of creativity. J.K. Rowling took the world by storm with the Harry Potter series. People love the world she created so much that they have reread the books obsessively, gone to see the movies obsessively, and visited Harry Potter World in Universal Studios … obsessively. Rowling has said that people don't seem to understand that she needed time to continue writing the books, and then to work on other projects: "I must guard my writing time as fiercely as a Hungarian Horntail guards its first egg," she joked. Creating a world that rich and deep and fantastic—in other words, any world that springs to life from a page—takes *time*. Creating a world on the page takes time and effort and discipline.

Furthermore, we are a society of success-mongers. We want our efforts to result in something successful. In some ways this is normal—we want an outcome for our hard work, like a paycheck—but for an artist, a writer, it can be deadly. Usually, if I'm trying to write something 'good,' something that will be 'publishable,' I sit and stare at the screen for a few days, hopelessly stuck. (That's what happened when I started this essay.)

But if I start instead from a place of play, from a series of questions—"How can I look at creativity differently? How have I nurtured creativity in my own life? How *haven't* I nurtured my creativity, and what can I learn from those mistakes?"—then words start coming.

Play Time

I recently read an article in an education magazine by a teacher who had been observed by a district administrator. The woman looked at the class schedule and sneered, "Choice time? What's that? These kids don't have time to *play*." She was visiting a kindergarten class. The teacher was horrified. She knew, for example, that one child who was behind academically shut down during formal lessons, but came alive during play time. Another child with autism used play time to develop his communication skills without the pressure of a teacher. In short, her kids learned through play just as much (if not more so) as through formal instruction.

How true this is for writers! I do my best work when I feel like I'm playing: I come up with the most creative ideas, the most innovative plot twists, the most intriguing character motivations. Play requires an absence of deadline—that carefree feeling that you have all the time in the world, even if you don't. And it requires the mental freedom not to judge the work that comes out, but to see it as the raw material for a sculpture. Of course, it is still hard work to implement all those ideas. I'm not discounting work. But perhaps we sometimes work too hard at the expense of play. We take ourselves too seriously, sure that our writing process must be serious to be taken seriously.

What does a writer's playtime look like? Try a writing exercise or two. Maybe you're trying to work on your novel but had a crazy dream about mince pies chasing you, and think it would make a great surreal short story or flash fiction piece. Go where the energy is. Eventually it will settle in one direction.

Maybe you feel burned out and have been stuck in the same room or house writing for days or weeks and just need to get outside. I used to work from home and sometimes would see only my spouse for a few days at a time. Then on the weekend we'd drive out to the city to see friends and I'd be amazed at the sheer number of people walking around. They were walking dogs, talking on the phone, sipping coffee: living their day-to-day lives, and I knew none of it for most of the week. Go where the people are. They're always doing something worth writing about.

Reading

Some elementary school teachers claim that it doesn't matter what kids read, as long as they're reading.

I disagree.

I've recently realized that the books I read fall into three categories: books that entertain, instruct, and inspire. The best books meet all three criteria. But if a book doesn't meet at least one, it goes back to the library (or sometimes to a well-meaning friend) unread. Who has time to read a book that's completely pointless?

The first two—books for entertainment and instruction—are relatively easy to find. Books for entertainment (*The Night Circus, The Hunger Games*) abound. These are the volumes I can't put down, the ones that I rush home from work to pick up and read. Books that provide instruction might be craft books (I loved *Burning Down the*

House), or they might be novels that are especially well written, books in which I feel I am in the hands of a master writer and I read in part to appreciate the work of art they've created. I feel this way about books like Barbara Kingsolver's *The Lacuna* and Karl Marlantes' *What It Is Like to Go to War*.

Books that inspire me take a while longer to locate. These books are about more than what they're about. They aren't superficial: plot, action, plot, character, plot. They struggle after meaning. They deal with people asking big questions—not just people to whom things happen. *Blue Nights*, by Joan Didion, is a perfect example.

On another note, I am appalled by the number of writers I know who don't read on a regular basis.

Scientists bemoan the fact that the human brain is losing its ability to focus on deep thinking because of the perils of technology. We're losing our ability to read and think deeply, because on a computer we jump from reading one paragraph of a news article to checking for new email to reading through our Twitter feed, clicking a link, reading the first paragraph of that blog post, and then going back to the first site and skimming down to its conclusion.

We can't think and write deeply if we can't first read deeply. And reading deeply is becoming a lost art. To me, reading a book—nowhere near a computer screen, my phone in another room—uses the same part of the brain as my writing. I need to feed that part of the brain, nourish it, if it's going to produce creative work for me on any kind of regular basis. Anne Lamott has described that subconscious part of the brain as a little kid drawing pictures who's handing the crayon drawings up to your conscious mind through a trapdoor. But you've often got to occupy the conscious mind with something wholesome, engaging, rewarding, before it'll let the little kid loose.

A Suspension of Cynicism

The final element that nourishes my creativity is a willing suspension—not of disbelief, but of cynicism. Sure, some of my characters are cynical. But I can't be cynical *about* them. I have to believe in them fully. Cynicism cuts down, and creativity requires us to build up. So I shut down the voices in my head that think what I'm doing—namely, writing a novel—is silly, or a waste of time, or possibly foolish. I try to be as generous with my characters—and with myself—as I am with my family and friends. I give them the benefit of the doubt. I forgive them. I assume that they're doing the best they can with what they've got. And when they're not—when they're being petty and mean (the characters, not my family, of course)—I probe the pain that is causing them to do this. It requires empathy, and empathy is always harder won than cynicism.

Creativity is a force to be used for good. It is structured playtime. It is words pouring onto a page that have the power to change us, if we let them. They have the power to change our readers. They require belief in the power of good.

Don't know where to start? Get outside and play.

*B*rooke reminds us to bring joy back into our writing lives, to play with craft. What happens if we need a push from outside ourselves? Who can—and who should—we trust to get us back on track? Our literary friends, of course. Rachael Basch teaches us more about leaning on the people who understand our issues best.

A Kinship of Fugitives: Why Writers Need Writers in Life and on the Page
—Rachel Basch

In a speech at a long-ago AWP Conference, I heard the novelist Scott Spencer explain that writers are simply people who sit around in their bathrobes all day and try not to smoke. I laughed. Every one of the writers in the three combined ballrooms of that hotel laughed, long and loud, a mass acknowledgement of the illegitimacy and isolation that are part and parcel of being a writer. Yeah, even a writer as commercially successful as Spencer.

Among the many reasons I enrolled in an MFA program was to legitimize my most secret desire. For the two years while I was in grad school that desire to write, one I'd been protecting and nurturing since before I could read, was not only accepted, it was honored. But the very stories that had seemed so promising to me in my final workshop, struck me only weeks after graduation as random, irrelevant. Whatever relief I experienced at being out from under the yoke of someone else's syllabus, was offset by the dread of a lack of context. On the far side of the program, the value of my work seemed to diminish daily.

Of course my loss of faith was continually fueled by the fact that most everyone I knew (non-writers all) had real jobs, jobs for which they got paid regularly (yes, this was a long time ago). It seemed to me that all my friends had to do was show up and not screw up, and they would succeed. The sole yardstick of success for me was publication, which was infinitely more difficult to accomplish than simply returning to the correct desk day after eight-hour day. And while my friends were busy ascending in what seemed like the real, quantifiable world, I spent my days, when I wasn't doing temp work, descending several flights of stairs in a sketchy walk-up so as to retrieve my own words coming back at me in a manila envelope, my own pathetically hopeful hand having written out my own pitiable address one or four or ten months before.

Painful though my predicament seemed to me, the remedy was magnificently simple. All that had to happen was publication. If I got even one story published, I'd be in. I'd have proven myself. Everyone would know I was on the right track, that I was for real, that all the years (time was passing) of temp jobs and rejected stories now made sense.

> "Being a writer is a commitment that needs to be renewed every single day."

And then after what seemed like forever, that happened, publication, even some money. And it was great. And it was great. And then it passed. Magazines have new issues. More books are published every day. Milk has a longer shelf life than literary fiction. And there I was again, fielding rejection, only now I was running down a different set of stairs in a different state, my SASE's sporting a different address.

I had stupidly thought publication would be like getting my driver's license or losing my virginity. Do it once, and your status is forever changed. I had no idea that the writing life would bear more similarity to taking religious orders than to punching a clock. Writing is about as far as one can stray from the path of least resistance. Being a writer is a commitment that needs to be renewed every single day. It was slowly dawning on me that I was engaged in a marathon, and I would require sustenance far more nourishing than external validation if I was going to endure.

I was making art in a society in which making anything other than money is considered transgressive, and transgression gets lonely. In the 25 years since I've been out of graduate school, my friendships with other writers have provided a sense of community, a kinship of fugitives. These friendships are like those forged in support groups, where people who for whatever specific reason feel injured, imperiled, marginalized and misunderstood, commune with others enduring the same sad fate. It is only with other writers that I can rip open a vein and describe the precise nature of my despondency, that yawning discrepancy between the novel I envisioned and the one I actually wrote. Only another writer can understand the sentence, "I'm not smart enough to write this book," a sentence I have both uttered and heard uttered by novelist friends. Only another writer comprehends that lunatic relationship we have with time, how we're as devoted to lusting after the precious stuff as we are hell bent on squandering it. Who but another writer would offer an empathetic and knowing nod as we describe the axis of desire and shame against which we so often nail ourselves?

"More than once I've cured what was wrong in my relationship to a character by spending an afternoon at The Frick."

When I feel fogged about what I'm doing and why, when the energy drains away from an idea that seemed so thrilling only the day before, when I confront the reality that I am an adult who spends inordinate amounts of time steeped in make believe, when the whole flimsy construct of this thing I call my work life causes me to tilt and swoon, I wave a poem under my nose and come to my senses. While writer friends are essential when we want to dish freely in our native tongue, art of all kinds can be the most supportive of mentors. More than once I've cured what was wrong in my relationship to a character by spending an afternoon at The Frick. The insistence in the musical messages of Lucinda Williams, Stephen Sondheim and John Darnielle, has repeatedly helped me to more keenly feel what I'm trying to articulate on the page. The poetry reading I went to last night sent my fingers twitching for a pen. The intensity and ferocity of Carol Ann Davis' work resounded like an exhortation to make meaning out of pain, beauty out of chaos. Stories and essays, poetry and novels, music and painting help me relocate my own artistic impulse when it gets misplaced in the triage of daily life.

Lewis Hyde said, "We are only alive to the degree we can let ourselves be moved." Surrounding myself with what moves me serves as a needed reminder that my writing is not about me. In his book *What is Art?*, Tolstoy wrote, "… the recipient of a truly artistic impression is so united to the artist that he feels as if the work were his own and not some one else's—as if what it expresses were just what he had long been wishing to express. A real work of art destroys in the consciousness of the recipient the separation between himself and the artist, and not that alone, but also between himself and all whose minds receive this work of art." When the "best-of-luck-placing-your-work-elsewhere" letters pile up and the email queries go unanswered, I turn to other artists, in person and on the page, colleagues and legends, living and dead and remember why I got into this racket to begin with—to connect.

*I*f you take inspiration from the authors in this chapter, you can re-commit yourself to the craft. You know to whom and what you can turn to get back on track with your writing. What else is there to do? Baron Wormser suggests that living and experiencing life is the best lesson we can learn. Let living inspire you to write..

Life Comes First
—Baron Wormser

I come from the old dispensation, the pre-MFA world, the long line of writers who learned from reading other writers and served their apprenticeships not in workshops but in silence, matching their efforts with what others before them had done and being humbled by the gap. It never occurred to me get such a degree. It's not that I distrusted it. It simply wasn't on my radar. I was pursuing a Ph.D. in English but after a year of that, it became clear that I lacked the temperament and I left. Meanwhile, I was drafted during my year of graduate school, took my physical in the fall of 1969 and was declared 1-Y, psychologically unfit. I was free to do whatever. Wooly life beckoned. When in my twenties I wound up living with my wife in rural Maine and starting a family and building a house in the woods and learning to take care of myself in elemental ways, the thought of how I might be a writer was not on my mind. I was writing but writing was something I seemed to have to do. It chose me more than I chose it.

I know no more now about how writing fits into the so-called world then I did then. That's not to say I haven't had plenty of dealings with the world beyond my pen. I have, but the connections have made only sporadic sense to me. In the nation of selves I can only be one more self. Some selves become well-known as writers, most don't. The crucial aspect—the esteem of writing as a living value—remains no further down the road in American society than when I was young. Many think it's gone backwards if it's gone anywhere. That may be. I was reading the other day a writer in the 1940s ruing how his father and grandfather's generations esteemed the written word much more than in his day.

What my life in the woods taught me as a writer is that the life comes first not the writing. This may seem a heresy. The focus on fine writing, particularly in poetry, is often an art-for-art's-sake end in its own right. That's understandable. Poetry is a terrifically demanding art. Even the most accomplished poets succeed only once in awhile. But what I mean is that without a lived life there really is no writing worth reading. The Romantics who insisted on the passion of the life were right. When we mock the likes of Shelley falling on "the thorns of life," we only reveal our own corporate lassitude. When we point at the manifest unhappiness of the mid-twentieth-century American poets such as Plath, Sexton, Lowell and Berryman and assume some stagey pathology was at work, we only show our unwillingness to acknowledge the genuineness of suffering. Living fully (and creating art fully is part of that living) may entail, as Shelley recognized, a powerful degree of suffering. It's not to be sought out but it's not to brushed aside with a quip either. Shakespeare, we recall, denominated a number of his plays as tragedies.

The issue is the same it seems to me whether one is going beyond one's MFA or one never got one in the first place—the lived life. There is no replacement for intensity of experience. There is no replacement for the uniqueness of experience. There is no replacement for taking in one's days on earth as fully as one can take them in. If most writing fails, it's not because writers can't write half-decent sentences. MFA programs help them to learn to do that. What the programs can't help them to do is live a deeply felt life.

The notion of the United States as a herd of individuals is one to be reckoned with and in a very real sense the MFA degree caters to that illusion—each of us brings something to the table. Each of us does; it's true. Joe is not Suzy; Suzy is not Billy; Billy is not Patricia. But beyond that putative individuality there can be the willingness to go further into the experience and bring back something worthwhile. None of us can say beforehand whether that will happen. None of us can say whether we have the imagination to transform the experiences. Imagination is dicey; that's what makes it imagination. The post-MFA world seems to me to be no different from any world we inhabit. We do this or that in the socialized realm but our true lives lie beneath that accommodating surface.

I don't in the least think everyone should go off and live as I did in a cabin in the woods. I do think that everyone who calls him or herself a writer owes it to him or herself and to anyone who might read that writing to not be afraid to go to the well of experience and drink as deeply as possible. In a mass society we often seek to make a virtue of our getting along. As social creatures, that's understandable. Yet though the writer pays taxes and is likely to sit through his or her share of pointless meetings, there is no getting along. There is only the path and going down that path. When we look at the lives of many writers, of someone for instance like Richard Yates who wrote an incredible novel in *Revolutionary Road* and then spent a lifetime listening to people ask him what he had done for them lately, we can and should recoil. It isn't right. The world doesn't get how powerful and precarious the endeavor is. Bearing up takes fortitude but there's no need for any of us to feel sorry for ourselves, no matter what we go through with publishers, critics and the Great Maw of Indifference. We get to live a life and write. (Consider someone from a society where writers are proscribed by the state.) We get to know some other people who feel about writing as strongly as we feel—surely a gift of MFA programs. What more could we ask?

Chapter *7*

PUT YOURSELF AND YOUR WRITING OUT THERE

edited by Michael Bayer

Some writers write purely for their own satisfaction and have no interest in finding an audience for their work. But, not many. Unless you're one of those few, you'll need to learn how to place your writing where the world can read it.

*W*ouldn't it be nice if writers could toil at their typewriter—or tablet—and create work that gets discovered by agents, editors, and the general public without any effort? That's the romantic dream of "discovery" that many of us had as adolescents. The reality, however, is just about the exact opposite.

Like in any field, a writer must go out and find success, rather than waiting for it with open arms. Agents must be tracked down, editors must be sold, and readers must be won over. Nobody will come find you. Writers must not only tolerate rejection, but they must seek it out. Only through rejection can a writer achieve any degree of success. That means constantly submitting your work, developing your personal brand, giving readings, and being open to success in all of its wonderful varieties.

This chapter highlights the tools and attitudes that will help writers begin to develop a platform, attract a following, and embrace the random happenstance that often gives writers their first big break.

If you want to write for yourself, keep a journal. If you want your work to be read by others, it has to leave your computer and fall into the hands of editors, agents and readers. The first step for any new writer is to get your work "out there" and cherish any reaction, even rejection. Mark Berry explains how the art of submission is basically a numbers game.

Putting it Out There: Persistence, Revision and Simultaneous Submissions
by Mark Berry

In the world of creative nonfiction, agents and editors demand a publishing platform from aspiring authors. In other words, nobody wants to publish you unless you are already published. What's the name of that famous book by Joseph Heller again?

It took three years and almost twenty articles for me to become listed on the *Airways* magazine masthead as a regular contributor and then as a contributing editor. These *Airways* articles are part of a broader memoir that I hope to one day publish as a 100,000-word book, with a built-in audience of 25,000 readers already aware of my story though the magazine.

John Krakauer built his audience writing articles about adventure travel for *Outside* magazine and then went on to publish his bestselling book *Into Thin Air*. His success is a great example of platform-building that eventually developed into a coveted book deal. Building a platform in a magazine doesn't even necessarily have to follow your genre of preference. For years Clayton Taylor wrote his nonfiction column "Both Sides" for *Airways* about both his airline pilot and air traffic controller jobs, and then introduced his novel *Flying in Circles* to his readership.

So how do you break into the publishing world and become a *have* instead of a *have not*? Regardless of your chosen genre, it helps to establish some publication credentials. One of the best resources for authors seeking literary journals, magazines, and contests that are open to unpublished writers is *Poets & Writers* magazine, which has an extensive section for upcoming deadlines and even more opportunities in their classified section. Duotrope.com is an online resource that used to be free, but switched to an annual fee model at the beginning of 2013. In addition to its seemingly endless list of literary magazines and journals with guidelines and direct links to the individual publications, it's also a great submission management tool. As for tracking submissions, I'm still an old school paper records keeper, but there's an app for that too. StoryTracker is a new submission management tool for smart phones; it's not even close to perfect, but it's a helpful tool that might be worth looking into for you gadget types.

There are two basic ways to find appropriate markets to submit your work. First is to find a publication seeking the kind of work you have already written. The other is to use the needs of a particular publication to inspire your next original work. I have done both.

My primary writing is about aviation, and I have deliberately sought out appropriate places for my aeronautically themed work. The Editor-in-Chief of *Airways* magazine learned about my writing from my initial submission that sat in his slush pile for over three months before he had the time to read it and then reply. But once he finally accepted that first article, I developed a working relationship with him and provided more stories for the magazine. I learned that it's a lot easier for an editor to turn to a trusted writer for a story than to sift through that daunting pile. But that's where most of us have to start out.

The other way to break into a market is to customize your work for it, as long as it fits your basic interests. The editor for *TARPA Topics* magazine wanted to reprint my first *Airways* article, but my *Airways* Editor-in-Chief requested a yearlong exclusive. Instead of disappointing the *TARPA Topics* editor, I offered to write a separate aviation article for him, and he ended up accepting it. It's definitely more fun writing when I know that an editor will read my work once it's finished, rather than writing on spec and sending it out blind with the hope of eventually finding a home for it. That's my next topic: multiple submissions and simultaneous submissions.

"Multiple submissions" means sending more than one story to the same publication during the same reading period. Many magazines and journals have a policy against this to avoid flooding their in-boxes. Some publications, especially those hosting contests, allow multiple submissions as long as each submission represents a different genre because different genres are read by different sets of readers and editors. Check a publication's website for specific guidelines.

"Simultaneous submissions" means sending the same story, essay, or poem to more than one publication for consideration at the same time. This used to be frowned upon, but has become standard practice. Publications that don't accept simultaneous submissions will say so in their guidelines. Prominent journals like *The Sun, The Threepenny Review* and *The Paris Review* traditionally don't accept simultaneous submissions and have strong enough reputations that they can demand exclusivity for unsolicited material. For publications that do allow it, most expect the author to mention that his or her work is a simultaneous submission in the cover letter, and that it will be promptly withdrawn upon acceptance by another publication. If you want to be published, be sure to take full advantage of this opportunity, but prevent burning bridges by also adopting the follow-up withdrawal courtesy.

In one year I simultaneously submitted a score of short stories and essays 115 times. Typically, I submit something somewhere every two to three days. My strategy includes answering each rejection letter with a new submission to that same publication. Then I revise the rejected work and re-submit it to a different publication. In other words, each rejection inspires two new submissions.

At first I suffered through a lot of rejection. This is like the pain of working out. Rejection, like aching muscles the day after exercise, is to be celebrated by authors. If someone turns down your work, it means you are actively participating in the process of becoming published. Also, like weight training, you'll get stronger as you keep at it. As I mentioned, I rewrite each rejected piece. Over a series of rejections, that piece keeps improving just as if it were being workshopped back in grad school. Eventually most of my pieces have found a home.

As writers, we must work as hard at finding homes for our writing as we did at creating it during our MFA program. Put it out there, embrace rejection, continually revise, and resubmit. Eventually you will develop a following and more publishing doors will open.

For more on simultaneous submissions and more ideas on other basic rules of publishing, see chapter 10.

t's not enough to put your work out there. You must put yourself out there, too. Reading your work in public can be a harrowing experience, but it is one of the most effective ways for a writer to find new readers and engage them using the full variety of human senses. Travis Baker describes all the drama, and how giving a public reading will exercise your theatrical – as well as literary – talents.

The Author Will Give a Public Reading
by Travis Baker

If there's one thing an MFA will teach a student, it's how to sit through a reading. Students become practiced in the ways of appearing attentive even after days full of workshops, presentations and, for those in low-residency programs, salad lines. But while students and faculty spend a significant portion of their time giving, receiving or zoning out of readings, little critical examination of the process of giving a reading exists. Perhaps by understanding the event from a critical perspective, we can greater appreciate its significance and usefulness to both the MFA experience and to literature as a whole.

To achieve this understanding, it seems useful to examine the component parts.

The Author...

The Author who shows up to give a reading is a different person than the writer of a text or the fellow student or the person who stands in line at the grocery store. When the author gives a reading, he or she assumes a performative role. The author, when stepping to the podium, becomes the Author, the embodiment of what the audience *perceives* as the author. We must do our best to live up to the godlike image our readers have created in their heads. This might get a tad confusing, but just as one must never confuse the narrator with the author, one must never confuse the Author with the person who sat at their desk plunking away at a keyboard. That's the writer. The writer writes. The author is the marketing construction of that writer. And the Author is the live show. It is the Author whom people come to see, to hear speak, to sign books afterwards. The Author is the physical presence of the imagined creator of a work. He or she will either confirm or surprise, elate or disappoint, based on the audience's pre-conceived notions of who the Author must be.

…Will Give…

Ownership is important. The work is the author's, and so too is the reading of it. While the selection to be read is most likely not the entirety of a work, and may not even be representational of the work as a whole, it is representational of the author: the author's style, language, themes and substance. The author must own both what is to be read and the reading of it, must prepare to give them away and to do so in a manner that keeps the audience interested, or at the very least, awake. When the author takes to the stage or podium, the author must inhabit the role of the Author, a creature capable of gestures, facial expressions and intonation.

When the Author actually begins to recite the text out loud to the audience, that action gives voice to the narrator and enters into a heteroglossia of discourse. Context replaces text. Voice, place, time, and social conditions converge to give unique meaning to the text, impossible to replicate at any other time or place, with any other voice. Magic resides in the place between Author and Audience.

…a Public…

> **"an Author is talking *to* an audience rather than just *toward* them."**

Way back when the story of Gronk Flintback and his defeat of the Great Snuffled Tusk Beast and how he won the hairy hand of Lonka Stonetooth was told around the fire, storytelling existed purely in oral form. What was lost when humanity started writing stories down was the physical interaction, the physical presence of both the storyteller and those who elect to listen. A great deal of the appeal of a public reading is the return to that ancient art and the intense and honest relationship that can develop when an Author is talking *to* an audience rather than just *toward* them.

...Reading

What is normally thought of as reading is a private act, one done in constructed seclusion. An individual goes to quiet places; he or she curls up on a couch or chair or seeks the anonymity found at a beach, library or café. Reading, the verb, is private and solo. *The* reading is a public event, a return to the days of wandering minstrels, yet it is also firmly of the modern. A literate society attends a reading not to be told a story they would otherwise have no access to, but as a performance of a work they have already read, or as a tease of what they very well might like to.

An Author takes the work and "hands" it to others through oration. The Reading is reading out loud, a return to the dispersal of language on the part of the Author by means oral rather than tactile. An audience is not reading a text, but listening to a voice. As the text is now performative, the author becomes a performer. A new appreciation of the work presents itself. By moving reading to the performative realm, an author may not only share the work that has been so long labored on, but create a separate type of work, one capable of reaching an audience in a wholly different manner.

uilding your personal brand requires investment. You may need to shell out a few dollars, but largely you'll need to dedicate the most precious resource of all: time. Lary Bloom shares a few pointers for writers who want to invest wisely for the future.

Indispensable You: Five Ways to Build your Brand in the Writing Marketplace
by Lary Bloom

More than a dozen years ago, I left full-time work as an editor to set up my own writing business. There was no handbook for this, just warnings. "You what?" asked an author friend who worried aloud that making a living this way was not possible unless your name was Stephen King or Danielle Steel.

He was right, in a way—I have been unable to buy a home in the South of France. But I have made a living by writing, teaching, speaking, and editing. I've done this by adding a new title: director of sales of Lary Bloom, Inc.

In this pursuit, I am selling, if you'll pardon the expression, my brand. I do this in a variety of ways that make it possible to make a living without depending on any single source of income to survive and flourish. Here are a few hints to help you do this yourself.

Devote 20 percent of your time to making no money. I know what you're thinking—it's easy enough not to make money. So how is this point helpful? What I am suggesting is a formal way to make no money that leads to ways of making money. That is, become a volunteer, for example, teaching writing at your local library, or become active in a community group in which you have an innate interest. This does at least two things for you: enhances your brand, and also heightens your sense of purpose and self-confidence. Word gets around about how smart and helpful and talented you are, and then someone has a job that needs to get done, and you're in the right position.

Learn to Become a Persistent (but Courteous) Pain in the Ass. I think of a particular writer who, for more than thirty years, has pushed hard to get writing jobs he wants simply by showing up and, when rejected, showing up again. When form rejections fill the mailbox, the easily defeated writer decides, "Well, maybe I'm not the hotshot I thought I was. The editors are right. I'm a fraud." Then there are the writers who understand that those who do the rejecting are not the ultimate authorities on your talent. I still wonder about what happened to the New York publisher who turned down Anne Frank's diary because he thought, "The girl didn't rise to the level of the material."

Not that you need to do Anne Frank-like work to succeed. I think of the novelist David Handler, author of 20 very pleasant murder mysteries, who, at the beginning of his career, returned to the publishers that had rejected his initial work, seizing on what they liked about his writing, and then pounding again on their doors after he fixed the manuscripts. One of them took him on. This takes gumption, drive, and the ability to put aside hurt and the inevitable damage to confidence that rejection brings.

Work for Maximum Wage. Let's say someone comes to you and asks for help with his or her writing—it will happen because you are qualified to help. Your instinct will be to give away the store. Don't do that. Charge what you're worth. In each case this will be different. But at the very least you should think about what happens when plumbers or electricians come to your house and leave with hundreds of dollars because they're able to fix things that ordinary humans can't. You have similar abilities, and similar (if not higher) monthly charges.

"think about what happens when plumbers or electricians come to your house and leave with hundreds of dollars because they're able to fix things that ordinary humans can't. You have similar abilities."

If you go to a high-end restaurant, you have no qualms about paying for a chef's expertise. Similarly, those who need first-rate writers and editors will pay for excellence. Recently I put in a bid to write the history of a company. I was told that my bid was twice the cheapest bid, and there was no way the firm could consider it. I noticed that the company had marketed itself as one that never cut corners and provided the highest level of customer service. Aha, I thought. So I went back to the company execs and used their own argument against them. Why would they want to produce something on the cheap, and that looked and read as if it didn't measure up to the message they were trying to send? When they called back, I held firm to my price. And they hired me.

Earn a Masters of the Market Degree. You've already done the hard and expensive part: earning a formal degree from a distinguished institution. Now you must become an expert at sales. All life is sales. This may not be easy for you. Shy you. But to be a writer is to be a salesperson. In a book proposal I wrote in 2012, the overview ran about ten pages, which is a typical number for this critical first section of a pitch to agents and publishers. But the marketing section—how the book would be promoted and why it would be attractive to a hefty percent of the reading population—ran even longer, an additional *twelve* pages. The proposal led to an offer from a high-profile publisher.

Your rule here. No business plan, of course, works for all. You have strengths that are unique to you. Play them. Through hard work and sacrifice, you've become a professional word maker. That's a rare—and valuable—calling.

When a writer is ready to take his or her personal brand to the next level, the best advice is Socrates' old maxim, "Know Thyself." Your personal brand—or reputation—can help attract an audience, but it must be an authentic representation of you both as a writer and a human being. It must represent your true values, goals and passions. Lisa Diane Kastner explains how a writer can develop an authentic personal brand strategy that will withstand the scrutiny of the social media universe.

Building Your Personal Brand
by Lisa Diane Kastner

Congratulations, you've graduated or are about to graduate. At this point you're probably wondering what you should do next. You know how to write. You've spent the last several years honing your craft. But how do you get the word out about you—the brand of you? Developing your author brand should be among your top priorities. The development, introduction, and maintenance of your personal author brand is a way to strategically approach the product of you. Your author brand is a means of defining and packaging your skills, values, and personality so that you can best target your audience (those who will ultimately purchase your work) and assists you in defining your differentiators, or what makes you different from other authors.

Why is an author brand so important? Because this is how people will come to know you. This is how *you* will define what agents, editors, and, most importantly, the general public should expect of you.

This article reviews the steps involved in creating and maintaining your author brand:

Define Your Goals

Identify Your Strengths and Leverage Them

Develop a Reputation as an Expert

Maintain Your Brand

Get Feedback and Adjust Accordingly

Reassess Your Goals

Never Forget Who You Are

All well-established authors have a brand. Stephen King is known for creepy horror, and Joyce Carol Oates is known for dark, deeply intellectual literature. JK Rowling is known for epic, young adult fantasy. What about you?

Define Your Goals

I know this step can be difficult, especially if you've just graduated or have been writing for only a few years. That said, before you delve into creating an author brand, you need to have an idea of what you want to accomplish as an author. When I decided to actively pursue creative writing, I had a long-term goal of becoming an award-winning and best-selling commercial literary author; I'd also developed short-term goals, like getting published by established journals, magazines, and other publications; writing engaging and thought-provoking stories; and building my network of both up-and-coming and established authors.

Friends who shared my aspirations conducted a similar exercise and decided they ultimately wanted to become literary agents or editors, so they developed short-term goals that supported this strategy. Your goal helps you find your niche and will act as a beacon throughout your career.

Identify Your Strengths and Leverage Them

How do you decide which parts of *you* will become your author brand? And how do you then reinforce this brand with the public?

Decide on what will define and distinguish you. In other words, determine how you are different from other writers. When you talk to your fellow writers, mentors, and readers, what do they note as your greatest strengths? Of these strengths, select those that can serve as cornerstones of your author brand and then leverage them to build your career.

For example, when I first started writing fiction, I had no idea what genre I wrote. I knew I had fun writing and I enjoyed the revision process, but I didn't know where I should concentrate my efforts. I attended multiple workshops and critique groups in an attempt to understand my writing style and find like-minded writers.

In workshops, horror writers didn't like my stories because they weren't bloody enough.

"You need to add a gun or a mass murder or a monster on page five. I like the writing though. Good imagery."

Romance writers didn't like my work because there wasn't enough sexual conflict.

"Why is she searching for her sister? Why not search for her high school sweetheart while she's in a broken marriage? Oh, and the sweetheart has to be dying of cancer or something. I like your themes and action. Those are cool."

Each one gave me feedback based on their specific genre's "rules" while something in my gut said the feedback didn't make sense for my goals for the piece. I asked myself, if I made the changes would I realize my vision for the story? It forced me to better understand my writing style and my true intentions for the story.

When I attended my first conference, The Philadelphia Writers Conference, my instructor pulled me aside and commented on how wonderful my literary short story was and how he had enjoyed the magical realism elements. He also provided invaluable criticism for revisions. His commentary made sense. It fit in with my vision for the story. This was my A-ha moment.

No wonder the other suggestions hadn't rung true. Through the process of elimination and gaining a greater understanding of my writing, I came to discover my strengths: literary writing style, imagery, themes, action, and use of magical realism. Later, I would discover additional strengths in revisions and editing.

Ask yourself, what feedback rings true? Your differentiators are often identified in craft workshops, in mentor feedback, and in readers' responses. At this point you should have a bevy of feedback from which you can determine your strengths. Take this information and build an author brand statement. This will form the baseline for your branding activities. Ask others to critique your author brand statement to help make it stronger.

As an example, this is mine:

I combine my passion for writing, knowledge of craft, gift for revisions and editorial feedback with strengths in magical realism, imagery, themes, and action to develop engaging and thought provoking literary prose.

In this statement, I reference the strengths that were identified through my peers, mentors, and readers. When you have yours, send it to fellow writers and mentors and ask them for feedback. If you're really brave, post the statement on your blog or Facebook page and ask for criticism. You'd be surprised at the responses that can help hone it.

Develop a Reputation as an Expert

A key to building your author brand is to build a reputation as an expert in your field. By obtaining your degree in writing, you have credentials that millions of others don't, so your degree is a differentiator. Have you performed a public reading? Taught or assisted with a workshop? Earned a fellowship? These are also differentiators to add to your biography and consider incorporating into your author brand. Once you have your author brand statement, differentiators, and long-term and short-term goals, it's time to let people know you exist and that you're available to share your expertise.

Submit your bio along with proposals to teach classes at schools, universities, and writers' conferences. If your goal is to be an editor, submit your bio to publishing houses and journals.

To help build your brand and reputation, obtain a job with a publishing house or a new publication, or even begin your own publication to gain credentials. These don't need to be paid jobs as long as they give you experience to strengthen your standing.

For example, I had a blog in which I chronicled my experiences as an aspiring author. I gained a following of other aspiring authors as well as agents and editors. Through this experience I was invited to be the Features Editor of the *Picolata Review*, a new online journal. My role was to interview well known authors and editors as well as vet and select submissions for publication. The combination of my blogging and editor role gave me a greater standing in the literary community and gained the attention of agents. I had taken a passion of mine (becoming a writer) and turned it into a forum (blogging) for others.

Please note: Did I get paid for my blogging? No. Was I paid for my work at the *Picolata Review*? No. But I gained experience, credentials and attention from publishing houses and literary agencies. If I hadn't understood my writing style and strengths, I might have made choices that didn't fit with my brand or my personal goals.

You want attention. You want people to know your name and have positive impressions of you so that you'll get more jobs that align with your author brand and goals. You want to be sure that whatever you do—whether in person or through social media—reinforces your brand and your image and will move you toward reaching your goals.

"Everything you do and everything you choose not to do communicates the value and character of the brand."
www.fastcompany.com/28905/brand-called-you.

Did I take every job offered? No. There aren't enough hours in the day to do so. I had to make decisions based on what aligned with my author brand, so I only selected opportunities that fit within these criteria.

When a blossoming agent approached me about writing an insider's account of the pharmaceutical industry (I used to work for a pharmaceutical), I passed. I didn't want to be known as a whistle blowing, non-fiction writer.

When a world-renowned agent who typically represents thrillers told me to ditch this silly literary thing and become a chick lit writer, I passed.

Why did I accept the editorial job at *The Picolata Review*? Because it aligned with my author brand by leveraging my knowledge of craft, revision, and editorial feedback while being directly applicable to my shorter term goal of building a network of up-and-coming and established authors.

So far, we've focused on how to enhance your "in person" presence. Now let's look at how this extends to your online brand.

How do you say what you need to say, and what venues should you use? Twitter, Instagram, Pinterest, and Facebook are all free venues for you to leverage. You can even build a free blog at venues like Blogger. But the information you convey through these venues must align with your author brand and goals.

I have Facebook, Twitter, Instagram, and Pinterest accounts. Do I post all of my activities in these venues? No. I think about which information and activities will reinforce my author brand, and whether or not I want this information to be available for eternity. I don't want my cat's sensitive stomach discussed on Facebook.

Maintain Your Brand

Once that you have your blog, author website, and social media accounts, as well as your gigs as editor, journalist, magazine writer, teacher or speaker, what else do you need to do (other than write)? You need to continue to reinforce your brand through blogging, tweeting, and other means of updating. Keep your brand in the forefront of your audience's minds by reinforcing your strengths and passions. For example, I am not going to write reviews on Avon romance novels because this activity does not align with my style of writing, which is an integral part of my author brand.

Get Feedback and Adjust Accordingly

Once you've built your brand, get feedback from your audiences. Learn from what they tell you. Are your classes/editing/writing/teaching valued? What's not working? What is working? Interact with your fans and peers. Post thought-provoking questions or links to articles to engage them. Celebrate your successes, such as having your book published or being asked to speak at a bookstore or conference. Ask for feedback on your publications and listen to them. Thank them for their engagement.

"It's the act of sharing not just the published book but also the wider spectrum of what it means to be a writer that helps to create that sense of a bond of togetherness between authors and readers." http://www.bluezoowriters.com/discover-your-authors-brand/

Now that you have both an online and in in-person presence, adjust your tactics based on feedback. For example, when I started Running Wild Writers Community, I recruited several authors to teach in their genres: mystery, thriller, romance, science fiction, and fantasy, and I taught literary. Of our course offerings, only the writers' workshops, editing, and world-building classes generated interest, and most attendees in the world-building class were literary writers. I heard my audience's silent feedback and changed the course offerings to focus exclusively on literary and cross-genre writing. This feedback also directly aligned with my author brand.

Reassess Your Goals

Now that you have your in-person and online platforms and means to reinforce your brand, what you may find is that as you evolve as both a writer and a person, your goals may change. This is normal. If and when you feel your goals have changed, rethink how you first defined your author brand and then how you are presently positioned to your audience. Adjust those messages accordingly.

For instance, when I started receiving requests to serve as an editor, I realized that I had been frequently teaching classes on editing techniques and had taken on a lot of editing work. I reevaluated the classes that I taught and added classes that were focused on other craft elements, which broadened the types of opportunities that came my way. I had actively changed my audience's perception of me.

Never Forget Who You Are: *In the End, the Only Person Who Must Live with You is YOU.*

When you wake up in the morning, do you smile because you love who you are and are happy with how you present yourself? Is the brand that you built something that you can live with five, ten, or fifteen years down the road? Throughout your life, the one person you need to make happy, above all others, is you.

Here are a few of the most popular online venues authors are using to build their personal brands. The best part? All of them are free of charge.

Facebook: www.facebook.com

Goodreads: www.goodreads.com

Instagram: www.instagram.com

LibraryThing: www.librarything.com

Pinterest: www.pinterest.com

Tumblr: www.tumblr.com

Twitter: www.twitter.com

*W*hile social media channels allow writers to engage instantly with their fan bases, an author's web site and blog serve as the hub for online marketing, Writing, reading, editing and marketing are more digital than ever before, so a writer who lacks a compelling digital presence is increasingly missing opportunities. Lisa Calderone simplifies the process of website and blog development for aspiring writers.

WWW: Writer Websites that Work
by Lisa Calderone

So you have a Voice and want to be heard. You're now credentialed as a creative writer and are ready to shout to the world that you're here. Today, establishing yourself as a new talent and developing a readership is attainable for every program graduate. All you need is a digital strategy, a website (or two), and a bit of courage. Since you picked up the latter simply through the process of earning your degree (remember the workshops, the readings, your seminar presentation?), this article will walk you through the first two items—your digital strategy and your site.

I learned the power of the digital platform back in the mid-1990's when I was writing my first nonfiction book. At the time I was empowered by my desktop publishing skills to self-publish, and had no interest in investing time and energy in the rejection process of shopping around my manuscript. I established HomeWord Bound Publishing, LLC, joined a listserv for small press publishers, asked a few pointed questions, and was approached by three publishers who wanted to finance my book. The concept of positioning myself online was planted. Mindful that there were real people and real opportunities behind the curtain of my digital presence, I focused my online efforts on community and relationship building. In 1999, the website I developed to promote my first book was named one of the "Top Work-at-Home Sites" by *Parenting* magazine, and by 2002, my spinoff book was featured on the *Oprah Winfrey* show.

What's the connection between establishing yourself online as a nonfiction writer and building your brand as a literary artist?

Positioning. And like it or not, when you develop a website, you're positioning yourself to the world—whether you're an essayist, a novelist, or a poet. How you do so can make or break your opportunities as an emerging writer. So take the time now—with your MFA degree freshly hanging on your home office wall—to build a savvy online platform before the world knows you've arrived.

Here are a few tips to get started, with examples of some MFA'ers (students, alumni and faculty) who are getting it right.

1. Know the difference between a blog, a publication, an author website, and a freelancer website.

MFA programs attract graduate students of all ages, industries, writing career stages, and professional aspirations. Who you are on the day of graduation, and who you want to become at the next stage of your writing career, should direct your website options. Have multiple goals? That works too—just create separate website identities, linking them together on a centralized site.

Blogs. Many new grads are aspiring writers who have not yet established a readership. Launching a dedicated blog is a proven technique to develop a readership for both fiction and nonfiction writers. Blogs are self-publishing ventures that work best when a single topic is at hand. In the case of a writer's blog, that single topic is YOU. Your thoughts, musings, and reflections are your connection with your growing readership.

For more information on blogs and where to register one see the blog feature section, edited by Erin Corriveau, at the end of this chapter.

"Just remember that blogs are a form of publishing, so be careful not to self-publish any piece of work that you intend to submit to edited publications."

A key difference between a writer's blog and an author site (see below) is that a blog commonly has a theme, whereas an author site is simply titled after the author. When you're first starting out, it's that theme that's going to help you build your readership; by the time you have a published work and have "graduated" to an author site, your name (not your topic) becomes the primary draw.

Just remember that blogs are a form of publishing, so be careful not to self-publish any piece of work that you intend to submit to edited publications. Most reputable literary journals expect first North American rights and you can burn that opportunity by publishing your own work first. That said, once you are published (elsewhere), make sure to include links to your published work from your blog.

Example:
Karin Diamond's blog has it all—a named blog, up-to-date posts, and a brief author bio on every page reflecting the heartbeat of her work:
Eyes Peeled Always: http://www.eyespeeledalways.blogspot.com/

Publications. Perhaps your post-MFA aspiration is to establish yourself as an editor or publisher. Using the same Content Management System as a blog (WordPress comes to mind), you can launch a literary journal in your genre—or across genres—aimed at advancing the literary arts based on your own distinctive aesthetic. The caution here is to avoid confusing your readers by posting your own writing—publications are about soliciting, screening, editing, and publishing the work of others.

Examples:
MFA grads Erin A. Corriveau's and Linsey Jayne's literary journal *Spry* features "undiscovered and established writers' concise, experimental, hybrid, modern, vintage or just plain vulnerable writing. This is a place for people who excel at taking risks, who thrive under pressure—for people whose words and rhythms are *spry*."
Spry Literary Journal: http://sprylit.com

My own capstone project in Fairfield University's MFA program was the launch of *Mason's Road* in 2010. Doubling as a learning tool for writers, this literary journal was a collaborative effort among the graduate students of the program's first and second cohorts, and continues to be run by a rotating editorial team of current students. For academic credit, I spent my third semester conducting research, pulling together an editorial team, publicizing our first Call for Submissions, overseeing the reading/selection process, and building the website. The latter served as my introduction to using WordPress both as a blog and as a more traditional website.

Blog: The Journey of a Literary Journal:
http://lisacalderone.wordpress.com/

Online Publication: Mason's Road: http://masonsroad.com

Author Sites. A lucky few writers obtain a publishing contract within a year or two of earning their degree. Author sites are primarily online brochures that establish the credibility of the featured writer, with the value-add of offering interactive opportunities with your readership. You know you're ready for this type of site when you have at least one book under contract or already out. At minimum, you'll need a home page, bio, description of published work(s), contact info, and reader engagement.

Example:
Annabelle Moseley's author site communicates at-a-glance that she's an established author. Her homepage features a quote in the graphic header that serves as a writer's statement, an artistic headshot, and a rotating news feed of her recent appearances and accomplishments.

Annabelle Moseley: http://www.annabellemoseley.com/

Freelance Sites. Many creative writers have several writing competencies and make their living through business, technical, news, and development writing for others. Some come into writing programs already established as freelancers; others leave with stronger writing skills than when they arrived and are looking to market their newfound proficiencies.

Example:

Christy Miles uses her name-domain for her copywriting and creativity coaching business with a sidebar link to her personal essay blog. Her blog then features tabs for "services" and "work with me." The two sites pull together under the same design and color theme. (As an aside, Christy, who holds an MFA from Columbia College Chicago, makes a particularly compelling case for the value of an MFA in the business world on her blog post, "What does an MFA get you? You might be surprised.")

rivermaker: http://christymiles.com

riverboxx: a container for thoughts | ideas | creativity: http://riverboxx.com

2. Grab your name for your domain.

If you're looking to establish yourself as a writer, your name is your brand. Grab your brand before someone else can. If it's not available, throw in your middle initial or middle name, or add the word "author" at the end. Whether or not you're ready to establish an author site, it's worth the $10 at a domain registration site to reserve and preserve your brand. Some providers will even register your domain for free if you purchase their low-cost, do-it-yourself website design services, offering writers a one-stop Web solution. Don't delay!

Some popular registrars are:

1&1 Internet: www.1and1.com

GoDaddy: www.godaddy.com

Name.com: www.name.com

Network Solutions: www.networksolutions.com

Squarespace: www.squarespace.com

Wix: www.wix.com

By the way, grabbing your name for your website URL is important, but don't forget about other online marketing venues. Is your name available for a twitter handle? A Facebook fan page? Cast a wide net and claim your turf everywhere you might someday want to promote your brand. If you decide against using twitter for the time being, that's fine, but at least you'll still have the option down the road.

3. Articulate your message at-a-glance.

So who are you (really) and how can you best share that online? There is something you need to shout out to the world, and that something needs the editor in you to articulate it in 50 words or less. Your website should capture the essence of that message and share it with the digital universe.

Again, I point to Karin Diamond's author box that appears in the sidebar of every page of her aptly-titled blog "eyes peeled | *always*." Here she has a photo of herself in a triumphant and joyful celebration of life, with the caption: *"My Peppe told me, 'Always keep your eyes peeled; you don't want to miss anything.' With eyes wide open, this is how I see the world—the world of a young adult cancer survivor."*

Her message—clear, concise, and credible—welcomes every new and returning reader, and is communicated *at-a-glance*. Once you are clear on *your* primary message, write it on a Post-It note and stick it somewhere in your peripheral view so it's readily accessible at all times during the design of your site. With every decision you make during your site build, ask whether you're supporting or diluting this primary message.

As you develop your site, remember that the landing (or home) page is most critical. Writers tend to care only about the content, but professional web designers know that functionality, graphic design, and navigation are all part of the message as well. You don't want your first-time visitors to be guessing where they are or why they should care, then leaving. At minimum, consider:

Defining the topic of your blog or site in your header through the use of titles, quotes, and/or taglines. Remember that your site has multiple pages, and readers can surf into any one at any time. Since your header appears on every page, make sure it defines who you are and what you're about, instantly.

Example:
Brooke Adams' "Books Distilled": www.booksdistilled.com

Using graphics to communicate before your words. You may be a writer, but it's still true that pictures paint a thousand words. Use them.

Example:
Christine Shaffer's "French Food and Me" features a graphic header and sidebar navigation that set the mood and topic of her blog.

http://frenchfoodandme.com

Paying careful attention to your menu options and navigation. Navigation—or what is referred to in the industry as "information architecture"—is about usability and functionality. Like it or not, visitors don't just come to websites to read, but to gather and/or "experience" information. That's why they're often referred to by techies as "users" rather than "readers." For strong organization of content, analyze the navigation of your favorite writer sites before coming up with your own. Try to limit your primary navigation to six to nine menu items to avoid overwhelming your users, tucking additional pages in the sub-navigation.

Example:
Annie Finch's primary navigation hits the basics—the bio (About), works (Writings), reader schedule (Events), media attention (Buzz), and so on—with a triple-tier architecture so there's both pull-down and fly-out menus for second and third-tier pages.

http://anniefinch.com

4. Engage with your audience.

Ever felt the desire to respond to a compelling piece of writing by conversing with the author? Now it's your turn to answer the gentle knock of readers who have been moved enough by your words to reach out. By throwing some lines of communication out via social media, commenting, e-newsletters, and more, you'll turn readerships into relationships and your platform into a dynamic online community.

As you plan out this piece of your site, however, be careful to balance managing your time with being responsive to your online audience. If you're establishing your readership for the first time, you may want to commit to writing a weekly blog, sending out a weekly e-newsletter with a link to that blog, and then setting time aside to check and respond to any comments that may come your way. (If you don't have time to respond to comments on your blog, don't turn that feature on!) If you are an established (and busy!) author, engaging with your audience may simply consist of a video about your latest work, links to your Facebook and Twitter profiles, and an Events/Readings Schedule page so your fans can meet you in person.

Example:

Karen Osborn's site features a landing page that is self-explanatory: she's an award-winning novelist with four titles, *Centerville* her latest. This is the "Why" you came to her page. Then a down-to-earth photo of herself welcomes newcomers, along with a video and prominent social media links. Her navigation is simple and appropriate, answering the rest of your questions—"Who," "What," "Where" and "How" to contact her. Done.

Karen Osborn: http://www.karenosborn.net/

5. Proof your blog posts.

Nothing screams unprofessional louder than a typo or grammatical error, even in the casual publishing medium of a blog. Remember, your audience is likely to be avid readers and writers who care deeply about words, phrases, sentences—in other words, text in general. And if you're expecting any traffic from an agent, reporter, publisher, or employer, need I say more? Resist the urge to hit the "Publish" button right after you've written your heart out in a 3 a.m. burst of creative energy. Proof your post the next day, after a good night's sleep.

6. Decide to invest time or money.

Want to know a secret? With today's user-friendly Content Management Systems (CMS) such as WordPress, every writer can publish an attractive and effective website, despite limited technical skills. I know it's hard to believe, but it's true. You just need to decide to commit the time or the money...

Time. Here are two resources you can use if you have the time:

Studiopress.com. This is where you'll find inexpensive but professional WordPress templates. With each purchase, you'll receive online tutorials and personalized message board tech support to walk you through a step-by-step build. If you have any experience with simply "WordPress," you're ready to step up your skills to revamp your site. Dare to learn; you will.

WordPress for Dummies by Lisa Sabin-Wilson. This classic tutorial book provides an excellent overview of your WordPress options and walks you through the entire process, from registering your domain name and selecting a web hosting service to customizing free themes.

Money. Here are two exceptional sites that showcase the value of hiring professionals to position you credibly and strategically.

Kelly Ann Coveney's "Evolve the Conversation" is an ambitious project that reflects the writer's aesthetic, builds community, and uses the technical and graphic design talent of others. For me, Kelly's subliminal message is, "Watch me. I'm taking the literary and arts world to new places." http://evolvetheconversation.com

Bill Patrick's author site brands him as a serious, courageous, and bold writer and teacher. Note the photo of him in uniform, the simplicity of navigation that calls out his published work as well as his commercial writing services, and the homepage set to his latest book that happens to capture his brand in the title. http://williampatrickwriter.com

Ready now to launch or redesign your website? Your blog, e-publication, or author site is your gateway to prospective readers and publishers, and you are its sole gatekeeper. Considering how much time, creative energy, and money you've poured into earning your degree, it's worth taking a step back to strategize, plan, and build an effective web presence before walking up to the momentous, virtual podium of the World Wide Web. There are real people and real opportunities out there. Beware, and be wise.

When you put yourself and your work out there, success and serendipity go hand in hand. Many writers have fantasies about a breakout novel or an award-winning essay that finally puts them on the map. Typically, however, success is a much more gradual and mysterious process. A.J. O'Connell advises writers to be wide open to success in all of its forms.

What's the Right Kind of Success?
by A.J. O'Connell

So you've earned your degree. You've got at least one draft of one project written, and undoubtedly you also have a rudimentary publishing plan, even if the details of that plan are a little fuzzy right now. That plan is the one mapped out for you by your professors and your role models: polish up draft, find agent, publish, sell millions of copies, become required reading for English majors. Sound familiar?

But what if something else comes up? Will you be able to scrap that well-worn (and difficult) publishing route and embrace what really happens? There are so many different paths to publication: e-publishing, serial novels, small presses, self-publishing, contests. They're all out there and they're all non-traditional ways of becoming a published author, but do they count? Is publishing an e-book or self-publishing a memoir the "right" kind of success?

I never meant for my first published book to be a pulp fiction novella, but you can't always plan out the details of your own success.

I feared that there was a right way and a wrong way to be successful. But it turned out that fear was a close relative of the fear that hounds us when we're actually doing the writing. If you're a writer, you know this fear well. It's the inner critic, the voice that tells you to avoid all modifiers, and wonders what your workshop will say about your character's motivations.

Part of the joy of an MFA program is that it teaches you to ignore that inner critic while you're in creative mode. But, that critic has a cousin whose specialty isn't writing, but publishing. This inner critic is the one that keeps you from succeeding. It's always pointing toward the "right kind of success," whatever that is. It keeps you from submitting to certain magazines, keeps you from putting yourself out there, and if you manage to outsmart it and snag a little success for yourself, it tells you why this success isn't valid.

So, you have to learn not only to silence your inner writing critic, but to silence your inner publishing critic as well. The problem is that your classmates and professors helped you muzzle the inner writing critic. When it comes to gagging your publishing critic, you're on your own.

Here's my story: I wrote a novella in 2004. At the time I was in my early twenties and working with my very first writing group. I was just learning to tell a story back then, and it was the first time I'd gotten any kind of meaningful feedback on my work. It was a learning experience, but writing the book was also fun for me, an escape from the journalism that consumed the rest of my life. I was mainly writing it for myself and for my little group of writers, and I was writing short because we could only read five pages aloud to the group per meeting.

It was my own little radio play. I read it aloud every two weeks, doing the voices, leaving room for the laughs, and always ending on a cliffhanger. I loved the story. I loved the group's reactions to it. And then I lost interest and abandoned it.

After that, the piece sat untouched for seven years, and I moved on to bigger and, I thought, better pieces of writing. Then I earned my MFA, and wrote the first draft of a novel. *This*, I thought, would be my first published book. If I were going to publish anything, it would be this literary opus, which had been conceived during the program, polished in workshops and approved by my mentors. I envisioned myself taking the traditional publishing route: I'd find an agent who would find me a publisher and then I'd have a novel out. It would be glorious!

What happened instead was much more organic: a friend of mine, who'd been a member of that writing group in 2004, started a small publishing house with some associates. The company was publishing a line of novellas and novelettes as e-books.

My friend remembered my novella, and, in 2011, she called to ask if I'd be willing to submit it. I was thrilled, but when I pulled my manuscript out of a drawer, less than a week after gradating from an MFA program that taught me to write and appreciate literary fiction, I felt my heart sink. The writing was definitely not up to my standards, but I could fix that. The thing I couldn't fix? It wasn't—and isn't—the sort of writing I'd been taught to produce in the MFA program.

Oh no, I thought. This isn't literary fiction. The tone of the prose, the jokes, and all those cliffhangers I'd been so proud of when I was reading it aloud now seemed like liabilities. It read like a noir, chick-lit thriller. And suddenly I was nervous about announcing this publication "success" to my peers.

I was afraid that no one would take me seriously as an author if my first published book wasn't literary fiction. I worried that I might be boxed into a genre, and that my literary novel, my baby, would founder in a drawer and never find a publisher. And what would my professors think of this first foray into publishing? I had visions of the faculty from my MFA program marching up my front walk to revoke my degree, wearing disapproving expressions, chanting "Have we taught you nothing?" I had visions of my classmates telling me that my publishing a book was a result of who I knew, not what I knew. Then I wondered if it had even been worth it for me to get an MFA because I was going to publish a manuscript that predated my degree. Was all the Graham Greene I read for naught? What about all those craft books? Why had I bothered?

All of these fears were ridiculous, of course; they were the product of an overactive critic. Opportunity had caused me to deviate from my plan and the inner publishing critic was reacting.

Not that making a publishing plan is a bad idea. It's not; we *should* make plans, and our MFA programs give us the blueprint for those plans. But we can't be afraid to be flexible.

Flexibility is what allows us to shush that inner critic. In my case, it took me a month to quiet the critic, and I finally managed that by accepting that genre fiction could have literary merit. I spent the month after graduation applying all the MFA craft lessons I'd learned to the novella; I re-read some of those craft books. I worked on character rather than plot, developed tension and wrote character bibles. I embraced the idea of writing genre, joining two groups devoted to genre fiction: Sisters in Crime and New England Horror Writers. But I haven't given up on my "serious" literary work either. Everyone has to start somewhere.

I still plan to get an agent, publish my "literary" novel and win the Pulitzer. But if something comes up, I'm no longer afraid to deviate from the plan.

That's not to say that my inner publishing critic doesn't pipe up from time to time. Her favorite thing to say now goes a little like this: "You're only published because you happened to know someone who needed the book you'd written."

The cure for this, I've found, is to remember that, just as we don't write in a vacuum, we don't publish in one either. Networking is key to almost anyone's success. We go to writers' groups and conferences and, yes, MFA programs as much to meet people as we do to perfect our craft. Treasure those relationships. You never know what projects your friends will start, or what they might need from you.

You never know how success might find you.

For more on different paths to success in publishing and different publishing options, see Chapter 10, edited by A.J. O'Connell.

*B*logging is an easy and effective way for a writer to reach new readers – and keep existing readers engaged – through personal, timely and insightful communication. Below is a list of helpful sources of information.

Blogging Resources for Writers
by Erin A. Corriveau

For writers who are hesitant about creating their own author site, **The Internet Writing Journal** offers advice through an essay, To Blog or Not to Blog. It's available at www.internetwritingjournal.com/nov05/cew4.htm.

The most popular blogging platforms include:

Blogger (www.blogger.com): Free and hosted by Google

TypePad (www.typepad.com): Free

WordPress.com (www.wordpress.com): Free

WordPress.org (www.wordpress.org): Must have a self-hosted website to use. Same software as .com

MovableType (www.movabletype.com): Fees required

An article on **ProBlogger** can help you choose the right platform. It's available at www.problogger.net/archives/2006/02/15/choosing-a-blog-platform/

Most author blogs are simply designed with clean lines and plentiful white space, since the content should be the focus. A sophisticated looking site, however, will appeal to more readers.

Thesis (www.diythemes.com) – A WordPress blog theme with many configuration options

Woo Themes (www.woothemes.com) – Various themes for various platforms

For measuring reader traffic and engagement on your blog, **Google Analytics** (www.google.com/analytics) measures which posts are the most popular, how readers are finding your blog and a variety of helpful statistics.

If you have a book available for sale, and are using your blog as a marketing tool, **aStore** (astore.amazon.com) adds an Amazon store directly to your blog, so readers can purchase your books instantly while visiting your blog.

inkPageant (www.inkpageant.com) is a blog content repository that aims to help writers improve their craft and reach their goals. The site allows writers to submit a blog post, and once the post is approved, inkPageant will publish it and provide a link to the writer's blog. The site allows writers to share advice, recommend books and sell books through their profile page, as well as announce book signings and events, share film or book reviews, etc. Approved posts are distributed to an interested audience to boost blog traffic.

Chapter 8

MAKE ENDS MEET (WHILE YOU WORK ON YOUR MASTERPIECE)

edited by Michael Bayer

Even the most famous authors and poets once did boring, grueling or just plain odd jobs before establishing themselves as literary giants or commercial successes. This chapter explores a variety of ways writers can apply their craft to pay the bills while allowing time to pursue their own creative work and publishing success.

The Ghost Life

by Travis Baker

Tuesdays and Thursdays suck the worst. I have to get up at 5:30 to make coffee, read the sports page, walk the dog, pack my stuff and be out the door by 7:00 and hope I don't get stuck behind a manure truck on highway 202 to get to my 8:00 College Comp class in Unity. After that class I have an hour off before the 10:00 College Comp class, which I usually spend in the library, tucked into the little table under Coleridge and Collins, grading papers. After the 10:00 it's back on 202 to try to get to EMCC by 1:00 for Introduction to Communications, or, as it should be called, How to Write a Sentence with a Verb and Everything!

Mondays, Wednesdays and Fridays aren't too bad because I only have two classes, the 9:00 ENG 101 class at University of Maine and the 12:30 Intro to Lit at Eastern Maine Community College. But Tuesdays and Thursdays definitely suck.

I mentioned this to Dave, my former Advisor. He took in air between his teeth.

"Yup," he said. "That's the life for awhile."

My three parking passes give me close to the door proximity at all three campuses, which is great in the winter when it's -5 without the wind chill factor.

I float through hallways like a ghost, drifting past the open door offices of the full-time tenure-tracked with their stacks of books, leaning back in their well worn chairs. I wish I had a coffee mug sitting on top of a filing cabinet like they do. Instead I have 152 papers to grade by next Monday and I forgot to pack my lunch.

In Unity, Brad wrote a story about how his father saved him when he fell through the ice when he was seven and then gave him a beating for doing something so stupid. At the U o' Maine, Marshall managed to connect Aristotle's model of argument with Anzaldua's "Wild Tongue." At EMCC, Shelly wrote a coherent paragraph. There is warmth in being able to write "Well done!" There is pride in seeing a smile.

I'm like a literary feather floating on the breeze. I have taught somewhere around 1,700 students and learned from 1,698 of them.

I'm an adjunct English Instructor.

*I*s writing a job or a passion? Is it professional or personal? For many writers, these lines are blurry. Some of us have found financial success in other fields, but feel writing is our true calling. Some of us have pursued a writing career since college, and embraced all the fears and insecurities that come with that. Some of us write freelance. Some of us teach writing. Whatever a writer's circumstances, the rent needs to be paid.

While it's tempting to envision our lives as either world-famous authors or starving artists, such a dichotomy is both impractical and unnecessary. Even in the absence of a blockbuster book, writing can be a stable – and even lucrative – professional field if you're willing to keep a low overhead, be flexible about the kind of writing you do, and maybe open your mind to teaching.

Many writers make the ends meet through some combination of freelance gigs, adjunct teaching positions, and grants or fellowships. This chapter highlights opportunities for writers to find gainful employment while they're still, or always, working on their blockbuster.

Freelancing is one of the most common ways for dedicated writers to keep writing while paying the bills. It can be stimulating, gratifying and lucrative, and the MFA degree is the ultimate academic credential that allows you to market your services. Abbey Cleland describes the ideal attitude *and* aptitude that will benefit aspiring freelance writers.

Yes, I Can Write That

By Abbey Cleland

The life of the freelance writer-for-hire is not a glamorous one, even if you write for glamorous people. Have you ever seen a billboard featuring Shane Halter's face? Would you spend a week's pay for Shane Halter's rookie card? Probably not because chances are you've never even heard of the guy.

You've probably never heard of Shane Halter because he is a utility player. And not just *any* utility player, but *the* go-to, "we can depend on you" utility player for my favorite baseball team, the Detroit Tigers, from 2000 to 2003. In fact, on October 1st of 2000, Shane Halter played all nine positions in a single game—the fourth in history to do so—and still you've never heard of him. How unfair is that?

See, in our society, we don't like to hunt about to determine who deserves recognition. No, we like it to hit us in the face, or in this case, we like the ball they hit to hit us in the mitt, should our mitt be four hundred feet from home plate. After middle school, few trophies go to the player who's most well-rounded. When was the last time your boss patted you on the back for your charming versatility? Probably never. Because you are an adult now, and adults specialize.

Well, specialization means death if you're new to the world of freelance writing. In order to survive as a new freelance writer you cannot hit a home run once every ten at-bats. You just need to get on base every time, and the way you get on base is by saying, "Yes I can write that," even if it means you go home and frantically Google "Angstrom compensation pyrheliometer" (which I learned quite a lot about during one assignment).

Simply, freelancers are the writing world's utility ballplayers. We must have the "can-do" attitude of a Marine and the heart of Notre Dame's Rudy. We must be impeccably punctual and fiercely self-disciplined, for our livelihood depends on it. Most importantly, we must be style chameleons, able to articulate ideas in every tone from clinical to flirtatious, and snap between these settings with the grace of a seasoned short stop.

Now maybe you're thinking, "Okay, I can do this. I can be versatile. I've got the discipline. Put me in, Coach." Great, glad to have you. But how do you go from the bench to the freelance field? And how do you ensure you stay a key player? (Sidebar: I promise, [probably, hopefully] no more baseball analogies.)

Here's your mission:

1. Create a killer portfolio.
While you may feel pressured to create a portfolio that is pigeon-hole-proof, meaning it wouldn't fix you into any one niche, genre, or medium, you should feel comforted that the grand versatility you must

possess does not need to be initially presented in your portfolio. For example, my first official writer-for-hire assignment was to adapt two binders packed with interviews and notes in prose and bullet-point form into a feature-length biopic screenplay. The subject was a real-life '60s jazz prodigy conman who, when he wasn't playing brilliant jazz, spent most of his time in jail, or buying, selling, and using heavy drugs (which warranted his return to jail). At the time, I was marketing myself as a children's writer, toting around an educational TV show pilot and pitch bible that would never be produced (if you're interested, give me a call; my mom and I still think it's quite clever). For some reason I may never understand, an independent producer read my children's work and thought I'd be a good fit to write this racy biopic. Since then, I have secured several other jobs using both the biopic feature and the children's educational TV show as writing samples, and hence learned this valuable, albeit obvious, lesson: good writing is good writing. This lesson yields another valuable, albeit obvious, lesson: good writers are good writers. So, if you hope to secure jobs writing grants, manuals, dissertations, business plans, screenplays, treatments, poems, and editorials, you needn't spend three years developing sample content for each niche. Simply write a few exceptional pieces and be convincing (through the confidence and composure you project in the interview) when you say, "Yes, I can write that."

2. Tap into the invisible resources around you.

In each of our daily lives (think dinner parties, the hair salon, charity events, PTA meetings), we encounter people who at some point need to write, but do not know how or just do not have the time. While trying to avoid morphing into some shameless self-promoter, acknowledge the quiet opportunities around you, especially while you're building your client base. Maybe you're waiting to hear back regarding a slew of submissions you sent to your dream publications, or maybe you need a little extra cash. You truly never know when one of these random "side projects" may grow to be your bread and butter, or a one-time-only jackpot. Once, purely by mentioning a ghostwriting anecdote at a holiday mixer, I was connected to an aging multi-millionaire who hoped to have his personal biography penned quickly. This casual conversation led to one of my most fascinating and lucrative gigs to date.

In that same respect, once you secure a job out of your realm of expertise (which, chances are, if you're good, should happen quite often), tap into your friends, family members, and colleagues as resources. Everyone likes to feel like an expert at something, and I assure you, most will welcome providing you with some insight into your topic du jour. That leads us nicely into our next task:

3. Research like your life depends on it (because it sort of does).

It can be difficult to sound convincing all of the time, right? In a single week, you may have to critique a red wine reduction sauce, write a retirement center's brochure, and polish a TV repair manual. But what if you're a thirty-something technologically challenged wine neophyte? Research. Research. Research. (And thank your lucky stars that Al Gore invented the Internet.)

4. Always appear to be in high demand.

Now, we don't have to get crazy with this one. No need to answer your cell pretending to be your fictitious, over-worked assistant, but number four should not go overlooked, either. No one wants to hire anyone who seems too eager for the work. If the potential client, publication, or employer discovers you are *always* available, they may assume others don't acknowledge your talent. This won't work in your favor, especially when you're just starting out. Also, on this note, should you maintain a "day job" while dipping into the freelance marketplace, it's best not to share this with the potential employer. If you expect to be paid professionally, then you must appear to be pursuing this as your primary profession. (Note: Some feel "freelance" is synonymous with "part time." This is a dangerous misinterpretation. "Freelance" simply means that you work for different companies at different times rather than being permanently employed by one company. To avoid confusion, I have come to refer to myself as a "full-time freelance writer.")

5. Always appear happy to write a variety of content in a variety of media.

No one likes to hear the prom queen complain about being asked to the dance by too many fellows, right? Doesn't exactly inspire sympathy. Some will find your freelance writing life to be a glamorous, creative way to make a living, and, as mentioned earlier, it is not. Not at all. So keep the whining about "today I have to write about this," and "tomorrow I have to write about that," to yourself. Your friends and family members won't want to hear it, and your potential employers *definitely* won't. Vent to your writer friends. We are your tribe, and we know what's really "behind the curtain": sweat, blood, pulled hair, vats of coffee, etc.

We get that sometimes upon hitting the final "send" button, you'll fight a tear, as you'll regret having to say goodbye to a topic that you enjoyed exploring so very much. We get that other times, you'll be forced to create incentives to fulfill the pettiest interim deadlines. At those moments, it doesn't matter that you can work in your pajamas. The assignment is miserable, which means your little writer life is miserable. Just yesterday I said aloud to myself: "Two more pages and you get to watch *Downton Abbey* and eat half a sleeve of Girl Scout Samoas." Do what you have to do (within reasonable means) to complete both your favorite and most dreaded gigs, and always keep in mind that, either way, they come and they go.

6. Never short-change yourself.

Most successful writers will admit that writing has always come somewhat naturally to them. It's understandable that one could feel uncomfortable monetizing what comes naturally. To make matters worse, by and large, we writers are a brittle, highly opinionated, highly insecure lot—a population predisposed to self-scrutiny. It may feel funny to demand $100+ an hour. For heftier, more complex and more time-consuming projects you may even have to propose some serious flat compensation figures. I'm telling you now, do yourself a favor and get over any reluctance immediately. Most people cannot write, though they can acknowledge when something is poorly written, and then there's a whole population of others who can write well but simply don't have the time. If relevant, don't balk at mentioning in your pitch that the potential employer could probably do a fine job tackling the writing of the project herself but that her time would surely be better spent focusing on different aspects of the business. This way, you acknowledge her intelligence, while emphasizing the time-consuming nature of the work—double win for you, especially if you charge by the hour.

Years ago, a friend of mine demanded to know my base pay. She flinched when I told her $80 an hour. "What are you, a frickin' neurosurgeon?" she said. (She's not my best friend.) Two distinctions must be made, and I hope you find this comforting: 1. *Unlike* neurosurgeons, at slow times freelance writers may work just five hours a week. And, more importantly, 2. *Like* neurosurgeons, the freelance writer is a high demand professional who provides a unique, rare skill, oftentimes with very short notice. Value yourself, value your skill, and don't work for anyone who doesn't.

So, should you create that killer portfolio, tap into the invisible resources around you, research like mad, appear busy *and* happy, and demand you remain valued all the while, I think it's fair to say you're doing everything in your power to excel in the wild freelance marketplace. Just remember to keep the phrase, "Yes, I can write that," on the tip of your tongue, and who knows, maybe you'll end up like unsung utility ballplayer Shane Halter, doing what you love from all different angles in the field. Would that really be so bad?

*S*uccessful freelancers must be curious and resourceful. Independence has its special privileges, but it also requires that freelance writers have the drive and determination to keep learning and keep their plate full of assignments. Just as a writer needs readers, a freelance writer needs clients. Sarah Z. Sleeper provides practical tips to keep your freelance business thriving.

The Business of Freelance Writing (Or, I Have an MFA, Now How do I Earn Money as a Writer?)
—*Sarah Z. Sleeper*

When I went to college, some twenty-five years ago, my goal was to become a writer, and possibly a literature professor or literary critic. One way or the other, I envisioned a literary future. After earning a degree in English, I made a key decision, one that I credit for bringing me much joy as well as professional success. I decided I would never take a non-writing job.

And for two decades I never did. My goal was to make a living as a writer and I did it. I have been a journalist, a ghost writer, a corporate writer, a marketing writer, an editor and a writing teacher. All along I honed my writing skills, striving to learn as much as possible from my superiors and my fellow writers. Writing for a living was excellent preparation for earning an MFA.

We MFAs tend to equate "writer" with "literature." And of course, we're right to do so. But don't limit yourself. There's a universe of non-literary writing work out there that can stimulate your brain, satisfy your creative spirit, hone your writing and editing skills, and pay your bills. It's a mistake to think that you compromise your artistic standards by doing non-literary writing. The truth is that any professional writing you do—for a corporate client or a mainstream publication, for instance—will make you a better artist.

Even though it's write-for-hire work, approach every article, press release and brochure as a story. As a professional writer with an MFA, you know the importance of taking readers through the beginning, middle and end of a narrative. That's how you keep their interest and that's what will set your writing apart and garner you repeat clients.

Cultivate an open mind

Successful freelancers are willing to try many types of writing. Everything from television scripts, to web site content, to local newspaper articles, to advertisements in magazines, to computer manuals—all can be written by freelance writers. Many companies hire freelancers, so don't assume that the software company you admire or the charity you support wouldn't hire you to write its press releases or newsletters.

The Internet has only multiplied the opportunities for freelancers. Popular magazines publish their content online, but also publish special online features and blogs to complement their printed material.

Online communication means it's completely reasonable for you to apply for a writing job in Germany, or Japan, or anywhere else in the world. The Internet opens up a universe of possibilities for freelancers. It's possible to write for a newspaper in Washington, D.C., from your office in San Diego, or to write for UNICEF in New York from your home in Connecticut.

Freelance Writing Jobs

Here are some types of writing worth your consideration because they often come with nice paychecks attached:

1. **Press releases**—Company news, financial announcements, new product launches, personnel/executive changes, award notices

2. **Advertising copy**—Special sections in newspapers and magazines ("Special Advertising Section"), copy for classified and display ads, copy for brochures and flyers, copy for television and radio ads

3. **Corporate web site content**—From the home page to the "About" page, companies need well-written online copy to attract and retain business

4. **Internal corporate magazines and newsletters**—Did you know that most big companies print these types of publications? Often they

are glossy, 100-page magazines. Sometimes they're small black-and-white mailings. Companies publish feature articles, Q&A interview pieces, editorials, industry news, biographies and more.

5. **External corporate magazines**—These are usually glossy, slick publications distributed to customers, potential customers and anyone in the corporation's particular industry. They publish feature articles, Q&A interview pieces, editorials, industry news, biographies and more.

6. **Annual reports**—These are a bit specialized because you must have solid understanding of financial fundamentals, but can be lucrative.

7. **Case studies**—From a one-pager to one-hundred pages or more, these require in-depth knowledge of the company and often the same type of knowledge about its competitors. Can be lucrative.

8. **Corporate books**—For marketing purposes. Sometimes ghost-written for CEO/CFO/CIO or the like.

9. **Non-profit documents**—Fundraising appeals, donor letters, pamphlets, web site copy and on and on and on.

10. **Editing of all of the above**—You can find a satisfying combination of writing and editing jobs. Doing a bit of both is good for your brain and helps improve your writing

Even if you've never published before, your MFA gives you an automatic credential and credibility as a writer. Be fearless! Be creative! Approach companies in industries you like, know about, want to learn more about. Think big! What's the worst they can say? You're a writer; you'll survive rejection! Just keep trying. Disney? Apple? Intel? Successful local companies? Give them a shot.

It's hard to know what to charge when you first start out, but I'd encourage you to ask for a professional rate, enough to allow you to support yourself. If you charge too little, your potential clients may not value you or take you as seriously as they should. Early on in my freelance career, I might have accepted a few hundred dollars for a short article in a local magazine. As you gain experience and publication credits, your rates should increase. You will earn the right to charge more over time as your skills and reputation improve.

You must be prepared to negotiate. You must believe in yourself as the writing expert, worth the fees you charge. Eventually, for specialized writing, such as corporate work, it's reasonable to picture yourself making $1,000 to $2,000 for a 1,000-word article, $10,000 for a 100-page book, $1 to $2 per word for a 500-word blurb, or $60 to $100 per hour for hourly work. Business writing tends to pay more than journalism. You may find that you can earn more money writing press releases for companies than feature articles for your local newspaper.

Keep in mind when you do business writing for corporations, you are probably doing "work for hire." That means the company will own what you write and you relinquish your copyrights. If you write journalism or literary work, make sure the publication contract does not give away your copyrights. You may be presented with a contract that asks for all rights, but you should negotiate. You can find more information about contracts from The National Writers Union, www.nwu.org.

Where can I get jobs now?

As you strike out as a freelancer, try local and national publications. Search online databases. Look into big companies and small ones, non-profits, professional associations, marketing firms, radio and television stations, e-zines, blogs and trade journals. Try querying consulting firms, research firms, PR and marketing firms. Be as creative in your job search as you are in your writing and you will find jobs!

Your MFA community can also be an excellent resource. When you're looking for work, mention it to your peers. Someone might know of a job or freelance gig that would be perfect for you. Put the word out that you are on the market. Post it on Facebook and LinkedIn. Talk about it in your writers groups and with your friends. Spend plenty of time online, researching the possibilities and examining your options.

Try consulting firms:

- www.accenture.com
- www.pwc.com/us/en/index.jhtml
- www.mckinsey.com/
- www.deloitte.com/view/en_US/us/index.htm

Try research firms:

- www.gartner.com/technology/home.jsp
- www.forrester.com/rb/research/
- www.idc-fi.com/

Try PR and marketing firms:

- www.edelman.com/
- www.burson-marsteller.com
- www. fleishmanhillard.com/
- www.ketchum.com/
- www.ogilvy.com/
- www.yrgrp.com/

Spend time on professional sites and job sites. In addition to those below, there are professional sites, organizations and publications for just about any industry you can think of, from horseback riding to microchips to fitness to medical device manufacturing. It's up to you to do the research.

- All Freelance Writing... http://allfreelancewriting.com/
- American Copy Editors Society... http://www.copydesk.org/
- American Society of Business Publication Editors http://www.asbpe.org/
- American Society of Journalists and Authors... http://www.asja.org
- Association of Writers and Writing Programs... http://www.awpwriter.org/

- Authors Guild... http://www.authorsguild.org/
- Elance... http://www.elance.com/
- Freelance Writing... http://www.freelancewriting.com/freelance-writing-jobs.php
- Journalism Jobs... http://www.journalismjobs.com
- LinkedIn... http://www.linkedin.com
- Media Bistro... http://www.mediabistro.com
- National Press Foundation... http://nationalpress.org/
- National Writers Union ... http://www.nwu.org
- Poynter Online... http://www.poynter.org
- Publishers Weekly... http://www.publishersweekly.com
- Society of Professional Journalists... http://www.spj.org and http://www.sdspj.org
- The National Press Club... http://press.org/
- Writers Market... http://www.writersmarket.com/

The last word

You have your MFA. You were already a writer, but now you've got the diploma to prove it. Go forth and write! Write your poetry and your stories and your essays. And if you want to be a freelancer, do it. It's completely possible to live a literary life and make a living, too. You might find happiness as a part-time poet and part-time journalist, or as a novelist and ghostwriter, or as an essayist and corporate editor. Can you create your own combination of writing work that works for you?

djunct teaching at the college level can be incredibly rewarding, incredibly frustrating, and everything in between. The experience isn't easily encapsulated. As featured in the opening of this chapter, Travis Baker employs a prose poem style to articulate the elusive, yet profound rewards of adjuncting. And, like freelancing, adjuncting is one of the most common ways for writers to attain gainful employment while maintaining the time, flexibility and energy to keep up their own creative writing. Talk to a hundred adjunct instructors and you'll hear a hundred opinions, but here Ioanna Pettas Opidee distills the adjuncting experience down to its bare essentials.

Surviving the Adjunct Lifestyle: Advice from the Cliff's Edge
—*Ioanna Pettas Opidee*

Before I earned my MFA in Creative Writing, I got an MA in English. To pay my way to that degree, I worked as a "graduate assistant," teaching freshman composition courses in return for tuition remission, and I fell in love with teaching.

This despite the fact that it was a classic sink-or-swim scenario. I received the mandatory textbook for the course about two weeks before my 45-50 students did, most of whom were just about three or four years behind my 21-year-old self in their schooling, and some of whom were old enough to be my parents. In terms of productivity, I did everything wrong—I stayed up all hours of the night, grading papers, planning lessons, to an unhealthy degree of obsessive perfectionism. I released my classes fifteen minutes early almost every period because I remained pretty shy about public speaking, but to make up for it, I spent an exorbitant amount of time conferencing with every single student. At the end of the semester, I received some validating—yet revealing—student evaluations: "Ms. Pettas is the best teacher I ever had" (which I found sad); "Ms. Pettas cares so much about all of her students" (which I found excessively true); "Ms. Pettas is always there to help. Even if you email her at 3 a.m., she'll respond within five minutes" (which concerned my faculty advisor a great deal). In short, I was driving myself crazy; I'd embarked on the road to burnout . . .

I wasn't there yet, though, and I wanted to keep teaching. I loved being able to test out an idea together with my students, to help illuminate the value of doing so, collaboratively; I loved coaching and motivating them through the processes of reading and writing, and deeply examining those processes together along the way. So near the eve of my graduation, when my faculty advisor asked what I thought I might do next, I said, "I think I'll try to adjunct."

"Oh, no," she said, "you don't want to do that." As a specialist in working class literature, I think she was particularly alert to what it means to be overworked and underpaid—as many an adjunct certainly is and may feel. She shared horror stories of her friend who motorcycled across New York City every day to teach eight classes at four different colleges just to make ends meet, riffling a stack of student essays like a machine processing bubbled-in Scantron sheets.

But it didn't matter. I wanted to teach, at the college level, and I wasn't in league for a full-time position, so I applied and was hired by three local universities, beginning my now-six year career as a part-time professor. A year in, I enrolled in an MFA program. While earning that degree, I worked as "graduate assistant director" of the school's composition program, in return for portionable tuition remission, and I learned a great deal about how writing programs are run, and how adjuncts are hired and managed.

At one point in all this time, I did reach bitter burnout—an intensely unpleasant experience for me and for those around me—and I quit teaching to waitress full-time. It was remarkable—and frustrating—to me that I could earn roughly as much teaching college courses as I could working a job I'd been doing since before my parents and I invested in three relatively expensive degrees (I attended Boston College as an undergraduate). On the other hand, there are interesting, and rewarding, crossovers between waitressing and teaching—particularly in the realm of *service*. (Teachable moments abound, too, when you can dispel certain notions and assumptions about servers and their levels of intelligence, education, and ambition.) At the end of the waitressing shift, though, there are no papers to grade; I could focus on my writing. And it was empowering to be able to make the choice to step out of the teaching cycle, to reflect on where my career was headed and what I wanted from it—what sort of balance I wanted to strike.

But I missed the classroom too much and returned after only one semester away. Since then, I've managed to crawl back up the hillside to a healthier equilibrium. From this state, and based on my own experiences and observations, I will try to offer a few thoughts on the matter of how to "survive" as an adjunct, in hopes that some portion will be useful to others.

1. Remember why you do this.

I teach because I'm a writer. I write, in large part, to learn. Teaching, for me, is a key source of learning, as it likely is for most teachers. I learn from my students—from the questions they ask, from the knowledge and insights they bring, and from the process of trying to understand and articulate what I know about a subject, or don't.

In more practical terms, I teach as an adjunct because it affords me the flexibility to write during the day. It frees me from a 9 to 5 schedule that I've found to be a drain on my creativity. But more importantly, I spend most of my waking, working hours thinking, speaking, and learning about reading and writing. While, admittedly, this in itself can be draining—can, in excess, drain the well of energy we can devote to these activities—I find that it ultimately creates a sometimes mysterious, often serendipitous synergy in my work and life.

Those are just my reasons, though. Whatever your own, I think it helps to keep those reasons (which will likely change and evolve) top of mind, especially in those dark, lonely hours when you may ask yourself—as you glance across the hall at the full-time, tenured colleague who earns triple what you do per class, or as you glare at a towering stack of student writing portfolios—"Why am I doing this?" My suggestion is: Try to answer that question for yourself, every time you ask. If you don't like the answer, it might be time to try something else.

2. Remember that it's a choice.

This leads directly into another thought that I've found helpful: Remember that you're not stuck. Or, perhaps, you're only stuck if you *feel* stuck.

One of the major drawbacks of being an adjunct—the often semester-to-semester contracts—can, in certain circumstances, be an advantage. You have the freedom to do something else, to *choose.* Full-time and tenured professors do, too, of course, but they have a lot more to lose. Adjuncts commonly take leave for one or more semesters—to devote additional time to writing, to attend a residency, to take on freelance projects, or even, as in my case, to waitress—and return to teach at the same school with no hard feelings on either end.

There is a risk involved, of course. Once you're off a program director's radar, it *might* be difficult to get back on it. New people join onto his or her faculty, and there may not be room for you during the given semester when you try to return. But if you stay in the loop and on good terms, decision makers may be more likely to reach out to you when a need does arise.

And needs, as far as I've seen, *always* arise.

Also, there are lots of schools out there. Some may be more aligned than others with your interests, needs, and approach to teaching. Developing relationships with multiple institutions in your area gives you more choices, freedom, and flexibility to take or turn down offers.

3. Cast a wide net, and maintain multiple relationships.

Whether you want to teach composition, creative writing, professional writing, journalism, or some other type of course, it's important to know which department or program these courses fall under and who does the hiring. Before you reach out to a new institution, do your research online. But don't be discouraged if the information isn't as explicit as you'd hoped; reaching out to the chair of a program or department for more information or with questions, I've found, is almost always helpful—they'll either answer your questions directly or immediately forward you to the most relevant person.

Don't wait for a job posting to appear online; many schools don't bother to list part-time openings but, instead, maintain a growing pool of current, former, and potential adjuncts that they can dip into at will. Instead, send out a simple query—briefly introduce yourself and what you're interested in, and attach your C.V. Unless you're replying to a specific job ad, I would avoid sending too much information—teaching philosophy statements, sample assignments, syllabi, etc.—until or unless they are requested. Asking to come in for an informational interview or to learn more about a particular program/department often works. When they're busy and hard-pressed to fill a slot, they'll be more likely to call *you* if they can put a face to a name on that glorious C.V.

Whether you're trying to land a gig at a new institution or at one where you've taught before, it's important to reach out at the right times—namely, when the aforementioned "needs" are most likely to crop up. While you don't want to bombard a program director or department chair's inbox, it's worth reaching out around mid-semester to inquire about their teaching needs for the following term. Because things often change at the last minute, it's also worth following up again in the few weeks right before a new term begins.

All of this is part of how you keep your options open, and possibly avoid feeling stuck. Remember that English departments and writing programs need you, as a reliable and effective adjunct, as much as (or *more than*) you need them. Value yourself and your time, while fostering good relationships.

4. Understand your rights and responsibilities.
Good relationships are founded, among other things, on mutual respect. In the adjunct realm, this means remembering that you are a professional, and as such, you are entitled to certain benefits (which, unfortunately, almost never include health care just yet) and rights, ranging from whether you'll be granted office space with access to a computer to whether you'll be represented in (or welcome at) department or university-wide meetings. These matters vary from school to school, so it's a good idea to become familiar with them. If an employee handbook is available to you, it's worth reading. If not, or if it's not specifically tailored to adjuncts, it's worth talking to and asking questions of your supervisors and colleagues.

Of course it's equally as important to understand your responsibilities. Are you contractually obligated to attend meetings or hold regular office hours and conferences with students? Are there certain curriculum standards or requirements that you must include on your syllabus and integrate into your courses? If you teach at multiple institutions, it can be difficult to keep track of all these, but doing so is essential to establishing a reputation for yourself as an adjunct who can be counted on. This, I think, puts you into a stronger—or, at least, less vulnerable—position.

5. Know, and communicate, your limits.

And then there's going overboard. Signing on for every "opportunity" to sit on a committee, or join a task force. Volunteering to work every "Come be an English major!" fair. Serving as an advisor for various students' honors projects or independent studies without compensation. Such activities can be professionally and intellectually enriching, and can also be a chance to present yourself as motivated and dependable. They can widen your exposure and showcase your value. But, in excess—and excess, I find, comes quickly here, as these activities have a way of compounding themselves—you may find yourself feeling stretched too thin, not to mention *broke*, and possibly on the road to bitter-burnout.

This applies, too, when you're suddenly offered more courses than you feel you can take on in a given semester. There's often a fear, for an adjunct, that saying *no* to a course will get you black-listed, or at least cast you permanently off an employer's radar. Perhaps this is a well-founded fear; however, I've found that explaining why you aren't able to take on the course, and following up at a later date (when you *are* more available), effectively avoids this issue. If you take on too many courses and end up flailing through the semester, it can be worse for your reputation and relationship than saying no from the start.

I, for one, am constantly forgetting my limits. So for me, it's not so much a matter of *knowing* my limits as *coming to know* them. I've learned to make a more conscious and reflective effort to do so, and it helps. I've also learned to better communicate those limits—to respectfully decline "opportunities," sometimes with a polite yet pointed reminder that, unfortunately, I have too many jobs and not enough time to take on this additional course, or that project I would otherwise love to complete. The reminder, I think, is important and useful to all parties involved.

While it's easy to feel embittered by the dearth of opportunity and the often utterly unjust circumstances, it may be helpful to recognize that important work is being done at various levels within academia to improve job categories and working conditions for adjunct/part-time/affiliate/pick-your-preferred-euphemism-for-*subordinate* faculty. Enough work? I'm not sure. But even within the *six* years I've been teaching, I've seen a noticeable increase in the national conversation surrounding these issues, within and beyond academia. It's good to keep track of this—follow the trends reported on in *The Chronicle of Higher Education*, *The New York Times*, and other publications, and maybe even take action and join the AAUP (American Association of University Professors). Because, in our excitement and desire to teach at the college level, it can be just as easy to wear rose-colored lenses (especially at the start).

Perspectives on and ways of handling the issues discussed above vary widely. The best advice I can offer is this: Pay attention; listen carefully to what others have to say, take stock of your options and, meanwhile, figure out what works best for you, your career, and your *life*.

*W*hile the role of literature in civil society seems always to be under threat, government and non-profit institutions still support writers through a variety of funding sources, but writers must be knowledgeable and proactive to access these funds. Carol Ann Davis explains the options available to writers who need an extra financial cushion to finish that time-consuming book or collection.

Grants and Fellowships: Where to Look, When to Apply
by Carol Ann Davis

The number of grants and fellowships for emerging writers has grown in recent years, and many include a chance to do a little bit of teaching and/or complete a residency as part of the award, all of which are an opportunity for professional development. Some residencies may not provide large stipendiary support, but support you in other ways, such as placing you in touch with an artistic community and offering additional professional preparation (such as editorial training). All grants and fellowships are accompanied by guidelines; carefully consult those guidelines to determine whether the grant is intended for an emerging or a mid-career writer, a writer from a certain genre or geographical area, etc. The following information was adapted from the websites listed.

Places to Look for Grants and Fellowships:
• A few grants and fellowships will be highlighted below, but there are a great many tailored to particular regions of the country, genres, or constituencies.

• Keep up with grant deadlines by consulting the Grants & Awards free directory offered by Poets & Writers magazine (http://www.pw.org/grants).

• For $12, the PEN Center offers an annual Grants & Awards listing that is definitely worth the money, and PEN is a great organization to join as well (https://www.pen.org/content/grants-awards-one-year-subscription).

• State and local arts council grants are available on the websites of individual state arts organizations; many private, local arts organizations exist to support local writers.

A few select fellowships and awards (not requiring residency):

• The National Endowment for the Arts Literature Fellowships: the NEA Literature Fellowships program offers $25,000 grants in prose (fiction and creative nonfiction) and poetry to published creative writers that enable the recipients to set aside time for writing, research, travel, and general career advancement. Grant guidelines stipulate a certain number of pages in genre must be published prior to application for this grant. (http://arts.gov/grants-individuals/creative-writing-fellowships#sthash.IAdY5NBK.dpuf)

• The PEN Emerging Writers Award: $2,500 is awarded to two promising new writers—one fiction writer and one nonfiction writer—at a crucial early moment in their careers. The awards are given to promote talented up-and-coming authors whose writing has been featured in distinguished literary journals across the country, but who have yet to publish book-length works. (http://www.pen.org/grants-and-awards/pen-emerging-writers-awards)

A few select residential fellowships for emerging writers that include residencies and financial support (adapted from websites; consult listed websites for additional information):

• The *Kenyon Review* Fellowship Program: This two-year post-graduate residential fellowship at Kenyon College offers qualified individuals time to develop as writers, teachers, and editors. Fellows receive a $32,500 stipend, plus health benefits. (http://www.kenyonreview.org/programs/fellowship/)

• The Stadler Center for Poetry Stadler Fellows (open genre): Initiated in 1998, Stadler Fellowships offer a recent MFA or MA in poetry the opportunity to receive professional training in arts administration and literary editing. Stadler Fellowships are designed to balance the development of professional skills with time to complete a first book of poems. Stadler Fellows assist for twenty hours each week in the administration of the Stadler Center for Poetry and/or in the editing of *West Branch,* Bucknell's nationally distinguished literary journal. Fellows also work as staff members and instructors in the Bucknell Seminar for Younger Poets in June. The Fellowship stipend is $20,000. In addition, each Fellow is provided health insurance, office space in the Stadler Center, and housing. (http://www.bucknell.edu/x3733.xml)

• The University of Wisconsin Institute for Creative Writing: Since 1986, the University of Wisconsin's Institute for Creative Writing has provided time, space, and an intellectual community for writers working on a first book of poetry or fiction. Each fellowship carries a $27,000 stipend, health benefits, and a one-course-per-semester teaching assignment in intermediate or advanced undergraduate creative writing. Fiction and poetry fellows are asked to give one public reading during the fellowship year. (http://creativewriting.wisc.edu/fellowships.html)

• Colgate University's Olive B. O'Connor Fellowship in Creative Writing: The annual fellowship is designed to support writers completing their first books. It provides a generous stipend, office space, and an intellectual community for the recipients, who spend the academic year at Colgate. In return, each fellow teaches a creative-writing workshop each semester and gives a public reading of his or her work. (http://www.colgate.edu/academics/departments-and-programs/english/creative-writing-fellows)

• Stanford University's Stegner Fellowships: Stanford offers ten two-year fellowships each year, five in fiction and five in poetry. All the fellows in each genre convene weekly in a 3-hour workshop with Stanford's creative writing faculty. Fellowships include a living stipend of $26,000 per year. In addition, fellows' tuition and health insurance are paid for by the Creative Writing Program. The Stegner Fellowship is a full-time academic commitment, and is not intended to be pursued concurrently with another degree program. Fellows must live close enough to Stanford to be able to attend workshops, readings, and events. (http://creativewriting.stanford.edu/about-the-fellowship)

• Fine Arts Work Center, Provincetown, Fellowships: The Fine Arts Work Center offers a unique residency for writers and visual artists in the crucial early stages of their careers. Located in Provincetown, Massachusetts, an area with a long history as an arts colony, the Work Center provides seven-month Fellowships to twenty Fellows each year in the form of living/work space and a modest monthly stipend. Residencies run from October 1 through May 1. Fellows have the opportunity to pursue their work independently in a diverse and supportive community of peers. (http://web.fawc.org/program)

$\mathcal{W}$e spill our minds and hearts onto the page, often instead of taking "real" jobs with benefits, but let's not forget that writers also possess physical bodies that need to stay healthy. The Affordable Care Act has created a new landscape for writers in need of affordable and reliable health insurance. Meredith Kazer explains how "Obamacare" has created new rights, responsibilities and opportunities for self-employed writers to manage their healthcare without going broke.

Health Insurance for Writers
by Meredith Kazer

Prior to 2014, self-employed writers had few options for health insurance coverage. Young writers might have received coverage under their parents' policy until the age of 25. Married writers were eligible for benefits under the policy of their spouse. Writers might also have received health coverage through writer's guilds if earnings reported by their signatory employer reached the minimum threshold for coverage during a period of four or fewer consecutive calendar quarters. Those writers who might have fallen below the threshold after a period of coverage or left a position with health benefits could elect coverage under the COBRA, which extended the benefits provided by the employer for a period of 18 months after employment was terminated. In this case, while subsidies were sometimes available to reduce the premium, the (former) employee was usually responsible for paying the entire premium. A final option might have been the purchase of a major medical plan that provided catastrophic health insurance coverage for major health issues, such as development of cancer or a chronic illness.

Since January 1, 2014, health insurance for writers is a whole new ballgame. The federal Patient Protection and Affordable Care Act (P.L. 111-148), also known as the Affordable Care Act (ACA) or *Obamacare*, was officially enacted on March 31, 2010. Under the provision of the ACA, self-employed writers now have greater access to healthcare insurance than ever before. American Health Benefit Exchanges now provide opportunities for individuals to shop for healthcare insurance tailored to meet personal needs. The health benefit exchanges are designed specifically for individuals and small businesses and are regulated by states to provide an organized method through which individuals can shop in a competitive marketplace for insurance.

Depending on the income status of the writer and his or her family, tax credit advances or refunds may be available on a sliding scale (according to income) to subsidize the premiums for those individuals and families with incomes from 100% to 400% of the federal poverty level (FPL) requiring coverage. Four levels of coverage are available ranging from Platinum (highest level of coverage), through Gold, Silver and Bronze (lowest level of coverage). Families at or below 250% of the FPL may be eligible to enroll in higher levels of coverage at lower costs.

The ACA defines health coverage comprehensively. In addition, pre-existing conditions no longer prevent writers from obtaining coverage, as the ACA makes it illegal for insurers to deny coverage or impose lifetime or annual coverage limits on benefits. In addition, young writers may now remain on their parents' health insurance until the age of 26, and writers who are covering families are now able to continue covering their children until this age.

Catastrophic coverage is still an available health insurance option for writers under the age of 30 and individuals for whom the premium of the lowest level of coverage exceeds eight per cent of their income. Coverage within catastrophic plans, however, is extended to include annual prevention benefits and three visits to a primary care provider each year. These are excellent benefits which will not only improve the health of the nation, but may actually decrease healthcare costs by allowing individuals to receive primary prevention interventions to prevent diseases from occurring or to detect illnesses at an earlier, treatable stage. If a writer qualified for health benefits through the Writers Guild-Industry Health Fund in the past, there is no evidence to suggest that eligibility for this coverage is changed under the provisions of the ACA.

While greater access to health insurance coverage is ensured under the ACA, minimum coverage provisions have been implemented in order to keep the system balanced. Self-employed writers, who have risked going without health insurance in the past, can no longer do so under the ACA without having to pay a penalty. In addition, the availability of an adequate number of healthcare providers to meet the needs of the newly insured population has caused concern. In other words, newly insured writers could have trouble finding a provider to care for them, despite the fact that they have adequate coverage.

Overall, the ACA is a step forward to improving the health of the nation, but writers must be proactive and knowledgeable to ensure maximum benefits from expanded coverage.

Group Plans and Resources
by Heather Zullinger

Independent writers might find the following websites helpful in researching options for health insurance coverage. As with any other long term financial commitment, education at the outset is imperative for maximum results, particularly in a changing marketplace such as this one. Review each site thoroughly to determine your membership availability and ascertain the best "fit" for your individual needs. It is also beneficial to re-visit the chosen policy on an annual basis and review for efficacy as your creative portfolio and compensation expands.

Below are a few select resources and options to assist with decision-making:

Healthcare.gov. The ACA website provides information on how to select and enroll in a health insurance plan that covers essential benefits, pre-existing conditions, and more. Links to statewide websites for health insurance coverage are also provided. (http://www.healthcare.gov/).

Internal Revenue Service. This website details information on required health insurance coverage and tax implications (credits and penalties) for coverage, or lack thereof, for residents of the U.S. It also provides links to a number of other helpful websites. (http://www.irs.gov/uac/Affordable-Care-Act-Tax-Provisions-Home).

The Editorial Freelancers Association. Paid membership provides access to varying levels of insurance coverage and discount plans. Membership is $145 for one year or $260 for two years, plus a $35 processing fee for new members. (http://www.the-efa.org)

Freelancers Union. Free membership provides access to health, dental, disability, term, liability and retirement insurance options. (https://www.freelancersunion.org)

National Writer's Union. Eligible writers have access to dental and vision insurance as well as a free prescription drug card with their paid membership. Membership is $120-$340 per year, dependent on income; half year memberships are available. (https://www.nwu.org)

Artists Health Insurance Resource Center. The goal of this organization is to "insure every artist by 2014." It contains a wealth of information on healthcare under the ACA, providing a variety of options and methods for obtaining plans. (http://www.ahirc.org)

Writers Guild of America. This organization, which is broken into two regional sections (east and west), is a labor union that provides resources for screenwriters. Through the website, writers can learn about health insurance coverage that meets the revised ACA requirements. For more information, visit www.wga.org (West) or www.wgaeast.org (East).

Chambers of Commerce. Many Chambers of Commerce offer access to health insurance with a paid membership. Membership pricing varies by state/municipality. Contact your local chamber for more information.

Alumni Associations. A large number of universities and colleges in the U.S. provide access to healthcare via their alumni associations. Contact yours directly or visit the Alumni Insurance Program site below. (http://www.alumniinsuranceprogram.com)

All organizations, guilds and unions listed above are transitioning to the new regulations stipulated under the ACA. Read carefully and contact the source directly for clarification and confirmation regarding any policy or plan purchases.

*W*hen in need of inspiration, and sometimes to escape depression, writers often study the lives of the authors we most admire. We hope to catch a glimpse of ourselves in their life stories, to learn that they too once held a soul-sucking or entirely unglamorous job to pay the bills. We need reassurance that success comes in infinite forms. Ashley Andersen Zantop had fun tracking down the former occupations of some of our favorite visionaries.

Before We Knew Them: Jobs our Literary Heroes Held
by Ashley C. Andersen Zantop

When you've paid your last bill, washed your last dish, signed up for health insurance, updated your prescriptions for glasses, contacts or anti depressants and find that you're still not sure if your life or your writing makes any sense, sometimes what you need is old fashioned encouragement. Maybe you crave some reassurance that even though life seems odd now, if you keep writing, it will make sense later. Learning about the near-surreal jobs held by literary greats throughout the years can help us realize that no matter where we start from, we can achieve our goals as writers. Here are a few of my favorites for inspiration or at least a good stress-relieving chuckle:

Douglas Adams worked the night shift as a hotel security guard. *The Hitchhiker's Guide to the Galaxy* always did make more sense at night.

Margaret Atwood served a tour as a coffee shop cashier, briefly. She reportedly began writing when she was six years old and decided at sixteen to make a living as a writer, so she didn't have much time to do anything else. For some of us, it's just that simple.

Roald Dahl worked for Shell and served in the Royal Air Force. Shot down over Libya and wounded in Syria, he didn't start writing and publishing in earnest until he was recovering from head injuries sustained during his service.

Charles Dickens worked in a shoe polish factory to earn money to secure his father's release from debtor's prison.

T. S. Elliot labored in 'Colonial and Foreign Accounts' at Lloyd's Bank.

William Faulkner was a mailman, reportedly an atrocious one who read all the magazines he delivered and played golf while out on his route.

Robert Frost worked in a light bulb factory handling filaments.

Dashiell Hammett made a living as a private investigator for the Pinkerton Detective Agency and practiced his hand as a nail machine operator.

Nathaniel Hawthorne was a shipping clerk before publishing *The Scarlet Letter*.

Zora Neale Hurston worked as a maid to a traveling singer before conducting ethnographic research at Barnard with fellow student Margaret Mead.

E.L. James was a television executive before beginning to write fan fiction, which became fifty shades of an international phenomenon.

Ken Kesey volunteered as a test subject in a CIA-sponsored drug study and worked as a janitor in a mental hospital. The two experiences reportedly served as the inspiration for *One Flew Over the Cuckoo's Nest*.

Stephen King worked as a high school janitor. It's been reported that cleaning the girl's locker room provided the inspiration for *Carrie*.

Harper Lee worked as an airline ticket agent.

Stanislaw Lem was a car mechanic, welder and active member of the Polish resistance against WWII Nazi occupation of Poland. He began his writing career as a poet before earning fame as a science fiction author.

Jack London reportedly stole oysters from oyster farmers to sell in local markets. Seafood pirate? Seriously? It figures.

George Orwell worked in the Imperial Police in India, and was promoted to Assistant District Superintendent. He became a writer after leaving the Indian Imperial Police, prompted by taking sick leave in England to recover from dengue fever.

Sylvia Plath was a receptionist at a psychiatric hospital. Some things just make sense.

J.D. Salinger was an entertainment director on a Swedish cruise line.

John Steinbeck worked as a caretaker and guide at a fish hatchery. His first wife attended one of his tours.

Mark Twain worked as a typesetter and riverboat captain, among other things. The term 'mark twain' (a pen name) refers to the depth of a river of two fathoms.

Kurt Vonnegut was reportedly an owner and manager of a Saab dealership on Cape Cod, MA.

This final writer deserves a place of distinction as the ultimate success in fantastic pre-authorial careers, so excuse the lapse in alphabetical order: A variety of sources report **Maya Angelou's** professional endeavors outside of writing as "pimp, prostitute, night club dancer and performer, cast member of the musical *Porgy and Bess*" and "coordinator for Martin Luther King, Jr.'s Southern Christian Leadership Conference." She wins. Hands down.

Chapter 9

PUT YOUR DEGREE TO WORK: CAREERS FOR WRITERS

edited by Ashley C. Andersen Zantop

Successful writers often hold meaningful careers while writing and publishing—they find a way to balance and manage both. Learn about a sampling of career options for which well-trained writers with degrees are uniquely qualified, and learn from writers who have navigated through the challenges of both developing a career and developing as a writer.

True Confessions of an MFA Grad
—*Steve Otfinoski*

January 4, 2011. I put on my cap and gown and marched into the stone chapel on Enders Island, a beautiful little island off the coast of Mystic, Connecticut, where I had spent five residencies in Fairfield University's MFA in Creative Writing program, fifty of the best days of my life. Now at last, graduation day had arrived. My name was called. And one of our faculty, a poet with a resounding voice, read a few lines of my deathless prose. Then a dean I had never seen before handed me a degree and the director of our program shook my hand. I walked out of the chapel and into the bracing winter night air a bona fide Master of Fine Arts ready to take on the literary world.

They told us that the MFA was a terminal degree. I didn't know what that meant, but it sounded impressive. Then someone explained to me that a terminal degree is a teaching degree. Aha! I thought to myself. Now I can earn my living as a teacher on some quiet college campus until the agent that has my novel sells it to a major publisher and I can retire and live off my royalties. So I went to the nearest university and met with the Human Resources person.

"I have a MFA," I told him.

"That's nice," he said.

"You don't understand," I said. "I have an MFA, and I want to teach creative writing at your fine institution."

"Interesting," said the HR man. "Why don't you come back when you have a PhD. Then we can talk. Maybe."

Undiscouraged, I went to the nearest community college. "I have an MFA," I said to the dean of extended studies, "And I want to teach composition at your less than stellar institution."

She smiled and handed me an application. "Here," she said. "Fill this out and then get in that line." She pointed to a long queue of middle-aged men and women down the hall. I filled out the application and waited in line for two hours.

"We'll be in touch," said the young man who took my application.

"When?" I asked.

"That's hard to say," he said.

"But you don't understand," I said. "I have an MFA."

"You and everyone's grandmother," he said.

"But I went to FU. FU!"

"Using obscene language isn't going to improve your chances of getting hired," he said. "Good-bye."

I decided if I were going to get a teaching job, I would have to think outside the box, the higher education box, that is. So I went to my local community center and told the lady behind the desk that I'd like to start a creative writing workshop.

"What are your qualifications?" she asked.

"I have my MFA," I said.

"Okay," she said, much to my surprise. "We'll put you in the catalogue."

"What's the pay?" I said.

"Pay?" she said, "This a community center. At a community center people don't get paid for teaching. They volunteer."

"You've got to be kidding," I said.

"No," she said.

"FU," I said.

"Excuse me?" she said.

"That's where I got my MFA. At Fairfield U."

"Oh," she said.

I asked her if there was anyone on the teaching staff who got paid.

"Yes, there is one," she said. "He's an author who published a novel. We pay him."

"I see," I said. "Then if I get my novel published, I'll be paid to teach, too." "Absolutely," she said.

So the next day I called the agent who had my novel. "Hello," I said. "I want to know if you've gotten around to reading my novel yet."

"When did you send it to us?" asked the agent.

"Six months ago," I said.

"Give us another six months and we'll get back to you. Perhaps."

"You mean you haven't read it?"

"Read what?"

"My fucking novel."

"Make that a year," he said.

"That's it," I said. "Send back my manuscript."

"Did you enclose a self-addressed, stamped envelope?" he asked.

"No," I replied.

And that's when he hung up on me.

I was beginning to feel a bit depressed. So I went to my neighborhood bar and ordered a single malt scotch, because that's what serious writers who get their works published drink. A very attractive brunette was sitting on the stool next to me. "You look depressed," she said.

"I am," I said. "But I'll get over it. After all, I have an MFA."

"What's that?" she asked, leaning forward on the bar with growing interest.

"It's a Master of Fine Arts degree."

"In what discipline?" she asked.

"Creative writing," I said.

"That's not a fine art," she said.

"Of course it is," I said.

"No, it's not," she said. "A fine art is painting or sculpture. Not writing."

"Is that true?" I said.

"Yes," she said. "You got the wrong degree."

"How do you know so much?" I asked her.

"I have a BA in English," she said.

I could see this conversation was pointless, so I downed my scotch, ordered another and moved down the bar next to a very attractive blonde.

"Hi," I said, gaining courage from the liquor. "Can I buy you a drink?"

The blonde sized me up, not unkindly. "What's your name?" she asked.

"That's not important," I said. "I have an MFA."

"*Ooo*," said the blonde. "That's sounds impressive."

"It is," I said. "Now what are you drinking?"

But before she could part her pretty lips to tell me, a man in a three-piece suit with silver hair and a distinguished forehead sat down on a stool on the other side of her. "Forget that loser," he said to her. "Let me buy you a drink, honey."

"Why should I?" she asked.

"Because I have a PhD," he replied.

"In what subject?" she asked.

"International relations," he murmured, beckoning to the bartender with one finger. I could see I'd been out-degreed. So I slid off the stool, slunk back to a table in the corner and drank my single malt in solitude.

I was more depressed than ever. I couldn't get a teaching job. I couldn't get my novel published. I couldn't even pick up a woman in a bar. There was only one thing left for me to do, one place for me to go, where I knew I would be loved and appreciated. My old residency home—Enders Island. Luckily, it was the middle of the summer residency and Alumni Day. I saw all my old writer buddies and my mentors. I sat in on a seminar. I went to the annual clambake and ate two lobsters. I drank wine. Lots of wine. I slept through the readings of three distinguished faculty members. I took a midnight dip in my underwear. I slept it off by the sea wall. The next morning I went to see the MFA director. "I want to come back," I told him.

"You mean you want to take a fifth semester?" he said.

"Do I have to pay for that?" I asked.

"Of course," he said.

"No," I said. "I want to come back as a mentor. So then you can pay *me*."

"What are your qualifications?" he asked.

"I have an MFA," I said.

He began to laugh. He was still laughing when I got in my car and drove back down Mason's Road to the mainland.

So that is my story. Sad but true. Be prepared fellow MFAers. You may be having a great time now in the program, but what lies ahead is heartbreak and disappointment. And yet the situation isn't hopeless. You see, I have a new plan. I'm going to go back to school, and I'm going to get an MBA. And then I'm going to get a good-paying position with a Fortune 500 company. And I'm going to make a lot of money. Then I'm going to self-publish my novel and sell it on Amazon. And it's going to be a best seller. And with my royalties I'm going to buy Enders Island and turn it into a home for old, out-of-work MFAers.

hapter 7 explores ways in which writers can use their craft and skill to pay the bills while working on their own creative endeavors. What about those of us who don't want to piece together our own creations with a collection of minutes stolen away from another job? What about writers who want to use their degrees to help them develop a career in a field suited to their skills and abilities? Writers love to commiserate that finding real jobs in our field is challenging— challenging being a euphemism for slightly less difficult than winning a trip to Mars. Well-meaning family and friends might joke that the only degree less employable than English Literature or Creative Writing is History.

Sure. If you're looking for a job at an Engineering firm.

Finding the right job in the right career track isn't easy for anyone, but there are a number of interesting careers for which talented writers and creative thinkers are the *best* candidates. Marketing, communications, advertising, journalism, publishing and teaching are just some of the fields that need the skill sets well-trained writers possess. Michael Bayer, a 20-year veteran of the marketing and PR industry discusses the value of creativity in today's workplace and how an MFA or other creative degree can uniquely prepare you for a career in this space.

What About the 'C' Word? Creative Careers in Marketing and Communications
—*Michael Bayer*

If you're like me, you've always been a writer. You slept with a dictionary from the age of three. You gathered siblings to workshop your annual letter to Santa. Bored in the pew, you re-wrote the Lord's Prayer with more narrative tension. And the moment you learned about the MFA in Creative Writing, gravity took over. You enrolled not to *become* a writer, but to remind yourself that you already *are* a writer.

The question of whether or not writing can be taught somehow feels soaked in self-loathing. The more productive question is "What do we gain by earning an MFA in Creative Writing?" Yes, our writing becomes more craft-conscious, and we encounter kindred spirits who actually care and appreciate that our writing is becoming more polished, more controlled, more free, more alive, more masterful.

We write. Then we write some more. It's tempting to assume the sole product of the degree is writing experience. But, it's for good reason that the degree isn't called an MFA in Writing. Writing is the technical craft, but creativity is the intellectual fuel. So, why do my classmates and professors never mentioned the "C" word? Are we all missing half the point?

I propose a less technical, less craft-biased understanding of the MFA in Creative Writing. What if the greatest asset of the MFA degree is a mind trained for creative thinking? While some might call for my hanging, I believe placing greater emphasis on the *Creative*, and less emphasis on the *Writing*, opens up the MFA-armed generation to a world of new, exciting possibilities, including many in the business world, where creativity has become the new global imperative, yet remains horrendously elusive.

Earning my MFA was an enriching and transformative experience, the benefits of which I shall never take for granted. It felt natural. I felt normal for the first time. And I'm a much better writer for it. But, I must admit that I also sensed an ever-present haze of ghettoization, as if my classmates and I shared an unspoken dismay, that there wasn't much we could *do* with this thing when we were done. I often heard faculty describe the MFA as a "teaching degree" or a "fine arts degree" (code for a teaching degree). One woman told me she enrolled because she felt the MFA was part of her "personal journey," which was a lovely concept, but I didn't want to measure the value of *my* degree simply through the literary quality of my journal entries.

I acknowledge that terms like "value" and "measured" and "quality" are hopelessly analytical and fan the flames of academic consumerism, which is anathema to the arts and humanities. But does the MFA provide no advantage whatsoever to a candidate who might wish to pursue a slightly more—prepare for gasps—*commercial* path? Does the MFA really exist only for my personal spirit and literary craft, and if I'm lucky, my imaginary future students?

To answer these questions, contrasting the MFA and the MBA is a helpful place to start. These two degrees represent nothing less than the war over human nature. While it's true they are antithetical in many ways, they also have much in common. Like the MFA, the MBA is relatively young, uniquely American, and infuriatingly vague in its intrinsic value. Unlike the MFA, however, the MBA is considered a *professional* degree, meaning candidates are in training for specific job functions, much like law or medicine. And writers, as we all know, are decidedly *un*professional.

The MBA has also benefited from a steady PR campaign funded by the wealthy institutions that offer the degree, which has helped it gain considerable, if dubious, prestige in the business world. After all, it was invented by Harvard a century ago to prepare the next generation to take the helm of America's relatively new multinational corporations, so it was essential to America's global competitiveness, to preserve our exceptionalism in the world. The degree of patriots! A fine arts degree never had a chance. Why train the next generation to create culture when you can train them to buy it instead?

The MBA caught on fast. Whether or not it had any discernible impact on a professional's actual leadership potential, it attracted hundreds of thousands of ambitious managers in waiting. These privileged MBA candidates learned hard skills like finance, accounting, and market segmentation, but also softer "skills" like ethics and leadership. They could specialize in areas like globalization, brand management, and financial derivatives.

Today, many professionals consider business school at some point in their careers. The tug is palpable. When I recall the MBA course catalogs I perused during my brief stupor of curiosity a dozen or so years ago, I don't remember seeing the word "creativity," nor any of its variations. I did, however, read a lot about something called innovation, apparently a business discipline that embraces and commercializes new ideas. So, innovators don't create the ideas. They make money off the people who do.

For those of you brave souls willing to peruse the MBA course catalogs today, I bet you'd see the C-word all over the place, as it seems to have finally entered corporate boardrooms without getting beaten up by bully words like "risk" and "return." In 2010, IBM, one of the world's largest employers of MBA's, conducted a survey of 1,500 CEOs from 60 countries and 33 industries. The captains of industry cited creativity as the number one leadership competency for the successful stewardship of corporations in the future. With the global marketplace more complex and volatile than ever, CEOs want more C-word, not less. Apparently, creative leaders are more comfortable with ambiguity, more willing and able to change their business more quickly, and inspire greater and faster innovation from their workforces.

This is welcome news for Creativity, the poor little guy. In most business settings, the C-word has been kicked around like a hot potato. Welcome in the office one day, ostracized the next, usually dependent on financial performance. "He's creative" could mean either "he's smart" or "he's flighty" or "he's gay." Congratulations to IBM for helping to nudge creativity out of the closet.

"Experts" have identified creativity as the hot new business mandate, and they have a point. Occupations that require minimal skills in conceptualization and ideation are under considerable threat today. Information technology has advanced to such an extent that a growing number of functions can be either automated or outsourced overseas. Non-creative jobs can be done cheaper and faster than ever before. Who needs a human to draw up a contract or update a balance sheet or assemble a radiator? Humans are so twentieth century. And for those mundane jobs that still require a human heartbeat, there are billions of heartbeats in Asia just a click away. And they don't expect health benefits.

These dramatic changes have spawned a small army of creativity evangelists. Author and columnist Daniel Pink claims that the American marketplace has rapidly evolved from an Agricultural Age (Grow corn!) to an Industrial Age (Bend metal!) to an Information Age (Go to college!) to today's Conceptual Age (Create something valuable!). Social scientist Richard Florida takes the creativity imperative even further, claiming that 38 million Americans already make up the Creative Class, including those who work in science and engineering, architecture and design, arts and entertainment, marketing and advertising, and other fields where big ideas are big money. Florida imagines the U.S. workplace as some kind of nuclear fusion reactor, in which a

"Super-Creative Core" of workers toils in the creative process all day, surrounded by a much larger pool of "Creative Professionals." I should note that Florida's definition of creativity is extremely broad. As long as you don't lay foundation or greet customers at WalMart, then you get to add the C word to your resume.

> "There's no such thing as a creative industry, or even a creative profession. There are only creative individuals."

Personally, I disagree with Dr. Florida's sunshine state of creativity in the workforce. The notion that 38 million creative visionaries are walking the halls of corporate America is silly. Florida lumps creative professionals into industries, but there's no such thing as a creative industry, or even a creative profession. There are only creative individuals, and, in my experience, very few at that.

> "Is there any academic credential that certifies creativity better than the MFA in Creative Writing?"

Have commentators like Pink and Florida done a disservice to the cause of creativity? On one hand, they've redefined creativity on superficial and meaningless terms. On the other hand, they've elevated the virtue of creativity out of Bohemia and into the boardroom, and we're the beneficiaries. Is there any academic credential that certifies creativity better than the MFA in Creative Writing?

For MFA graduates interested in pursuing more than artistic or academic endeavors, some industries, to varying degrees, are known to seek out exceptional creativity, exceptional writing skills, or both. These generally include publishing, media and entertainment, fashion and what is fantastically called—by highly creative Wall Street analysts—*marketing services*, a term meant to encapsulate the outside agencies that provide services like advertising, PR, communications, design, branding, and digital marketing to corporations and institutions. This last category is by far the fastest growing, and the sector in which I believe MFA graduates stand to benefit from a tidal wave of opportunity.

Every organization in the world with more than a handful of employees has a marketing department, even if the Vice President of Marketing had until six months ago served as receptionist. (I have seen this more than once). And every marketer in the world will agree that creativity is the lifeblood of successful marketing. Things on Earth change really fast, especially when it comes to the tastes, needs and preferences of irritable human beings, so anyone engaged in marketing needs new ideas delivered constantly and nearly intravenously.

The textbook definition of "marketing" spans everything involved in getting your product or service into a customer's hands. So, in theory, a sophisticated marketing department does almost everything. It researches and anticipates changes in consumer behavior. It coordinates with R&D and manufacturing on product demand and development. It manages wholesale and retail distribution networks. And it builds and manages the brand. However, I have never encountered a marketing department that actually does all these things. Instead, the CEO typically calls up the marketing department with the following concern: "Hey, I saw our logo on a bus and it looked kind of orange-ish. Shouldn't it be red?"

Out of the 1,012 corporate-side contacts I worked with over the course of my 22-year agency career, two of them were creative. That's because corporations—Apple, Google and Amazon notwithstanding—are where creativity goes to die. Imagine being an idea inside a large corporation. You'd envy a fruit fly's life expectancy. First, you have to tunnel your way into someone's brain. Then you have to catch a wave of speech and hold on tight until you become an utterance. Then you have to sustain a half-dozen rounds of rejection and laughter, mostly from colleagues who are pissed off that you didn't tunnel into their brains instead. Then you have to climb up a massive ladder, your feet ceaselessly yanked backward by co-workers on lower rungs, to someone who has the authority—and the budget—to keep you from dying. Then you have to endure several rounds of due diligence and risk mitigation from accountants and lawyers, who despise everything about you. Then you need someone willing to beg and plead on your behalf, until you win final approval from the CEO, who is excited by your potential but will be terminated by the board of directors momentarily because revenues have dropped two quarters in a row.

That's why the real action, creativity-wise, is in the agency world. These are the advertising, PR, digital and branding firms whom corporations, governments and non-profits hire to be creative, presumably so they don't have to be. So, why shouldn't creative agencies have their own advanced degree? Just as the MBA is widely held by bankers and consultants, the MFA in Creative Writing could and should be widely held by those who work in marketing services. As the only graduates whose degree even contains the C-word in its name, MFAs have gained skills in ideation, abstraction, collaboration, criticism, problem-solving, and perseverance, not to mention a masterful way with words.

The more MFA graduates that storm the creative agencies, the more the degree's prestige will rise. If you're interested in joining the cause, here are some things you need to know.

Entry level titles at these agencies include Assistant Account Executive, Junior Account Executive, and Account Coordinator. (Do your best to negotiate the word "executive" in your title because it looks better on your LinkedIn profile.) Should you be so lucky to obtain one of these coveted positions, don't expect anyone to ask you for your creative ideas right away. You'll be asked to book travel itineraries and order food and beverages for the next client meeting. If you're widely seen as a rising star, you'll be asked to conduct research.

And the person asking you to do these things will have an otherworldly, impressive title like Super Senior First Executive Vice President of Global Accounts. She might only be four years older than you, but her LinkedIn profile will be a hundred times more impressive.

You should not wait to be given a writing assignment. You should offer, loudly and frequently, to write every ad, every commercial script, every press release, every memo, and be delighted to write it at night over a glass of discount white Zinfandel if necessary. If you're an exceptional writer, you will be noticed, and you will quickly become everyone's BFF because nobody else wants to be writing at night over a glass of discount white Zinfandel. Just know that your first draft will be butchered throughout the editing process, and the final product, which someone may be so kind to share with you weeks later, will be completely unrecognizable to you.

Here's the thing: Great writing is always welcome at creative agencies, but adequate writing is all too easily accepted. I have witnessed the flame-outs and dismissals of some wonderful writers because they prioritized perfectionism over expediency. As a creative writer, your tendency will be to treat that press release like a work of art. It's not art, it's just work. And you must accept that.

The greater value of your MFA to creative agencies will be that C-word. You have a diploma, scripted in gorgeous Latin, which certifies you as a creative thinker. Demonstrate that you possess a superior creative mind, and you just might get noticed. There is only one rule you need to follow to achieve this: Attend every brainstorm.

Brainstorms are the boxing matches of agency life. Here's how they work:

1. A junior account executive will circulate an e-mail message inviting everyone in the building to attend a brainstorm session for a very important client. To reinforce the client's importance, this e-mail message will make use of purple font and a minimum of twenty exclamation points, and will most certainly promise lunch or snacks as a reward for your attendance.

2. Upon arriving at the conference room, you will find a variety of children's toys (Slinky, Etch-a-Sketch, Play-Doh) strewn across the long mahogany table. These objects are rumored to inspire creative thinking, but they will have no human contact throughout the session.

3. To start, one senior manager will inarticulately explain the strategic purpose of the brainstorm, reciting an inventory of the client's marketing goals. For maximum confusion, he will draw columns on a large white board, with the assumption that the group simply needs to fill them in. The columns will never be re-visited.

4. Immediately, attendees will commence throwing out random ideas, sometimes in the form of single syllables, one or two of which may actually contain a degree of relevance to the session's objective. Two attendees with particularly thunderous voices will talk over all the others, eschewing all guidelines for professional courtesy.

5. Throughout the session, three attendees will articulate all of their ideas in the form of taglines, utilizing rhyme and alliteration to form memorable catch phrases that have no tangible application. These people are informally called "tagline savants."

6. Invariably, the idea with the greatest potential will come from a twenty-two-year-old unpaid intern who recently graduated from Fairleigh-Dickinson University, and proudly shares that she and her college classmates nicknamed the institution "Fairly Ridiculous."

For a creative writer, however, the ultimate fantasy is to participate in a rare variation on the brainstorm called the "name-storm." These sessions, most frequently found in branding agencies, are aimed at coming up with a new name for a company, product or campaign. In name-storms, the Slinky and Play-Doh on the table are replaced by an eight-inch thick dictionary, an even thicker thesaurus, and a torn volume of Bulfinch's mythology. Attendees are also encouraged to bring their tablet computers with Wikipedia and a Latin dictionary open in the browser. The facilitator will introduce a long-winded and well-intentioned methodology for arriving at the ideal name attributes and phonetics. He will encourage the use of fancy-sounding language devices, such as metonymy, mimetics, and onomatopoeia, but this methodology will invariably disintegrate within seconds into an orgy of words, sounds, grunts, acronyms, goddesses, inventors, historical figures, chemical elements, and, if you're lucky, an occasional literary reference.

Brainstorms are the most tangible exercises of creativity, but the C-word permeates almost every interaction, meeting, document and project inside these agencies. That's why I encourage anyone with an MFA in Creative Writing to march into your local ad agency or PR firm and wave your diploma with zeal. You've proven, academically at least, that you have the creativity that these firms so covet and promote to their clients and prospects.

Now, here comes the sobering part. If and when you land the job, you will still ache to write poetry all day long. Even though you'll be writing Web site copy and name-storming for hours on end, it will feel like showering in a SCUBA suit. It will not satisfy your literary cravings. You're bound to feel inauthentic, in the existential sense, like an imposter in a world of corporate naturals. No matter how successful you become, embrace this feeling always! It's the pulse of an artist. It's the call of your past and your future. You are a human being, and you want to write about human things, not about toothpaste or vodka. You must sell your time and your labor, at least for now, but you should fear success as much as failure. As Lewis Hyde wrote, "a gift can be destroyed by the marketplace."

I had a blast working for creative agencies, and the financial rewards along the way allowed me to retire at the young, creative age of 42. But, despite the economic rewards, the fabulous perks, and the intensely exciting experiences, every day I longed to be reunited with my writer-ghost. If you pursue an agency career, your writer-ghost will become smaller and quieter as the years go on, and it might even fall overboard for a while. The more successful you become, the greater the sense of loss. One day, however, you will spot your writer-ghost alive on the horizon, a speck floating across the setting sun, waiting patiently for the dramatic rescue. Throw out a life raft. Maybe you already have in the form of an MFA.

> **"Creativity is the opposite of death, so learn how to fill your life with it. Train your mind to be wildly alive."**

If you're enrolled in—or are considering—an MFA program, know that you're there not just to learn how to write. You're also there to learn how to think and how to see. Creativity is the opposite of death, so learn how to fill your life with it. Train your mind to be wildly alive. Re-imagine not just your story and your characters, but also the chaos and horror of the world in which they live. While you exist on this accidental planet, your creativity is the only purpose you'll have. It will be enough. Fortunately, in today's world, it will be marketable too.

*I*f brainstorming, name-storming, soft launches, web copy, press releases and collaborating on innovation projects are not for you, consider other career options for writers. Here, A.J. O'Connell, a journalist and educator, explores how writers can get started in the field of journalism.

Your MFA and the Fourth Estate
–A.J. O'Connell

So, you want to make a paycheck writing. Why not try your hand at journalism? Many great writers were also journalists: Ernest Hemingway worked as a foreign correspondent for the *Toronto Star Weekly* while he wrote *The Sun Also Rises*. More recently, Anna Quindlen worked as a reporter and later, a columnist, while working on her novels and memoirs, and Matthew Beynon Rees used his experience as Jerusalem bureau chief for Time Magazine as fodder for his first novel, *The Collaborator of Bethlehem*.

Graham Greene, Mark Twain, Charles Dickens, Hunter S. Thompson… the list of writers who worked in journalism before becoming known for their creative work is long and impressive, but—and this is a big but—the trend you notice is that many of these writers made their living as journalists *before* they started selling novels and essays.

You, with your MFA in creative writing hot in your hand, may have to approach the field a little differently, but that doesn't mean you shouldn't break into journalism. You're just going to have to do things a little differently than Ernest Hemingway did them, and with good reason. The field of journalism today is not what it was in the 1920s when Hemingway gallivanted around Spain, telling stories about trout fishing and bullfighting. Most newspapers no longer have money to throw at foreign correspondents.

In fact, this essay merits a warning. Journalism is often not a money-making proposition. News organizations are struggling and journalists lucky enough to score a full-time gig at a local paper make little to no money and work long hours.

However, if you play your cards right, you can do well for yourself in journalism. You just need to have the right attitude.

Turning creative nonfiction into freelance gold:
If you want to turn your MFA into a decent journalism living, your best bet is a career as a freelancer for magazines or websites that require long-form essays or columnists. This approach will work well for people who have studied creative nonfiction, and are familiar with the lives and careers of writers like Joan Didion, James Thurber and David Sedaris. Essayists with talent, drive and connections have always been able to make money by selling pieces, both long-form and short-form, to periodicals. This can mean a humorous essay for a magazine like the New Yorker, as with Thurber and Sedaris, or it can mean long essays that involve some reporting, like the work done by Didion for Rolling Stone in the '60s. Best of all, if you've written essays while you were working on your MFA you may be able to use those to impress an editor for whom you want to work.

How to break in:
Unless you're super-lucky or very connected, you're probably not going to be able to start a glorious career in journalism at The New Yorker or Rolling Stone, but thanks to the Internet and advances in blogging, there are an unending number of ways to break into this market. Be warned, however, many of these methods may involve writing for free for a while. Bear with me.

Jenny Lawson is probably best known as The Bloggess, a blogger whose acerbic, self-deprecating humor and style of writing won her thousands of followers online and an eventual book deal. But Lawson began her writing career at a newspaper's site, writing a parenting column.

The Internet has made it possible for local newspapers to open up their sites to more guest bloggers and columnists than the papers might have been able to support during the pre-Internet age. A column is a great opportunity for a writer. Essentially, a columnist is an essayist who writes about a given subject once in a certain period of time. There are weekly columnists, monthly columnists and even some columns that run less regularly (every two weeks, for example). Depending on a company's policy, a columnist may publish exclusively on the Internet, or may once in a while be featured in the paper itself. Some of these columnists are paid, but some columnists and bloggers write for free. What do those volunteer columnists get in return? Experience, name recognition and a portfolio of clips. These will be all important when you apply to your next freelance job, one that offers better pay and more exposure for your work. In journalism, as with any other job, you generally have to work your way up.

So how do you get into that first job as a columnist?

No matter what you think of your local paper, that will be the easiest way to break into journalism and possibly get paid. So call your town's weekly, daily or news site and offer your services as a columnist or a blogger on their site. Make sure you offer to write about something you know well and enjoy writing about, because if you have to produce a column or post every week or month, you'd better be a font of information. Also, do your research before you call. Make sure someone's not already writing about the topic you want to write about. Identify a hole in the paper's coverage and point it out.

Conversely, you may want to start on the Internet. There are many struggling webzines out there looking for original content. Read one, and see if you have something to offer them. If so, email the editor and say you'd like to write for him or her. Once again, you may end up writing for free for a while, but this will pay off in terms of a portfolio of published articles.

How you leverage that published work to get a paying gig as a freelance essayist or columnist is up to you.

Making the leap into the world of hard news:
I have heard it said that most news reporters are either Woodwards (they're addicted to the news itself) or Hemingways (they're in the business for the prose.) I'm assuming that, since you are reading

this essay in a guide for creative writers, you're a Hemingway, and are considering journalism so that you can pay the bills until your masterwork is published. However, I could be wrong.

If you're passionate about both prose and current events, news reporting may be the thing for you.

Before I leap into a discussion of the world of hard news, I want you to consider a couple of things. First of all, if you go into straight news reporting, you will have to unlearn many of the things you've learned as a student of creative writing. The object of news reporting is to tell a story—without bias—using the fewest number of words possible. This means that you will have to learn a new style and bid adieu to things like modifiers, the Oxford Comma and conclusions that tie an essay up with a neat little bow (most news pieces are written into a format called the inverted pyramid, which is designed to place all the pertinent information at the top and then trails off at the bottom of the piece). You will also have to learn a specific news style. Most news organizations follow a specific school of newswriting, which helps them with consistency. For example, many media companies use the Associated Press Style. The New York Times uses its own style.

> **"nothing teaches you to ignore that inner critic like having to turn in 15 inches about the evening's city council meeting in the next half hour"**

If you're up for all this, news writing can actually help your creative prose. How? Well, nothing strengthens prose like omitting unnecessary words, and having to write for a news organization—which only has a limited amount of space or time for your story—will certainly teach you how to write a story in the fewest words possible. Another benefit to your writing? You will learn how to write on a deadline. In journalism, if your story has to be done by midnight, it has to be done by midnight or it doesn't get published. This gets you in the habit of turning things in when they're due, and it also teaches you how *not* to agonize over every single word you're committing to paper. Most writers struggle with an inner critic that paralyzes them with a need to produce perfect prose. Let me tell you, nothing teaches you to ignore that inner critic like having to turn in 15 inches about the evening's city council meeting in the next half hour.

How to break in:
Want a job on the local paper? A national paper? Any newsroom at all? The best thing you can do is call the editor and ask about openings. The news side of journalism is all about being forward; as a reporter you will have to cold-call people you want to write about and you will have to get comfortable with pestering sources for comments and information. There is no better way to get into the industry than by showing an editor you aren't shy about calling and asking for what you want.

You may, however, need to show that editor clips, or articles you've written previously, because he or she is going to want to make sure you're good before hiring you. Your MFA may impress an editor, but it won't be enough and the creative work you've done won't necessarily impress a newsman. This means you might need to volunteer your time and skills at a smaller paper or a website, writing a few articles for free and learning how to report, before you approach a paper you want to pay you.

Once you have a few decent clips under your belt, you're ready to make that call. Don't be afraid to be persistent. There aren't a lot of openings in the news business, and competition can be fierce. But if you're really after a career in news, you should be fine. Persistence is part of the job, after all.

You might also try freelancing for a news organization rather than trying to get on a staff. Many organizations don't have the money to hire staff members, but will work with freelance reporters instead. That will also leave you open to freelance for other kinds of publications at the same time, and a properly managed freelance career can allow you to make a living. A word of advice, however: don't freelance for two competing organizations in the same market. Editors tend to frown on that.

Conclusion:
Journalism will not make you rich, but you can get a paycheck for your writing when you're writing as a member of the media. There are other perks too: Columnists gather a following and news reporters get to see or do something different every day. It's an interesting way to make a living, and it will change the way you write and the way you look at the world.

Whether you're a Joan Didion or an Ernest Hemingway, journalism may be a way for you to make practical use of your MFA. Your facility with prose will put you heads and shoulders above candidates without a creative writing background. As long as you're willing to learn a few new things and as long as you aren't shy about putting yourself and your work forward, you can succeed in journalism.

Has your training as a writer taught you just as much about how to read critically, with an eye for craft, detail and style, as how to write well? If your answer is an emphatic yes, perhaps consider a career path in one of the multitude of options in the publishing industry outside of the press. Consider the options of literary agent, publicist, marketer, editor. A confounding array of today's most popular publishing genres are in need of skilled editors. Fiction, nonfiction, educational, trade and consumer. As with journalism, you may need to produce well-crafted samples and start in entry-level positions, but if you're willing to try genres outside of our own reading tastes, publishing jobs are available. Justin Scace explores the success and the sacrifice of launching a career in one of the several rapid growth segments of the publishing industry.

Listen Up! Put Your MFA to Work in the Audiobook Industry
—Justin Scace

So you've achieved your MFA, and while you make your plans to take the literary world by storm, you're probably also thinking: How can I put this piece of paper to work for me? The unfortunate truth of the matter is that most of the time, writing alone is not going to pay the bills. While you can employ your new degree in almost any industry if you play it from the right angle, many of us end up closely eyeing two paths post-graduation: teaching or publishing. In the publishing industry, where I found myself shortly after obtaining my MFA, there are many different roles available. I am currently employed in the fastest growing (yet most often overlooked) arm of publishing: audiobooks.

Books on tape were once very à la carte products, and only the greatest bestsellers were thought to be worth the investment. Narrators were paid top dollar to work on a book, and production was nearly as complicated and regulated as making a movie. But today, because of advancements in technology, the advent of digital audio, and an incredible spike in consumer interest, you will find that almost any book has an audio counterpart, from the latest Stephen King novel to a decades-old self-published pamphlet written by an obscure conspiracy theorist.

Digital audio in particular has had a game-changing effect on the industry; consumers are moving away from buying physical CDs or MP3 discs, and more often are downloading full books to their portable electronic devices. Digital products cost less to produce, can be quickly and easily distributed to a worldwide public ravenous for the next good story, and they have made download sites such as Audible.com into audio publishing juggernauts. The downside of this is that narrators (as well as all the production folks behind the scenes) are getting paid less for producing more content in order to keep the whole venture as profitable as possible; the upside is that audiobooks have become a billion-dollar-a-year industry, and that means job opportunities.

I began working in audiobooks less than two months after receiving my MFA, and have been lucky enough to find success in three unique production roles in the business. In my nearly three years at an independent audiobook publisher, I have worked as an audiobook proofer, an editorial assistant, and a production associate, my current job. Here's a bit of information about each one:

Audiobook proofer is the position that I was hired into initially. This job entails sitting down and listening to the first draft of an audiobook from start to finish, comparing what you hear to the script, and marking any mistakes for the narrator to correct. It entailed (among other things) researching pronunciations, listening for audio glitches or distracting background noises, doing some simple audio editing, and also critiquing the overall artistic and professional merit of the performance. It was nice in the sense that I was essentially getting paid to read/listen to books. However, while the job was amazing when you were spending a week immersed in a good book, it was torture every time you had to sit through an awful one. Also, while there were small ancillary tasks that popped up, your day basically consisted of sitting at a desk, listening. For eight-plus hours. Every day. Monotony and boredom (not to mention numb hindquarters) had the potential to be a daily challenge.

After about six months as a proofer, I spent some time working as an Editorial Assistant. In this job, I was responsible for creating recordable scripts for narrators from material provided to us from authors, agents, or print publishers. I had to create these files for as many as 10 full-length books a week or more, always keeping an eye out for language that needed to be re-worded for audio (for example, the phrases "see below" or "on page 12" means nothing to someone who's listening to an audiobook), and also correcting textual or continuity errors on the fly (you'd be amazed what makes it past some print editors). This responsibility was also accompanied by editorial functions that you'd find at any publishing company, including the creation and proofreading of retail jacket copy and marketing materials, and the creation and editing of bonus materials such as pictures or graphs that would accompany an audio edition. The pros and cons were similar to audio proofing—I got to work on some fantastic books, but I got some truly heinous ones as well. And while there was routinely something new to learn or a new problem to solve, boredom and mindless routine continued to lurk.

In my current position as a Production Associate, I research newly acquired titles to cast them with the right voice, coordinate the script delivery to voice talent, help the narrators with any issues along the way, query after text from publishers for use in script creation, and keep an eye on projects as they proceed through audio proofing and post-production—basically a little bit of everything. At a company producing 60+ titles per month, it's not always an easy job, but in that deluge of information, I have learned a great deal along the way. In this essay, I'm happy to pass along what I've gleaned from the journey, and provide advice for those of you who might be interested in pursuing this career path.

While I will use the words "publishing" and "audiobooks" interchangeably in this brief guide to landing (and then surviving) a job in the industry, I should point out that there are a couple of important distinctions between audiobooks and traditional publishing.

- First, in audiobook publication you will typically not be creating (or even necessarily copyediting in-depth) original content; you will be taking existing content produced by authors or publishing houses and then facilitating that material's transition into the audio medium. For example, you know all those nonfiction books with graphs and charts? Yep, there are audio editions of those—and somebody needs to take that raw material and make it friendly to the ear, either through editing out references altogether, finding a way to craft a useful description, or connecting them to bonus material (companion documents and the like).

- Second, audiobook production moves FAST. While in traditional publishing it might take up to a year to bring a completed manuscript to publication with editing, a marketing platform, etc., it is not unheard of in the audiobook industry that you need to take a book from the licensing agreement all the way through text editing, narration, and post-production (and also build your entire marketing strategy) in the course of 30 days. Seriously. In fact, we often joke in our office that if traditional publishing had to move as swiftly in the marketplace as we do, they might not be in so much trouble.

Keep these things in mind as you continue reading; if you're looking for a position where you can create content or take a long time to work and re-work the written word, you may want to look at print publishing rather than audio.

I'm not going to pretend that it will be easy to get a job in the audiobook industry; the ever-changing landscape of the business, along with the consumer's constant demand for lower prices, forces companies to increase content while using more and more spartan resources.[1] However, while it won't be easy, it is most certainly not impossible, as the presence of audiobooks on the market is swiftly expanding, with new opportunities popping up every day. Here are a few tips for landing the job.

1. A job in publishing is not acquired by an MFA alone. Got other skills? Put them to work alongside your MFA. A hiring manager may raise his/her eyebrows at the MFA in the "Education" portion of your resume, but unless you can showcase other abilities that will help you succeed in a publishing environment, your application may be destined for the filing cabinet.

---

1 If that statement has you thinking you might like to pursue a career on the other side of the microphone as a narrator, more power to you—however, expect even stiffer competition, against narrators ranging from A-list actors to an ever-growing pool of amateurs with a merely competent grasp of the English language (but who will work on the cheap). Statistically speaking, it probably pays the bills about as consistently as a career solely based on writing.

Just a few of the skills that you will want to highlight, should you have them: computer literacy (this is a big one), work ethic, problem solving, and language and research skills (these are very helpful in a business that depends on pronouncing words accurately). Emphasize any foreign languages you have studied, even if your knowledge of them is only intermediate. Also, if you have done any volunteer work, be sure to bring it up, no matter how relevant to the job you are pursuing. Employers want to see candidates who like to be busy, think beyond themselves, and for whom financial compensation isn't necessarily a top priority.

Also, keep in mind that there are a ton of jobs that you can find within an audiobook company, not just those on the editorial/proofing/production side of things. Marketing, sales, rights and acquisitions, IT, graphic design, manufacturing—areas that you can find in any other industry. If your marketable skills point you towards an area perhaps not completely connected to the expertise you developed while earning your MFA, go for it! Your MFA will get you in the door, but your other skills will make sure the door isn't a revolving one.

> **"I have actually heard hiring managers insinuate that they are less likely to consider MFA candidates because 'they'd want to do something creative.'"**

2. Tailor your resume and your interview strategy with the understanding that this is business...NOT art. I feel that there is a widespread misconception that working in the editorial world is very similar to writing itself—you show up with your Starbucks coffee, sit at your desk, smith words on the anvil of your genius, and the worst thing you have to worry about in terms of social diplomacy is making an embarrassing gaffe at the office Christmas party.

Not so (at least not in my experience). While the industry does have its more solitary, independent, or "artistic" positions, even in these you will have to be efficient, quick to make informed decisions, all while being diplomatic to multiple people across multiple departments, just like any other job. Hiring managers, while they won't say it, will probably be more impressed by the fact you made the deadline for turning in your thesis rather than what it was about. They don't care if you're a "free spirit"; free spirits don't show up to work on time. I have actually heard hiring managers insinuate that they are less likely to consider MFA candidates because "they'd want to do something creative."

In order to overcome this stereotype, you need to be business-minded from the get go. Do a little research on what makes a successful resume and cover letter in today's market, and after you write yours, edit and re-edit them. Then edit them again. No misspellings, no odd formatting, and do not get conversational or familiar in your cover letter. Research your potential employer, and then emphasize what you can bring to the company, and why you're the only one who can bring it. Show up to that interview five minutes early (no earlier, and DON'T be late), be alert and tidy, and when the interviewer asks if you have any questions for them, you'd better have some good ones ready.

These things may seem obvious, but it's easy to assume the details won't matter as much if you've got that graduate degree on your resume. It's also easy to assume that in an industry that produces art, it's your artistic side that will make you stand out. Both assumptions are false. While any audiobook publisher wants to make a quality product, in the end it's not about good craft, writing-wise. It's about what can make money. More on this later in my #1 point in surviving the job, "Expect frustration."

3. Keep in mind that taking a job doesn't mean it's the job you'll end up in. So you've marketed every skill you have, nailed the interview with a business-oriented approach, and you get a call back from the company...offering you a totally different job than the one you wanted. If you really do want a job in the audiobook publishing industry, TAKE IT. I myself was hoping to be hired as an editorial assistant when I was offered the job of audiobook proofer. In the end, not only did I eventually move into the editorial job I had initially been gunning for, but I gained an incredible amount of expertise and new knowledge during my time as a proofer, not to mention a broad range of experience across departments that propelled me into my current position.

Even if you're offered a job at a lower tier within the company than you had hoped for, you should seriously consider accepting it rather than declining and looking for other options. Think of it this way—the lower you start, the more you have the potential to learn along the way.

Now we get to the nitty-gritty. Once you land that job in the audiobook industry, you will have a well-deserved sense of accomplishment, not to mention a great deal of relief if you really needed that steady paycheck. You will enter a honeymoon period with your new career, and I'm not going to be cynical about it—enjoy it, and learn every new thing you can while you do. However, as with any new and exciting experience, reality will sooner or later begin to intrude. Here are some tips and advice to prepare you for surviving the job.

1. Expect frustration...and prepare to feel overqualified. Times are still tough, not just in your home state, not just in the U.S., but worldwide. In the workforce, upper management will often take the attitude "you should just be glad to have a job", and the audiobook/ publishing industry is no exception. You may have an MFA, and it's a very worthy accomplishment, but do not be surprised when your higher level degree does not quickly propel you into a management position. You may also find yourself doing a great deal of work (if you work in editorial/production) without a proportionate level of financial compensation or recognition. Such is the nature of publishing in general, not just audiobooks.

In addition to feeling overqualified and underpaid, also expect to take issue with some of your projects. Right or wrong, publishing is based on trends, and once one has started, you can count on that cow being milked for as long as it continues to be lucrative. When the latest trend starts flinging itself across your desk, it can inspire anything from boredom (copycats of the latest Man Booker winner), to tongue-in-cheek derision (remember Twilight?), to downright disgust accompanied by existential crises regarding the state of our culture (thanks a LOT, *Fifty Shades of Grey*). At first it's easy to make light of the ridiculousness of the latest trend, and it can be great fun to discuss these crazy books with co-workers. After a few weeks without a break from them, it just stops being funny.

The nature of the work some days would be enough to anger anyone. MFA graduates have the potential to feel even more righteously indignant when we see great works set aside in order to pander to the lowest common denominator, when we realize that our own work (while we may not claim it to be a masterpiece) is being overlooked in favor of what is absolute drivel, written by individuals who have obviously not learned the proper use of a period, let alone the finer points of grammar, syntax, or plot development.

Be aware that this frustration will find its way to you if you work in this industry—and you will have to learn a way to negotiate it.

2. Know that you will be working with (and most likely be taking orders from) folks who are not "book people". While this can be tied pretty closely to #1, it is definitely worth mentioning on its own. With the publishing industry changing more rapidly than ever, competition in the form of small presses and self-publishing around every corner, selling books is more about the bottom line than about what's between the book covers.

In every department I've worked in, I have met individuals who are truly "book people"—they care deeply about content and pairing the perfect voice with a project, and they experience disappointment at some of the more moronic (but depressingly lucrative) books that come across our desks. However, when you reach some of the upper echelons of the publishing industry, tiers at which many decisions are made regarding the type of work you will do and how this work is done, you may develop the impression (not unjustly) that they are staffed by men and women who would be more accurately described as "bean counters" than "book people". This can be difficult, especially when you perceive decisions of an artistic nature being made by individuals who do not have any form of artistic integrity.

My best advice for dealing with that kind of aggravation is this: realize that, in many cases, it could be that "bean counter" who's keeping your paycheck steady...and making sure the numbers on it don't go down.

3. This WILL affect your writing and inspiration, sometimes for the better, very often for the worse. If you're a writer with an accounting job, or a construction job, or a bartending job, you are lucky enough to say that your work is just that: a job. You come home, and the worst obstacle standing between you and your writing is physical exhaustion. When you work all day in an industry closely connected to your craft, it can be a real inspiration vampire. After vetting your fifth poorly written erotica novel in a week for possible acquisition, skimming through a New York Times bestselling book whose author clearly went nuts at the latest comma store sale, and then finishing off the day with a slightly vitriolic interdepartmental meeting, when you get home you may not even want to LOOK at a book, much less write one.

Sometimes in the course of your work you will get inspired to create ("This gives me an idea for a story" or "I just thought of the best metaphor" or "Hey! I can write better than this clown!"), and you will just want to sit down and start typing away. Too often though, you will then look at the clock and realize it's only 10 AM—by the time 5:30 rolls around, you'll probably find your inspiration less writing-centric ("Oops, I need to put gas in the car" or "I could really go for a glass of wine."). That feeling of missed opportunity can be discouraging. You may not think that this will apply to you as you're graduating with your boundless hopes and endless inspiration—you will write between midnight and 2 AM if that's what it takes! I know, because that's exactly the way I felt.

This essay is the first new piece I've written to completion in the last two years.

The audiobook industry can offer a world of opportunity for those of us looking to put our MFA to work. It can be a rewarding career path, but it is accompanied by a very unique set of challenges that mustn't be ignored prior to starting down that road. In all likelihood, accepting a publishing job will not make you immediately abandon what your MFA stands for, and even if you do put your writing on the back burner for the sake of making a living, there is always the opportunity for re-examination and change. If you have considered all the angles and believe that you're willing to accept the challenge, I wish you the very best of luck.

ait. What? Actually use my MFA in Creative Writing to spend my career *writing*? Although it's encouraging to read about all the potential career opportunities open to creative thinkers and skilled writers, it can be depressing that more of them don't involve actual writing. But, Freelance writing does.

Does freelancing even count as a career? The answer is Yes, it does, if you make it one. The lesser-sung truth is that many successful writers don't just pay the bills freelancing, they make meaningful careers out of it. Steve Otfinoski, a writer who has built a substantial career as a *writer*, of all things, explores this opportunity.

My Career as a Freelancer
by Steve Otfinoski

Unlike many of my fellow students, I was a published author before I began my MFA and continued to be after I graduated. I'm not bragging. Although the number of books I've published is climbing toward 160, I've yet to make my debut as a bona fide novelist, although I'm working on my fourth novel (number three was my thesis). You see, I'm a freelance writer and have been at it for more than 35 years.

What exactly is a freelance writer? As I like to point out to students on author visits to public schools, the term originated in the middle ages when knights roamed the countryside on their trusty steeds selling their services to the king or lord who would pay the highest for them. Their lance and sword, in a sense, was free, not tied to any one employer for long. And so my pen and computer is also for hire, although most of my roaming is done by phone or email.

I didn't set out to be a freelance writer. I sort of fell into it. My first job out of college was as a town reporter for a daily newspaper in Hartford, Connecticut. It only took me a year of covering zoning board and selectmen meetings to realize that I wasn't cut out to be a journalist. So I quit and soon landed a job at Weekly Reader Corporation, then owned by Xerox Corporation, in Middletown, where I lived. After a stint in the mailroom, I was hired as an assistant editor on *READ*, a secondary language arts magazine. In the economic turmoil of the late 70s, I was laid off after a year and a half and began freelancing for Weekly Reader Books. And I haven't held a regular job since.

My specialty became young adult books, supplemented by textbook writing and such ancillaries as workbooks and teacher's guides (often uninspired work, but usually better paid per page than the books). "Young adult" is a bit of a misnomer. The age range, depending on who you talk to, is roughly 8-14, although I've written picture books for younger readers and reference books for high school, college students and even adults.

You can buy my books on Amazon, but don't look for them in your neighborhood Barnes and Noble. The publishers of most of these books are in the school library market, selling their wares through catalogues directly to school and public libraries. Many of the books I write fit into a series (states, presidents, explorers, animals) and are published by a handful of publishers or in some cases, packagers, who hire writers and package books for publishers too busy or understaffed to do the work themselves.

The pay for writing school library books isn't great, but the work is often steady. Once a client sees what you can do and likes your writing, he may assign you book after book. A freelance YA writer rarely needs an agent; publishers work directly with writers and the advances are modest enough that you wouldn't want to share 15-20 percent of them with an agent. Writers' royalties were once standard in this industry, but in recent years have largely disappeared. While the royalties I made on most of my books were not huge, they were a welcome income booster, and I miss them.

As a freelancer I enjoy a lot of freedom. While earning my MFA, my work schedule allowed me time to write my 15-20 pages a month for my mentor, and I never had to worry about getting enough vacation time from my boss to go off on my ten-day residencies twice a year. I already knew the thrill of being published and had the discipline to write regularly and stick with it. While writers of children's school library books don't get the respect or financial rewards of best-selling authors and literary novelists, they make a living at writing, which few of my fellow MFA colleagues can say.

But there's a downside for the MFA grad who is a freelance writer. Writing for a living drains some of the energy away from your more creative projects. When you write all day for work, pushing yourself to work on your own stuff on nights and weekends can be a challenge.

Unfortunately, that living, at least for this free lancer, is becoming more and more precarious. The advent of electronic books, kindles and database publishing has put the educational publishing industry into a tizzy. One of my steady clients has largely stopped publishing books. Another one just went out of business. Among the remaining school library houses, most of them have ended writers' royalties and have reduced flat fees to save costs in an uncertain market. With fewer outlets for work, the competition has become keen, and writers are willing to accept work for low fees that they would have turned down a few years earlier.

For this freelance writer, teaching has become a second career. My terminal MFA degree has helped me to find adjunct work at several colleges, including the university where I earned my MFA. I also teach continuing education and writers' workshops in the evenings. By supplementing my income with teaching, I have managed to survive financially in these difficult economic times. And then there's my wife's full-time salary as a teacher that pays most of the bills and provides us with health insurance.

Of course teaching takes preparation and then there's grading papers, student conferences, and faculty meetings. If I thought I had less time to write my fiction because of freelance deadlines, it has become even harder with the added teaching load. However, as one of my MFA mentors is always saying "a writer must write," and it's your job and mine to find the time in a busy work schedule to finish that damn story, novel, memoir or poetry collection.

Freelance writing is a career that will appeal to anyone who loves to communicate through the written word and get paid for it. Like any career, it has its ups and downs, its cranky, unreasonable editors and its tight deadlines. But it also offers the writer the opportunity to see his work in print (often), set his or her own schedule, take time off for that writer's retreat or conference when needed, and, hopefully, set aside time to work on that great American novel that's percolating upstairs.

reelancing is to publishing as what is to academia? That was one of the logic problems on my SAT, I'm sure. How *does* an adjunct make the move to a tenure-track position? Is it even possible today? If you love writing and love teaching, yearn to be an educator, a professor of anything literary and are prepared to make the commitment to both your writing and a challenging career path, consider this exploration by Carol Ann Davis of MFAs and tenure-track careers in teaching.

Into the Afterwards; On Landing Tenure-Track Teaching Jobs and Diving into Your Post-MFA Life
by Carol Ann Davis

By fate, by work, or by luck—and my money's on luck—I am the full-time tenure-track writer and colleague who has an office across the hall from many diligent and hardworking adjunct colleagues, separated by so many invisible barriers we each daily cross, though often in my myopia or hurry I'm not able to offer my bit of professional insight or help. Even when I can and do stop to chat, what insights I offer on my own path to whatever small, seemingly safe harbor in the academic seas I've found may seem so particular as to not be useful to anyone graduating—or entering the teaching profession—today, nearly twenty years later. What I mean is that as soon as one graduates from the MFA and embarks on whatever journey will take him or her into the wilds of balancing avocation with vocation, writing with work, one's story quickly becomes irrelevant to the next generation, who graduates into ever-more challenging times and into realities not anticipated by their teachers or mentors.

That's why I will give only a rough sketch of my own path, and then spend some time talking not so much about how to land that tenure-track job, but how to find ways to sustain your work in the meantime; it's my experience that the attention you give your own work early on is never, ever wasted, and it's sustained attention to your work—composing it, mindfully and energetically promoting it, following it where it takes you—that eventually leads to "the job."

The job I refer to is the coveted tenure-track creative writing teaching position, though I have reservations, which will be noted throughout, about whether such positions are necessarily right for those graduating today. I certainly hope those reading will not have "the job" as their goal, but rather the accomplishment of a writing process that will sustain them over time. In my experience, it is only through such a process that "the job" emerges anyway.

Much of what I have to offer may seem a simplistic, pie-in-the-sky bit of Monday morning quarterbacking from the luxury box, but the truth is that if you have not done the work you need to do to make your writing the central driving engine in your life, then even when you get that dream job, you may be unprepared to keep your writing on track. It's not as if the work lets up when the tenure track job is undertaken—it only increases, and sometimes in unappetizing directions. So, my advice is aimed toward assisting in the effort to understand what it is you can do now to nurture and support your work and find those avenues of support that are available to you, in preparation for a time in which you may be offered a tenure-track position, and in preparation for a time when accepting that position will find you well on your way to establishing a promising career in your genre rather than snowed in by new duties and bereft of a true writing practice. First and foremost writing must remain the goal.

As I began to write an article on finding tenure track employment severally from a chapter on finding grant-and-fellowship-related support, I realized that they are integrally related; one is the cart and the other is the horse. The cart (a dream job) moves nowhere without the horse (a continuous focus on a writing practice). I recalled letting my graduate school teacher know five years out from getting my MFA that I had been offered a tenure-track position; I said to her, "I thought it would take longer. I was just settling in to writing poems for their own sake." To which she replied: "It's because you were focused on your writing that you got the job." I had, you guessed it, been adjunct teaching in the intervening years, publishing pieces in magazines, and applying for fellowships; I'd recently received a $35,000 fellowship from my alma mater, Vassar College, and this had been the tipping point for me. I was offered a position at the College of Charleston; it would be another seven years before I had a book, and five subsequent years until I published my second book and made the move to Fairfield University, where I hope to stay. Calling it a long haul doesn't really do it justice.

For more on finding grants and fellowships, see the article by Carol Ann Davis in chapter 8.

Yet it was the poems I first wrote for the fellowship—and also the "surrender" I consciously made to writing those poems for their own sake and for no other reason—that tipped the balance in my favor and gave fate a chance to smile in my direction; it was my continued commitment to writing for many subsequent years that that led me where I am, on the way to being happy and fulfilled. This fulfillment, in my case, arrived on the tenure-track, but it is a larger project, a spiritual exercise that must constantly keep envy, self-doubt, and cynicism at bay long enough to get the writing done for the day. It is also the voice, private, interior, that requires the writing to take precedence over teaching preparation, committee meetings, advising, and all that comes with a full time teaching job. Then there are the professional distractions: there is someplace else that looks better, like a better job, prize, fellowship, publication. In reality, there is always someone across the hall (or across the country, or in that magazine, or at that press) who seems to have more, or have it more together, than you do. That is not, unfortunately, the exclusive province of adjunct teaching. I mention that now in case anyone thought, as I did, that getting a tenure track job would alleviate the self-doubt endemic to the writing tribe. That's with us to stay.

> **"There is always someone across the hall (or across the country, or in that magazine, or at that press) who seems to have more, or have it more together, than you do."**

I hope the above thumbnail sketch of my path to the tenure track gives you some indication that I passionately care about how writers embark on and shepherd their professional careers. The good news is that there are resources available to emerging writers; availing yourself of them will only prepare you for the job—in academia or elsewhere— that is always just on its way to coming to you. Below I will hit on some of the main resources, any of which contribute to your looking extremely good to that tenure track hiring committee, and all of which will make you a better, more fulfilled writer (which is really the long-term goal and prize). Here goes:

1. If you seek a pleasant peninsula, look about you...
Okay, that's the state motto of Michigan, but it really is the first rule of finding resources for your work as a writer. All of us live in a particular place, and in that place there will be grants and fellowships available only to residents. State art commissions have individual artist grants. Many cities do as well. The Rose Fellowship, the large award I received that gave my tenure-track candidacy traction, was a fellowship from my alma mater exclusively for students who had pursued creative work as undergrads. Scour your own undergraduate institution's career site for similar opportunities; do the same with local, regional, and state newspapers, the websites for local and state art and cultural commissions. Also, consider volunteering at festivals, workshops, or events in your town or city. Get involved. The more people you meet, the more will know of your work. Invitations for readings may follow, as well as editorial work, and, of course, those state grants I mentioned.

2. Define communities broadly, and seek out support from those with which you are a natural fit (there are bound to be a few).
Communities can be local or virtual, and even ones not near you geographically can provide support networks, sources of funding, or a community of practice. Outside of your direct geographical location, consider the ways in which you might belong to communities more broadly. I recently discovered a grant for writers who are parents; I

shipped my kids off to school and quickly applied. The fact of the grant's existence reminded me that there are other writers struggling through balancing home and work life, and that there are those working to establish a community that includes me, the one with the Cheerios in her hair, in it. Likewise earlier in my career when I began to be interested in literary outreach and poets in the schools programs, I found a vast network of online resources from those who'd done that work before I did. Female writers will find many magazines, websites, and online communities specifically tailored to them, as will those in other identifiable groups. As with the previous bullet, the key here is getting involved. Your willingness to be present in a community or communities will knit this big bad writing world a bit closer together, and closer to you. Another important source of community are the professional organizations you can join.

> "Your willingness to be present in a community or communities will knit this big bad writing world a bit closer together, and closer to you."

3. Join professional organizations and avail yourself of their listings. PEN America has a very good database of current grants and awards available for writers. So does *Poets and Writers* magazine, and the *AWP Chronicle*, the magazine of the Association of Writers and Writing Programs. Those are a few of the largest and best known, but there are many others. Read all the listings, even those for which you are not yet eligible. Doing so allows you to dream big—I'm still happily aspirational for the day I will be ready to do more than read the Guggenheim Foundation's guidelines, for instance. Reading these listings and publications also allows you to see that you are not so isolated—it really is a beautiful peninsula, and it is all "about you."

4. Consider doing a residency or short teaching gig, even if the pay is poor, the scheduling inconvenient, and the distance far. Okay, this goes back to personal biography again, but I once quit a bookstore job in Northampton, MA, and left my just-moved-in-together boyfriend to go and live in the senior dorm in a small Virginia women's college. Four months, $1,200, an eleven-hour drive between my intended and me. I'm old, but not so old that that was a lot of money, or even gas money, then. But it was an important experience for me, it gave me a "line item" on my CV, and I met a much more established poet (also stranded in the same town albeit on a much more lucrative residency) who became an important source of support and advice for two decades and even blurbed my first book.

5. And speaking of professional connections: stay in touch. Of course you are going to need to ask your teachers and mentors for letters later, so you want to keep in touch, but there's a more important reason to do so, alluded to in the previous paragraph, and that's the feeling of being part of a community. A writer just starting out needs to feel connected to a lineage, part of something larger, and those who are a little farther along are usually quite generous in expanding their circle to include you. Of course they like hearing from you; postcards are best, don't require a reply, and allow you to practice the fine art of concision. You can and will ask for a letter of recommendation—and when you do, upload it to an online service such as Interfolio so you don't have to ask again and again, but only update every other year or so—but more importantly, accept that you are entering into a community of writers. Step into that by taking responsibility for your part in things. The teacher-student relationship is transactional, one-sided, and awkward. As you graduate and move forward, the give and take should change; repay others' generosity with your own, whatever that may mean. I've sent flowers, postcards, pralines, oranges in season, each time out of the blue (rather than on the occasion of a thank-you for a recommendation) because the thought of someone's support moved me to gratitude. And, giving gifts makes me feel close to those about whom I care a great deal, no matter the distance. That sense of connection is be part of what has sustained me and my work over time—I highly recommend it.

6. Go for the bigger, more prestigious fellowships and residencies, too. So you heard about my sad-sack Virginia-on-a-shoestring version of the writer's residency, but there are plenty that pay well and add real prestige to your CV. (See sidebar) There are residencies for every time of year and in many regions of the country. Go, even if it's inconvenient. You will get some time for writing, and you'll further expand the community of artists that will sustain you through all those job seasons to come. Maybe some of them will even trade work with you, or read in your city later, or invite you to read! And the same advice on keeping in touch applies here too: follow up with truffles, postcards, the occasional praline. A former student of mine started a hand-made truffle business and you wouldn't believe his mailing list! After year three it read like the board of the Academy of Arts and Letters. I still dream of his salted caramels, and I'm guessing more than one Pulitzer Prize winner does too. And that reminds me of my next little tidbit:

7. Make time to develop additional interests: I was serious about the truffle business. That same student, a poet now with a book and a teaching job, had a garden blog, a small magazine (sent with the truffles, of course), and a baby in the decade we were in close touch. In other words, his life went on in all kinds of rewarding ways. This may seem obvious, but you enrich yourself—and your work—by engaging fully in your life. It's not all striving; some of it's changing diapers or picking strawberries on a freakish warm January day in Charleston. My interest in working with kindergartners as my son's preschool led, in a crazy curvy line, to work I did at an underserved high school, and that led me to my current academic position at a Jesuit institution that values that type of service. Your avocations have a way of leading you to good choices; listen to them. And of course additional work, such as community engagement, teaching or experience in an applicable field such as publishing, may make you additionally competitive for tenure track positions.

8. Don't focus so much on "the book," or if you do, do so because you are compelled to write it, and spend your time *writing it* rather than worrying about the market. All too often I hear graduate students mentioning that they want to "get a book" so they can "get a job." For me, this is anathema to my mentor's remark upon hearing of my first hire. Hiring committees are, I can lamentably report from actual hiring committees on which I've served in the last few years, deluged by candidates with books. One committee on which I served had 250 applicants, of which 150 had books. This was startling to me, as I had heard such truisms during my years in graduate school as "get a book and you will get a job" and "you can teach full-time if you're willing to move away from the east coast." Of course, at this point, a cursory look at the numbers of MFA graduates—not to mention the growing pool of PhD candidates in creative writing—tells a very different story. The numbers game is almost too discouraging to think about; precisely for that reason, I advise all emerging MFA graduates to work on that which they can control—their own writing lives, habits, and processes—and leave the rest up to the gods (whoever they are, they're not appearing on hiring committees, I assure you). That said, most full-time hires will have books accepted or in hand; it's simply that having a book alone does not make one competitive for the small pool of positions available. The better part of virtue in such a situation is to work on the book as you are compelled to, and to write the book that you are meant to write rather than the one that will fit a trend that seems to be developing in job ads or in the fickle landscape of trade publishing. Oh, and that reminds me:

9. Protect yourself from job-ad and blog malaise, accompanying cynicism, and/or fatigue: A major peril of the digital age is that what was once a "job season" each fall in which jobs were posted at one location on the web is now a perpetual cycle, attended by innumerable wikis and blogs trying to unpack or unearth the secret behind landing the perfect, or even a decent, job. I remember having to wait until the second Friday in September before the jobs were even posted, and by the time most of them closed December 1, the long wait to hear results meant I had about two months to—you guessed it—get back to my writing. Beyond putting applications in the mail, I had my writing life to myself. No midnight trip to the fridge was attended by a quick check on whether anyone had posted news to the Wiki for creative writing jobs, about their being notified for interviews or the perils of the inside candidate that meant no one should have bothered in the first place to apply. These days every spare minute could be spent analyzing an understandably tough and inscrutable job market. Resist the temptation and get back to your writing desk.

10. Keep submitting your best work to magazines you truly admire. Magazine publications look nice, especially as they begin to pile up on that CV, but the real reason to submit your work is to keep on trying and to knit yourself more deeply into the community of writers that surround you (that beautiful peninsula again). Presumably you are reading work in the magazines to which you're sending, and you're learning a lot about your own work from the responses you get and (maybe) even more from all that reading you're doing. No matter how many rejections pile up, or how the job search is going, you can always send your work out into the clear blue and wish it well. Doing so stretches the soul, and the soul of the work.

> **"No matter how many rejections pile up, or how the job search is going, you can always send your work out into the clear blue and wish it well."**

11. Weigh very strongly whether academia is the only place for you or whether you could be happy doing something else (and still write). Many of us have been told for so long that a tenure-track position in creative writing is the ultimate prize that sometimes we forget to check in with ourselves about it. There are many aspects of a full-time position in academia that are rewarding, but there are other aspects that can seriously interfere with the serious work of writing.

Adjunct teaching will let you know whether you love teaching, but this is only part of the equation. Consider whether or not you would like to tie your literary success to your professional success or whether you would like to keep them separate. If the answer is the latter, try another field, something that will leave time to write. I recently heard of a famous poet who gave up a prestigious chair at a major university to become a midwife, and I understood precisely. I think we'll see more and better writing from her for her having made that decision.

12. If academia is for you, accept that it's a long trail. If after all of this discouraging news, you still feel that academia is for you, go for it. Hopefully you will be writing a lot, publishing, and going on the occasional fellowship or residency. You'll have made a few connections that are authentic enough to survive into useful correspondences or even friendships, and the support they provide will help you through any dark days. It's only at this point, after you've developed a writing practice that survives the travails of baristaing, adjunct teaching, bookstore retailing, and whatever else you find for work that you might, if you already have the MFA, consider applying for the PhD. I don't say this lightly, as I dislike the codified, pro-institutional nature of today's creative writing PhD programs and many of their semi-wacky meldings of the study of writing, theory, and literature, but I also can't see the future. It's possible the PhD really will prevail over the MFA as the degree of record and you'll need to have one to teach at the tenure track level. The jury is still out on that, though I know what my vote is. At any rate, if you can protect your creative work and still attend such a program, perhaps you should consider it (she said reluctantly, in closing, and only when pressed).

So that's it. The path to the job you will have will be different from every other writer you know, different from mine and from the truffle-maker's and the happy exile midwife. What we will have in common, if we're lucky, is that twenty years from today, no matter what else we're doing for work, we'll still be writing. When you get to the end of the long trail, drop me a postcard. I'll do the same!

*W*hat if you are compelled to write but love your career? What if you can't or *don't want* to quit your eight to six but still want to write and publish successfully? If you don't have the option to cast aside gainful employment for a minimum wage job that allows you time and mental energy to crank out your bestseller, or if you actually enjoy your career, take heart. Here's some inspiration and encouragement (and a few new role models) for when the path to victory is littered with the obstacles of daily life.

More Than One Calling

by Ashley C. Andersen Zantop

Car salesman, window washer, portraitist, ticket taker, security guard, cashier, cowhand. The stranger the better. It's the struggling author's professional car crash we can't turn away from. Writers are fascinated by the day jobs famous authors held before scaling the peaks of notoriety and success. Just do a quick internet search for 'famous author day jobs' and you'll discover an abyss of results yawning more than a thousand articles deep from almost every major periodical in the world and a host of obscure ones, too. Maybe it makes us feel better, encouraged somehow, to know that most famous authors weren't born that way; they had to struggle for it just like every other aspiring word smith—savants with first paid publication at the silly age of 11 or 14, Ray Bradbury-style, excepted, of course. For those of us who do love the spectacle, the guilty pleasure of gawking at the car crash, by all means, gawk away. Turn to the end of chapter 8. You'll find a healthy list of authors with outrageous resumes.

Fascinating and amusing to be sure, but ironically, I've always found these lists and accompanying editorials a little depressing, too. Like a steaming, mangled highway wreck, the ones that get the most attention are the ones that spotlight the extremes, the gaping disparity of the most obscure beginning juxtaposed with a shockingly famous end—or present. The most often circulated of these lists fawn over rags to ridiculous successes of *New York Times* bestselling authors who started as cemetery caretakers or night shift janitors. The utterly discouraging part is the inevitable editorial about Mr. Famous Author who took a job as a nighttime security guard in the world's quietest town because it gave him time to write his first bestseller while on the clock. Or you hear about writers who chose assistant or clerical jobs that burn less than a fraction of their mental horsepower not because of circumstance but to ensure themselves time and opportunity to work on their debut novels while they're in the office. The manager in me swallows a trickle of bile every time I picture this.

What about those of us who have real jobs, or dare I say it, careers? What about those of us who don't have the option of joining the circus so that we can work on our memoir or poetry collection between shows? What's inspiring about learning that Don DeLillo had such a boring job as a parking lot attendant that he started reading and writing and eventually became a great American novelist? Many writers don't have or want the option of taking a low-paid or low-demand gig so they can spend time getting paid very little for one job while working on what they hope will be another. Hey, and here's a new thought in this context, what about those of us who actually (mostly) *like* our jobs and are committed to careers outside of writing? Can we still be successful authors too? Who are *our* role models?

Although you don't read or hear about them as often, or don't realize it when you do, literary greats and bestselling authors, alike, have a long tradition of maintaining meaningful and satisfying careers while writing and publishing their works. In fact, some use their careers as a way of fueling their writing lives, some of them use writing as an outlet to make sense (or fun) of their workplace experiences. Some of them use their jobs to help ignite their creativity and provide credibility to their writing. In fact, this may be the most practical option of all, given the odds of making a living solely as an author. In 2010, *Publisher's Weekly* reported that only 3% of authors make a living on their writing alone. Here's a look at a few writers who maintain, or maintained, successful careers while writing and achieving success as authors:

Sir Arthur Conan Doyle is most well known for his Sherlock Holmes mysteries, but he also wrote short stories and nonfiction magazine articles. He was a physician and served as ship doctor and surgeon on several voyages. Also a professional athlete, he played football, cricket and golf—his own brand of Renaissance man.

Benjamin Franklin was a printer, newspaper editor and publisher, most notably and profitably, *Poor Richard's Almanac* and *The Pennsylvania Gazette*. He was also a widely recognized scientist and inventor, founder of the University of Pennsylvania, president of the American Philosophical Society, diplomat (American ambassador or 'minister' to Paris) and governor of Pennsylvania. He was the author of countless articles, essays and self-published much of his own work in *Poor Richard's Almanac* under pen names. His autobiography was published after his death. His greatest achievement? With a CV like this, hard to say, but perhaps his work as editor of and signatory to the shabby little publication best known as *The Declaration of Independence*.

Heather Gudenkauf is the modern embodiment of commitment to literacy in all it's forms, with nearly one million copies in print between her three bestselling novels. She began as an elementary and middle school teacher and is now a Title I reading coordinator in the Iowa public school system.

Khaled Housseini is the celebrated author of bestselling titles *The Kite Runner* and *A Thousand Splendid Suns*. He trained and practiced as a physician for more than a decade before accepting a position as a Goodwill Envoy for the United Nations High Commissioner for Refugees and he also provides humanitarian assistance to Afghanistan via his Khaled Housseini Foundation.

Garrison Keillor is a renowned radio personality and long-time host of the radio show *A Prairie Home Companion*. Keillor is also a bookseller, as proprietor of Common Good Books in St. Paul, Minnesota. He's done a wide range of voiceover acting for commercials and films. Keillor was also a journalist and advice columnist, writing for publications such as the The Atlantic *Monthly, Salon.com* and *The New Yorker*. He's also authored novels, collections of essays, works of poetry, penned a screenplay for and starred in the 2006 film titled after his radio show directed by Robert Altman.

Kathy Reichs is one of 82 certified forensic anthropologists by the American Board of Forensic Anthropology and professor of Anthropology for the University of North Carolina at Charlotte. She's written academic papers and books, but is perhaps most widely known for her bestselling crime novels, the first of which was published in 1997, featuring the character known as Dr. Temperance Brennan. She and her work are the inspiration for the television series Bones that aired for the first time in 2005 on the Fox network.

It's heartening to read just a few paragraphs about these extraordinary lives. But, is there a middle ground? What about those of us in between? We want and need real jobs to support ourselves, our family and our intellectual curiosity, but we'd be glad to leave the world of "real work" some day to be a full-time writer. Does that sound right to you? After reading those blurbs, maybe you're thinking, *hmm, why don't I cultivate my career until I've reached that certain level of success as an author, and then I can retire form my meaningful career to a rewarding second career as an author?*

Good plan—if you leave aside that 3% statistic. But, surprisingly, there and plenty of solid role models and sources of inspiration for a two-part career journey. Perhaps these examples are the most inspiring for those of us who can't or don't want to leave our careers now, but dream of writing full-time one day. In fact, it's even easier to find examples of successful full-time authors who once held jobs and careers before "retiring" to write full-time. Here are a few:

Isabel Allende worked for the United Nations Food and Agriculture Organization, was a translator of novels (reportedly fired for making unauthorized changes to make the female protagonists seem less ridiculous), worked in news media as an editor and columnist and served as a school administrator in Venezuela.

Robin Cook was trained as a physician at Columbia and Harvard Universities, he practiced and taught medicine for many years. He is also credited with being a co-founder of a software company and a real estate investor. He's a bestselling author of medical thrillers, with reportedly over 100 million copies in print.

Patricia Cornwell began her career as a journalist, covering crime reporting, then became a technical writer for the Office of the Chief Medical Examiner of Virginia and then became a computer analyst there. She also volunteered with the local police department.

(John) Michael Crichton is a doctor, producer, director as well as screenwriter and bestselling author. Crichton directed the film adaptation of Robin Cook's *Coma*. Several of his own novels have been adapted into successful films.

Graham Greene was a tutor and journalist, editor, book and film reviewer. Greene's critical review of the Shirley Temple film *Wee Willie Winkie* resulted in a libel lawsuit for the magazine he co-edited, and subsequently it closed.

John Grisham was a lawyer specializing in criminal defense and litigation of personal injury cases, he also served in the Mississippi state House of Representatives. His works total nearly 300 million copies in print, and nine of his novels have been made into films. His first novel, *A Time to Kill*, was initially just a modest success, reportedly only 5,000 copies on the first print run, but his second work, *The Firm*, became a *New York Times* bestseller and launched his career as a writer.

Jayne Ann Krentz is the bestselling author of numerous romantic-suspense novels. She began her career as an elementary school librarian before moving on to become an academic and corporate librarian. Her titles reportedly have over 35 million copies in print.

Salman Rushdie was an advertising copywriter, rumored to have worked on accounts like American Express, until he published his second novel and became a full-time writer; He also worked at Emory University.

This list literally can go on an on. These talented and versatile professionals should serve as a reminder that we don't need to give up on our dreams of writing just because we love (or can't leave) our careers. We're smart, we're motivated. We'll find a way to do both, even if neither is perfect. Our writing may be better for it.

Chapter *10*

PUBLISHING OPTIONS (AND SOME BASIC RULES TO FOLLOW OR NOT)

edited by A.J. O'Connell

From the slow expansion driven by the advent of desktop publishing decades ago to more recent advances in short run printing, social media and mobile devices, the number of potential paths to publication has exploded. Explore a sampling of your options in this chapter.

large press or a small one? A physical book or an eBook? And what about self-publishing?

The path to publication can be an intimidating one. Luckily, there are many routes to publication these days. Within this chapter, you will find several sets of rules and guidelines that will help you achieve your literary goals. Just remember, getting published isn't always about obeying the rules. Don't be afraid to break one here and there if that's what works for you.

Maybe you're interested in self-publishing. Maybe you've written several short pieces that you want to place in an assortment of literary journals. Or you may want to look into your options when it comes to publishing houses, because there are many different kinds of publishers: the publishing giants, small presses and academic presses. The following essay explores some of these options, with a focus on the small press.

Small Press? Large Publishing House? Both? Neither?

by Alan Davis

You've written a book, maybe as a thesis for an MFA program, maybe as night work to escape from the daily grind of a full-time job. You've put your heart and soul into it. It means almost everything to you. While writing and revising, you've applied every bit of craft that you know. You've had some success placing individual stories, essays, excerpts, or poems at literary magazines or journals. You've been applauded when you've read your work aloud. Further, you've found a few faithful readers or mentors and they've told you that it's time to submit your work in its entirety to a book publisher.

What do you do now? Publish with a large press, a small literary press, or self-publish? Here are some down-and-dirty observations that I hope might be helpful as you decide what to do.

There have never been so many publishing options available to writers. You can submit your work, once you've prepared a query letter and a synopsis, to agents in hopes of placing your book with a larger publishing house, few of which will consider unsolicited manuscripts that haven't first been vetted by an agent. Doing so makes sense if your book is mainstream fiction, a compelling memoir driven by trauma, or genre work—a literary mystery, for example, that might have commercial appeal.

If that's not the case, if you've written a collection of stories or essays or poems, or if your novel is experimental or driven more by language and character than by plot, you might find a publisher more quickly if you decide to submit your work to small (often not-for-profit) presses, where most editors are primarily interested in literary quality, can make decisions without the approval of marketing executives, and will keep your book in print once it's published regardless of sales.

If you decide to try your luck with small presses, you still need a query letter and a synopsis, but you don't need an agent. (It's worth noting, however, that at New Rivers Press [NRP], where I'm senior editor, we receive more agented manuscripts each year; that fact probably says more about the sorry state of commercial publishing, where genre fiction is king or queen and literary fiction can be a hard sell, than about anything else.) In fact, most small presses prefer to deal directly with a writer, who can contact a small press directly. Since there's not much money in play, either actually or potentially, an agent's negotiating expertise isn't required, either; if you're offered a contract and find yourself worried about signing away your rights, a lawyer can assist you with your contract if it's complicated or you can contact an organization like The Author's Guild for assistance. See chapter 12 for more information about publishing contracts and where to go for help.

Small publishers like New Rivers Press often have limited windows when they read general manuscripts. (At NRP, for example, we read open submissions in April, May and June.) You can often email a small press editor for information, but you should follow protocol and be courteous when doing so: don't email an attachment, for example, without asking permission to do so. In addition, visit a publisher's website to glean information before you contact them, then either mail or email your query to a particular editor.

It's never been easier to gather such information, thanks to numerous databases, search engines, and the internet. *Poets and Writers* has a good database of publishers, as does *newpages.com* and several other sites. Where do your mentors publish? Your peers with books in print? Take a look at a publisher's front list (books most recently published) and back list (all the titles in print) to see if your manuscript is compatible with such work. Do the research while you're proofreading your manuscript and preparing query materials; make a list of 50 publishers (or as many as you can manage) that might be suitable. If you can, get hold of representative titles and evaluate the quality of the actual book: cover design, typeface, aesthetic attractiveness, readability, etc. Who's the distributor for the press? Do titles get reviewed? Have they won awards?

In short, would you be proud to be included on a given publisher's list?

Very often these days, a writer, once accepted, collaborates with a small press publisher—sometimes has input on cover art, for example, if that's important to you. If you're middle-aged and want to make certain that the font is suitable for easy reading in dim light at a coffeehouse event, you can make such a request at a small press and be taken seriously.

Because small press budgets are limited, you should be prepared to collaborate with such a press on a marketing and publicity plan. If you want to do a reading tour, for example, you'll have to pay your own way, but the press's managing editor or an intern will contact bookstores and arrange for shipments of your book. (Just as often, you'll buy books at discount directly from your publisher and lug them with you to a venue like a coffeehouse where books aren't sold.) Some small presses ask, either directly or indirectly, for subventions (financial assistance of some sort) to help with costs associated with the publication of your book; this sort of thing has long been a common practice at many academic presses (though it's seldom spoken of) but now it occurs more frequently at not-for-profit presses, too. When a small press chooses a book through a contest (see below), they usually require writers to pay an entry fee for each submission.

At a large publishing house, you might feel at home or you might not. At a small press, if you're published, you become part of the family. You'll be contacted during fundraising drives and asked to contribute. You'll be invited to social events at conferences and your work will be put on display at book fairs. The book will be available at all the major online vendors for purchase (and, if so arranged, as an eBook). Most small presses have an established public relations and distribution system in place; they'll send out review copies, for example, and take care of any number of annoying details to make your book available to as many potential readers as possible. You can trust that your book will stay in print. You have to remember, however, that your editor or intern is probably wearing several hats, not only editing and marketing but also teaching and writing and otherwise filling her day with a to-do list that never gets done. There are few specialists at such presses, so don't expect a sophisticated marketing campaign; find out exactly what can and can't be done for your work.

If you decide instead on self-publishing, I have a few cautionary tales to tell you. These days it's easier than ever to publish your own book; if you publish it electronically, it's easier than ever to make it available through online vendors like Amazon. A great deal of genre work is published in this fashion these days. Think carefully, however, about how much time and energy and expertise you have. A friend (and former student) self-published a novel, for example, good stuff but work that wasn't edited or professionally prepared when it appeared in print. Her book was available electronically but also in print via POD (print on demand—books are printed only when they're purchased). She had no distributor, no publicity except what she herself could drum up. She decided, later, despite the fact that she works professionally in the technology sector, that she couldn't do justice to the novel and wanted to find a traditional publisher for it. It was too late; the book had an ISBN number, identifying it as a book in print, and she couldn't convince any publisher to republish it.

On the other hand, one of our former interns at NRP, Ryan Christiansen, who has also worked in the technology sector, decided to found Knuckledown Press, not to publish his own work but the work of others: "Knuckledown Press publishes literary fiction and creative nonfiction titles in English for worldwide distribution in electronic formats. Our authors enjoy high royalty rates and retain their rights to publish their works elsewhere in print. Knuckledown Press utilizes professional editing services to prepare titles for publication." We were so impressed by what he was doing that at NRP we've appointed him as editor of our new Electronic Book Series, which publishes "popular fiction titles with literary value from new and emerging authors in the genres…" The first book in that series will be available soon.

In short, publishing is a brave new world these days. If you want to publish with the larger publishing houses, don't wait for permission. Prepare your manuscript and accompanying materials and go for it. Let prospective agents tell you whether or not your book is right for such a market. If you want to try to publish with a reputable literary small press (and you're the judge who decides which press is "reputable" for your purposes), you should send the same kinds of materials to such presses (simultaneous submissions are fine until an agent or press makes a commitment or requests exclusive rights). For more on simultaneous submissions, see chapter 7.

You should also enter your manuscript selectively in contests and competitions like the AWP Award Series or NRP's Many Voices Project. Though such competitions almost always require entry fees and have long odds, they're worth your attention; many writers have achieved recognition when their manuscript was chosen for publication.

If you prefer self-publishing, do the research before making the decision.

Whatever you decide to do, ask the right questions. Talk to mentors and peers and those who've done what you hope to do. Take chances, make mistakes, keep writing, and learn in the process. Go for it, and whatever you decide, keep in mind what the poet E. E. Cummings advised: "Listen; there's a hell of a good universe next door: let's go."

*O*f course, publishing a novel, memoir or collection is not the only way to get your work out to the reading public. Often a writer can make a big literary splash if he or she has a story, essay or poem published in a respected literary journal. Sometimes an author is also interested in finding homes for pieces that may be included in an upcoming work. If that sounds like you, read on for a list of suggestions that will help you submit your work to journals and magazines.

The Pirate's Code of Submission Absolutes
by Linsey Jayne

My first submission was probably an editor's worst nightmare. I'll set the scene: as a 19-year-old girl, during an independent study in poetry as an undergrad, I asked my poet laureate professor what the next steps for my manuscript might be. My professor cryptically responded[2], "You submit." He told me many stories of submissions gone wrong for an abundance of reasons. Sometimes they failed to adhere to the submission guidelines. Other times, they were accompanied by a grotesquely long cover letter, one that perhaps embellished too much, or was—perhaps as a defense mechanism—bleeding with humility. This was, of course, not to mention the times that the stationary was not to the editor's liking—"Please, Linsey, remember: no puppy-dog stamps, no scented paper, no purple pens allowed." I shook my head very seriously, made detailed notes in all capital letters: NO PUPPY-DOG STAMPS.

So there I was, an apprehensive poet with a 2008 edition of *Writer's Market*, furiously highlighting magazine titles and trying to decipher what any of what I was doing really meant. When I had finally decided on a mantra ("Aim artificially high!"), and selected a journal whose guidelines were readily available online, I triple-checked each piece for blindness, wrote the most straightforward cover letter I could muster despite my nerves, and mailed them my third draft pieces, with no return address, and a blank SASE.

---

2 Please note that while the results of this interaction were the same, the events described may have been hyperbolized or otherwise misremembered, as memories tend to be. Puppy dog stamps were, however, fervently discouraged.

Crossing the threshold from privately writing, or even writing for a class, into submissionhood is wacky, and it probably happens differently for everyone. The same is true for the editorial experience—no two editors swim the same stream, and each of us could suggest a thousand different things to consider when we talk about the "Ideal Submission." But you already know that—you've probably ventured into some copies of the *Writer's Market*, or tried to sift through the pages upon pages of magazines in various forms that you can find on *Duotrope*, or in *Poets and Writers*. So, while it would be impossible to write an editorial bible of absolutes for you, what I *can* provide is the pirate code edition. Why *pirate code?* Like literary journals, pirate crews each had a specific code of conduct. The codes would vary between crews, but often addressed several staple behaviors, and appeared to follow similar outlines. So, while I can't advise you on gambling, or tell you when it's appropriate for you to leave your ship and go ashore, I can absolutely provide you with an outline of things to consider while you're submitting. Know that these are strictly guidelines, but they're certainly going to be more helpful than submitting to the impulse of throwing wild copies of your poems or stories directly at editors on the streets and shouting *"Love me, dear god, why won't you love me?"*. Oh, you weren't planning on doing that? That was just me. Again, your experience may vary.

The Pirate's Code of Submission Absolutes
I. Research like your life depends on it

Because it does, in a way—at least, your writing life may. And it's important to research in the broadest sense of the term—do enough reading to know your own writing, and do enough research to know which publications are looking to house writing like yours. Research enough to know which are in print, and which are online-only. Separate your options into tiers—have an a-list of high-level aspirations, and maybe a b-list and a c-list, too. Make sure they're all publications you'd be proud to be accepted by—don't simply look toward any old journal just because you think you can get in. As an editor, the people whose motivation is publication for publication's sake are more obvious than perhaps they intend to be, and they can unintentionally have the effect of insulting a magazine—hurting the chance of even the best piece of writing getting placed.

Research enough to know what you like and dislike about the journals you're submitting to. That's more for your personal benefit than anything, but sometimes it's helpful to include notes about this in dialogue with the editorial staff (especially in cover letters). This will help you create your lists, too, and ensure that the packet of writing you put together is the best fit possible for the magazine.

II. Read the submission guidelines

This is a big one—and probably the most frequently ignored tip of all. The submission guidelines are the place where editors spell out, as best as they possibly can, what they are looking for in their submission. These can vary from place to place, but they often address the following questions that most writers would ask when putting their manuscripts together. This is where you learn if your submission should be *blind*— meaning that it should contain no identifying information on the body of the submission itself—or *nonblind*. If they specify the latter, this is where they'll likely tell you what information they are looking for on your manuscript—whether it be address, full name, page numbers, or any other sort of organizational information they might seek. It's where you'll find out how long your prose should be; how many poems or flash pieces you can submit. Where you'll learn how long, on average, it might take for you to hear back about your submission. And, of utmost importance, this is where a magazine will tell you whether they accept simultaneous submissions or previously published work. Ignoring that last rule can, on occasion, put a potentially strong relationship with an editor at risk, and has caused even some well-known and talented writers to be blacklisted from publications altogether.

III. Simultaneous Submissions

In an article entitled "What Editors Want; A Must-Read for Writers Submitting to Literary Magazines," The *Review Review* addresses this one best. "If you simultaneously submit, it should be in groups of magazines you think are equivalent. You are going to have to live with the first acceptance you get." This, this this this *this*. I cannot stress this enough. There is no conversation that is going to be more awkward between a writer and an editor than the following:

Editor: "Congratulations, you've been accepted into *This Pretty Cool Journal.*"

Writer: "Uh, hey, thank you! But unfortunately, I think I got accepted into *This Even Cooler Journal than Yours*, and I want to give it to them instead."

Editor: "...."

(I'm sure you can imagine what comes next. Denial, anger, bargaining, depression, and finally, acceptance of another piece in the former piece's stead.)

IV. Re-read your cover letter

There are few harder slaps in the face, from an editorial standpoint, than opening a cover letter addressed to someone else's journal. That's not to say that we're ignorant of reality; we know that our submitters are almost certainly submitting their work to multiple journals. And, of course, it's easy enough to make a mix-up like that, especially given the newfound ease that submission managers have granted online publications. But somehow, despite this, it's hard to shake the bad vibe that you get when you see another journal's letter by mistake. It's not unlike accidentally stumbling upon a love note to your boyfriend from his high-school girlfriend. Yeah, you know that stuff happened , but it's nice to remain unaware of the whole mess. So, when you think you're finally ready to submit your work, you aren't. Read everything over once more time. Check for consistency, check to make sure you follow the submission guidelines, and *check to be sure your cover letter is addressed to the actual place your work is being sent.*

V. Ask questions!

This is my fifth and final point, because it seems like the easiest one to overlook. A lot of the problems and questions that submitters face when preparing to send off their work can be answered by the editorial staff. So if something isn't addressed on a publication's website or in their submission guidelines, you should never hesitate to find their contact info and send them an email *before you submit.* Sometimes, as editors, our priorities are so set on building our sites up, or going through our submissions, that we neglect minute details that would be truly useful for those who haven't yet sent in their work. Don't be afraid to ask! The likelihood is that you'll get your question answered, and in the worst case, you won't get a response. (In the instance of the latter, you can rest assured that the editorial staff is inundated with whatever's going on, and it might be better to wait until the next submission period to look into this further, or just find another place to send your work.)

The process of submitting work to a journal is equal parts stressful, and exciting. Some days, there's no better feeling than knowing that you've just put out a fresh batch of work, and now can eagerly await a (hopefully positive) response. If you stick, even loosely, to the guidelines above, you can avoid any *what-if-I-forgot-to...* negative feelings, and rest easy, until that unread email appears in your inbox. As for the nature of that email? Well, everyone's results may vary. No need to worry—write boldly, dear friends!

*W*hile you should always have your work edited, editors themselves (the kind who call the shots and have creative control over your work) aren't for everyone. Some writers like to retain control over their prose and verse, some would rather bypass the snarls and delays of traditional publishing and some like the idea of not having to share royalties with a publisher. Self-publishing provides an alternate route to publication for these writers. The following essay will give you some perspective and some pointers on what's become a fast-growing segment of the publishing industry.

Self-Publishing: An Overview and Some Insights
by Mark L Berry

This is a hot topic, and a hot potato. Magazines such as *Writer's Digest* and *Poets & Writers* cover this subject every month, and for good reason. It is a game-changer, it is growing, and nobody knows its limits or potential. I can't promise that self-publishing is the right choice for every author, and I'm not rejecting the traditional publishing options. The advantage of self-publishing at least one title is that it offers you, as an author, the opportunity to create, publish, and distribute your original work into the world. Then you can put as much or as little effort into its growth as you choose.

There are many reasons to self-publish: it's a shortcut to a finished product; it allows for increased control over the final product; and it offers increased percentage of royalties over traditional publishing. I chose to self-publish my first novel *Pushing Leaves Towards the Sun* because I wanted to increase my readership. I created an inexpensive eBook version, and then I also recorded a free podcast audio version to give away.

Does this promotional model really work? Seth Harwood spoke during an AWP seminar during 2012 about giving away all of his work—noir detective fiction and his collection of essays about growing up—as recorded podcasts. He claims that giving away an audio version of his work increased the eBook and print sales of his same titles by eleven percent. His role model is Scott Sigler who also gives away all of his work as podcasts and Scott is a *New York Times* bestselling author. Scott also now has corporate sponsors for his podcasts so he is earning revenue even though the end consumers don't have to pay to listen.

Increased sales or not, both Seth and Scott have huge followings. Seth calls his fans *Palms Daddies* and Scott calls his *Junkies*. Before I gave away my first novel as an audiobook, I called my readership *Dad*. Soon after my novel was released, I received congratulatory notes from friends. Now I occasionally receive fan mail and reviews from complete strangers, and that is an indication that my work is finally traveling beyond my direct reach—a significant landmark for any author.

Self-publishing used to be considered vanity publishing. It was a place of refuge for the wealthy (it used to be expensive, but it no longer is), and for those prospective authors who were not willing to put in the vast effort necessary to attract a literary agent and a traditional publisher. Self-published books have long held a stigma of inferiority to traditionally published books. Even the best ones could be identified as such by their ISBN numbers, if they even had one. This made finding reviewers, blurb providers, and every aspect of a traditional marketing plan more challenging for self-publishers. To self-publish was to tattoo your own face.

Then, not so long ago, self-publishing developed a following in a couple of niche markets and began shedding its outcast persona. Green, or ecology-minded writers began embracing it because of its P.O.D. model. Print On Demand means that books are only produced as they are ordered, saving trees, oh so many trees. This production model is more expensive than traditional publishing where large print runs drive down the individual unit cost, but it saves the enormous up-front cost necessary to produce an inventory of actual books, and it prevents filling your own basement with unsold books.

The other self-publishing niche is filled with experts of all kinds. People wishing to sell or market their experience often demonstrate their expertise by self-publishing a book. The book becomes as much of a resume enhancer as an actual product to sell to their target market. If I tried to write and sell a book titled *The Seven Secrets to Self-Publishing*

Success by Mark L Berry it would hide in a Google search among a slew of other books with similar titles.

Herein lies the major problem of self-publishing. You, as the publisher, become the entire marketing arm of your printed work. There is no Simon & Schuster to put your book into retail shops. There's no Random House to procure a review from other authors under their roof. And there's no HarperCollins to secure an ad or review in *The New York Times* while you dream about appearing on their best-seller list.

The self-publishing model works for experts who are using their book as a symbol of their expertise. This is a more difficult road for literary authors who want to actually sell their books to a mass audience. Self-publishing promotion also demands energy and effort that you may have to sacrifice from your coveted creative time.

But fear not, because as I stated in the beginning, this is a rapidly changing environment. The birth and expansion of the eBook market is the largest factor contributing to self-publishing's recent gain in popularity and credibility. First, producing an eBook is far less expensive than producing a physical paper book. The potential buyers have already paid for the physical production costs in the form of Kindles, Nooks, iPads, and a host of other electronic media buckets just waiting to be filled with content. Once the author's book becomes available electronically, there are virtually no further production costs.

I wrote a report during grad school that addressed actual facts and figures of eBook market growth, but two years later those numbers are already meaningless. By now you'd be hard-pressed to find anyone who still believes that e-publishing is anything other than mainstream. I will share one number with you. A friend of mine, Leland Shanle, Jr., has put the first two of his historical fiction trilogy novels out on Amazon so far (*Project 7Alpha and Vengeance in the Pacific*), and he says that his electronic sales greatly exceed 25 to 1 of his physical book sales. His mantra is only to produce enough physical books to send to potential reviewers and blurb providers. His sales and marketing strategy is strictly online oriented.

That brings up the big question: How does an author get the word out for his/her self-published book? Social media is providing this opportunity. The bottom line is that through Facebook, Twitter, email, and just about every other computer social media medium, new authors are reaching out and finding readers. Results may vary, but at least you can exercise your marketing skills in your pajamas.

One appeal to self-publishing is pricing. Traditional publishers eat a big chunk of the pie, leaving authors to nibble on a small slice or even the crumbs. Granted, they are able to make a much bigger pie to begin with. As I write this, Amazon pays self-published authors royalties of 70 percent of sales on their eBooks if priced between $2.99 and $9.99 with a smaller percentage for books priced outside of that margin. An Amazon author may sell fewer books, but make more money per book, and Amazon is available on everyone's computer, tablet, and smartphone. Other retailers such as Barnes & Noble have similar self-publishing structures.

Amazon has also made the self-publishing market more mainstream and acceptable. How successful? That's open to wide speculation, but their dominance in the eBook market has led to recent lawsuits from traditional publishers. When the legal guns are loaded and pointed, we know that the market share is worth fighting for.

Another appeal of self-publishing is the hopeful trend that the best in the minor leagues are sometimes called up to the majors. The NaNoWriMo (National Novel Writing Month) novel *Water for Elephants* by Sara Gruen began as a self-publishing success before traditional publishing house Algonquin Books acquired it. Many new authors hope that self-publishing will become their road to a traditional publisher as well.

The effort required to break into traditional publishing is often a frustrating *Catch 22*. Agents and publishers today are far less willing to take on a client who doesn't already have a strong sales platform. One "super agent" once told me that if I were the right client for him, he would be looking for me instead of me reaching out to him. A modern query letter is incomplete without a sales and marketing plan as well as an established quantifiable readership. As writers we enjoy the creative aspect of our art, but the publishing industry is first and foremost a business—a reality that is frustrating to many creative people. Self-publishing allows an author to begin swimming in the shallow edge of the publishing pool, and practice sales and marketing techniques with the hope that our book will somehow go viral.

Even if it's a long road and a long shot, self-publishing offers an author the opportunity to begin reaching out and developing a following. With electronic publishing's popularity and increasing market share, you have the potential to reach out worldwide from your home computer. Putting it out there is no guarantee of a success, but nobody ever won the lottery without a ticket.

Finally let me add that although you may spend two years of grad school developing and polishing a single book, it is extremely rare that an author's first work becomes a best seller. *The DaVinci Code* was Dan Brown's fourth novel and the second with Robert Langdon as the protagonist after *Angels and Demons*. If you plan to become a successful writer, you should plan on producing many books over your lifetime while you develop an increasing following with each one. I recently spoke with bestselling St. Louis author Susan McBride and she told me she had written ten books before a major publisher acquired her. If I am shattering your illusions of a rocket ride to the top, then perhaps the next three books you read should not be of the fantasy or fairy tale variety. It's OK to dream. Fairfield University's MFA alumna Deborah Henry's first novel *The Whipping Club* became an Oprah pick the first summer after its release. If your first work launches your career in a spectacular way, I offer my deepest congratulations. Publishing miracles, though rare, do happen—but let's be realistic and prepare for a longer road to success just in case the publishing gods are sleeping during your initial book launch. Short of divine intervention, you can still make it as an author, but you must prepare yourself for an extended journey to success, and self-publishing is one way to begin widening your circulation.

Finally, I want to talk about giving something away for free. Some of my writer friends abhor this concept. They justly want to be compensated for their hard work. I suggest that you take a broader view. Human nature makes most of us reluctant to try new things, and if potential readers have to open their wallets to learn about your writing, they'll be even more cautious. By offering a sample of your creative writing for free, you have the ability to build an audience that may eventually buy your later work. This is why I chose to turn my first novel into a free audiobook. It's not selling very well on Amazon as an eBook, but 37,000 individual episodes have been downloaded for free so far on iTunes as an audiobook, and it has been listened to in 40 countries. No matter what else I write and try to sell in my lifetime, I will always be able to tell potential readers to try my audiobook out for free, and then buy my new work if they like my writing style.

*S*elf-publication, as Mark points out in his essay, has not always been a respected route to publication. Many in the industry still struggle with the stigma attached to self-publishing which, though fading, is still present. If you're considering self-publication but are concerned that you may not be as successful (or taken as seriously) as your traditionally-published peers, read on. This essay by writer and teacher Heather Frizzell both examines several self-published authors who went on to mainstream fame and fortune and the author's views on the quality of the work that resulted from that process.

Self-Publishing to the Mainstream Spotlight: a Tale of Internet Fame and Fortune
by Heather Frizzell

There's no denying that the publishing industry is changing. Much like the crisis the music industry underwent in the early 2000s, the digital revolution has buried its claws deep into what many considered a stalwart and unshakeable publishing process. With the advent of e-readers, books can be transferred and spread as quickly as mp3s. With the rise of Amazon.com, writers can publish their own work, cutting out a sea of middlemen and, as evidence as shown, can gain large-scale success. Self-publishing is losing the stigma attached to it: it is no longer exclusively regarded as a last resort for authors whose inferior literary work would never have seen the light of day if they hadn't gone through "proper" channels. As a writer, however, publishing yourself does not guarantee your book will become commercially successful. The same holds true for going the traditional way: getting an agent who markets your book to a major publishing house. In the old days, publishing companies would factor money into the budget of marketing your book, but in these dire economic times, that simply is no longer the case. This begs the question: which is superior, traditional publishing or self-publishing? Or, rather, *is* one method superior over another?

Since the publishing industry is still in such upheaval, the answer to this question is complex and not entirely definitive. There are, however, several self-publishing success stories to take into consideration when one might be entertaining alternate publishing routes. But within most success stories lie cautionary tales as well, and it would behoove you to weigh the pros and cons of both.

Before the Advent of Internet Publishing, There Was *Eragon.*
Ah, *Eragon.* When the young adult fantasy epic swept the nation in 2003, there was a lot of buzz about the author, Christopher Paolini, and his young age. At the time *Eragon* was published, the author was sixteen. I was around the same age, and in a fit of jealousy I refused to read it. I was hard at work writing too, and no one was publishing *my* stuff! What made Christopher Paolini so special?

Seven years later, with two more books in the series out, I caved at the insistence of a friend and read *Eragon.* With maturity I had lost my reservations and tried to give it an honest shot. I was terrifically underwhelmed. The pace was slow, the characters poorly developed and unmemorable. The plot was an obvious mash-up of *Star Wars* and *Lord of the Rings.* In short, it read like a fifteen-year-old had written it. Which he had, of course.

But how had something that probably should have stayed on Christopher Paolini's hard drive gone on to become a huge commercial success? The answer, to be perfectly honest, seems to be luck. Paolini's parents owned a small press called Paolini International— and they don't seem to be around anymore, or else do not have a findable website—and put out the first book in the series themselves. Afterward, they devoted all of their time and attention to promoting the book, going to bookstores all over the country. Even then, the book didn't catch on until famous author Carl Hiaasen bought a copy for his son, who loved it. Hiaasen got in touch with the right people, Paolini switched his work to a major publisher, and boom.

While this story, with its fairytale quality success, shouldn't be considered the norm for self-publishing—or publishing in general— there is an important lesson to be taken from Paolini's experience. Not only did Paolini have outside support, but the resources and dedication to market the book once it had been published. These days, the burden of promotion of books is falling to the authors, so a smart marketing plan can only benefit you once your book is out there, regardless of the means. You may not have to stand in bookstores dressed in medieval garb like Christopher Paolini—although it might be fun—but there is something to be said for pushing your own work, especially if you're passionate about it. And eleven years after *Eragon's* initial publication, writers have far more resources at their disposal thanks to the internet and the social media phenomenon.

A final word on going the route of *Eragon*. If your parents/ other assorted family members/best friends happen to own a small commercial press and are willing to publish your work at any time, make sure your manuscript is polished. I often wonder how *Eragon* might have read if its author had been just a little bit older, just as I wonder if the other books in the *Inheritance* cycle have evolved as Paolini has grown older. Has he ever looked back on that first fateful book and wondered what it would be like if he could only do a rewrite now that he's no longer a teenager? I know I sure would. I'm also glad none of the stories I wrote in my teen years will ever see the light of day. It will save me a lot of embarrassment.

Fifty Shades of Green: Cash Cow Extraordinaire.

We need to talk about *Fifty Shades of Grey*.

I know. None of us want to. But if we're going to analyze self-publishing trends, we'd be ignoring the huge elephant in the room if we didn't give E.L. James's recent smash hit its due.

Simply put, *Fifty Shades of Grey* and its success would not exist if not for the internet. It would also not exist if not for the rampant popularity of the *Twilight* franchise, but how Stephenie Meyer's teen vampire saga rose to fame is not the subject of this essay. Before *Fifty Shades of Grey* was on the shelves in bookstores and elsewhere (I've seen it at BJ's Wholesale) and on e-readers, it was on the internet. It was not called *Fifty Shades of Grey*, but the much more ambitious-sounding *Master of the Universe*. It was also *Twilight* fanfiction.

That's right. The characters were not E.L. James's (back then she called herself Snowqueen's Icedragon, a flashier moniker all around) but Stephenie Meyer's. Instead of the central conflict of the story being about Edward's vampirism and Bella's unconditional, confounding love for him, James's version featured the mysterious hunk as a business tycoon and the blushing, inexperienced female first-person present tense narrator as a journalist for her college newspaper. And the dark, dangerous society "Edward" was a part of was not that of vampirism, but the lifestyle of BDSM. (Because obviously the two are practically interchangeable—a myth any Google search could dispel in under a minute flat.)

I'll admit, having begrudgingly read the first *Twilight* book and gawked at commentary on the others, that this plot line sounds nothing like anything Meyer would write. Which is precisely why James did, I'll wager. She was filling a void in a franchise with a huge following: that is, for a series read rabidly by hormonal teen girls and repressed housewives, there just *wasn't* enough sex.

Fan fiction is a phenomenon that does not get much acknowledgment in literary circles. However, since I grew up in the internet generation myself, one of the many factors by which I gauge commercial success is how much of an online presence a fandom has. *Twilight*'s is huge. In these sorts of circles, fans cater to other fans, going so far as to pick up the slack they feel the author dropped, writing their own version of events, other imaginings of the same universe. And yes, sex. Often lots and lots of sex.

As the old saying goes, "Imitation is the sincerest form of flattery." Fan fiction is the ultimate embodiment of this adage. Of course, fan fiction is not officially publishable due to copyright infringement. However, James's story garnered so much popularity it inspired James to take it off the internet, change the characters' names, rework some plot structure, give it a better title and use a vanity press to publish it herself. Having an established following helped immensely, as did reviews on book blogs and word of mouth. Its success was so widespread that *Fifty Shades of Grey* was acquired by Vintage Books, an imprint of Random House, originally founded by Alfred Knopf. In the UK, it became the fastest selling paperback book in the first week at 100,000 copies, beating out both *Harry Potter* and the *Twilight* series, according to the Telegraph. Today it has sold over 70 million copies worldwide.

There is a lot that can be learned from *Fifty Shades of Grey*. Most importantly, never underestimate the power of an internet fan base. If James hadn't gathered fans when the series was *Twilight* fan fiction, it's likely the series never would have seen the light of day. Whether it *should* have seen the light of day is another question entirely. I meet people who are very angry about the existence of this series, claiming that better and more substantial writers have been shunned for the likes of James's inaccurate depiction of erotica. Personally, my problems with the book don't lie with its origins. I'm awed by how far James was able to propel herself thanks to self-publishing. Likewise, I don't find fault with its starting stage as *Twilight* fan fiction. If all she had to do was change a few names, it's clear she never intended to stay true to the spirit of *Twilight* to begin with. That's her prerogative, although as someone who believes derivative works should at least uphold the original creator's intent, I think this may speak against James's own artistic integrity.

No, my problem with *Fifty Shades of Grey* comes in its production value. This is a common pitfall of self-publishing, when a writer is able to release work without a seasoned editor to comb the manuscript with him or her. I haven't read the entire first book or the sequels, but I have read excerpts and spoken with people who have, and the consensus is plain: the writing just isn't very good. I don't refuse to read *Fifty Shades* because I shun fan fiction or want to avoid taboo topics like BDSM. I simply don't want to waste my time on a work with writing so shoddy it will only make me angry. James's careless use of language is my favorite example. Despite being set in Seattle, Washington, the book is rife with British slang, put there by its British author. Ostensibly the setting is Seattle because *Twilight* takes place in Washington state, but given the freedom to make the book stand alone as an original work, couldn't James have just switched the setting to London and be done with it? I suggest this solution because it seems she is not enterprising enough to actually research American slang to begin with, so going through the manuscript and eliminating the unrealistic Britishisms was clearly too much work.

Tales of Terror and Internet Fame

The aforementioned phenomena might seem like a grim omen of what is to befall the publishing industry. However, it should be stressed that not all instances of self-publishing success are the result of an increased need for poorly-written erotica or even a lukewarm re-imagining of the classic fantasy tale told by a teenager. The important thread to be taken from both *Eragon* and *Fifty Shades of Grey* is that self-motivated widespread exposure of a work can only boost its success. Furthermore, the use of the internet to build a fan base before the finished product is available—or even using the internet publication *as* a finished product—can aid the author farther down the line. Integrity need not be entirely compromised for an author to use this in his or her favor. There are several other examples the internet aiding a creator's jump to mainstream publication, all with varying degrees of success.

The first example is the young adult author Cassandra Clare. I've had her work recommended to me by a friend, and although I haven't had a chance to read it yet, I was intrigued by her origin story. Clare started out as a fan fiction writer who wrote huge, sprawling works that became wildly popular in the Harry Potter fandom. If this sounds similar to E.L. James's story, that's because it is. Clare, however, actually predates James—she wrote her fan work, *The Draco Trilogy*, in the early 2000s, at the height of the Harry Potter franchise. Her success led her to signing a hefty book contract with the YA imprint of Simon & Schuster, Margaret K. McElderry Books, for a trilogy of original work. *The Mortal Instruments* has gained popularity in its own right, and currently a movie adaptation has been made. After she was published, however, Clare deleted her fan fiction from the internet. In my research, I found this curious. If her fan fiction had helped her get where she was, why deprive people of it? Wouldn't it continue to serve as a way to channel readers toward her published fiction? While Clare herself called it "juvenilia," I thought that a bit unfair, considering she probably would not have gotten where she was without it.

Digging deeper, I found out what may be why. All official channels bore no mention of this, but once I delved into reviews of fans, I discovered a disturbing pattern—the use of the word "plagiarist." In writing circles, that is the worst accusation anyone could make about a person's work. And, while I think the use of the word is hyperbolic in this case, a writer wouldn't want this type of discussion to continue.

Obviously, no cross-referencing can be done, but suddenly the deletion of Clare's online work seems less like distaste for immaturity and more like an attempt to put an end to something unpleasant. I personally don't think what is described by some of these reviewers is plagiarism, because in writing, all works are inevitably derivatives of literature that came before. Clare's attempts to mask it may have been sloppy, and the deletion of her fanfic may seem incriminating. But if the plot is her own, and the character archetypes are common enough—and Harry Potter has received its own accusations of borrowing too much from existing lore—then there is nothing that can stop her. In the long run, all it can do is alienate certain fans. Which I'm certain no author wants, but if the demand for Clare's work is any indication— she has published three trilogies set in *The Mortal Instruments* universe—she isn't hurting too badly.

On a side note, I find it fascinating that E.L. James has made no attempt to hide that *Fifty Shades of Grey* is *Twilight* fan fiction with the names changed and no one has accused her of plagiarism.

My second example edges away from the fan fiction debate, probably much to everyone's relief. Jason Pargin, the editor-in-chief of the well-known humor site Cracked.com, maintained a personal blog site for years, confidently titled Pointless Waste of Time, where he chronicled the fictional exploits of his alter ego, David Wong, and his best friend, John Cheese. Part comedy and part horror, the webserial garnered a dedicated group of followers since its inception in 1999. In 2006, he was approached both with a book deal and an offer to buy movie rights, so he compiled the blog posts into what is now a published work called *John Dies at the End*. Shortly thereafter, his blog was assimilated into the site Cracked.com. The *John Dies at the End* movie was released in 2012 and a sequel to the book titled *This Book is Full of Spiders: Seriously, Dude, Don't Read It*, also at one point viewable online at johndiesattheend.com, was released by St. Martin's Press in October 2012. About the experience, he writes in the afterword of *John Dies at the End*:

Word of mouth. That's all it was. No one 'discovered' me, I didn't get some big break out of the blue. It was a slow advance of strangers from around the world, passing around the link and loaning out those sad homemade copies. These are the zealots who would later buy copies, loan them to friends, then buy more copies when those never came back. Hundreds of passionate strangers whom I've still never met – they're responsible for the edition you hold in your hands. I wish I could thank all of them by name. (Wong 469)

And, on the following three pages, he does just that.

Pargin's story is certainly encouraging. Although, having read *John Dies at the End* in book form, I couldn't help but think of how disjointed the narrative is. The writing is strong, the situations at times achingly hilarious, but the characters and the plot often seem all over the place. One event does not necessarily lead to the next, and there are large gaps in time and logic that never quite get explained. When I learned much of the book first existed as blog posts, I understood. The disjointed quality is one a person might expect, reading an account of one's life, told from far in the future, recalling the crazy events of the past and perhaps revising them in hindsight. If I read it as a fictional blog, I might have enjoyed the story far more than I did, having put all the expectations of the novel form on it when I started.

This begs an important question of the self-publishing model, particularly on the jump to the novel from the internet platform: is it really so easy to adapt one medium to another, when removing the online component? I haven't read *John Dies at the End's* sequel yet, but I'm curious to learn whether knowing it would end up as a published novel changed Pargin's approach to the narrative at all; will it *feel* more like a novel and not a serialized offering to an online audience? The novel writer in me hopes so, but obviously your mileage may vary.

While we're on the subject of online mediums, I'd like to end with one more example. In this instance, we depart from book publishing and delve into hybrid storytelling—both film and narration, told entirely using online social media. The story starts on the online forum SomethingAwful.com in 2009. In a particular thread, discussion participants wanted to create a new horror mythos, based around a singular, although vague idea: an absurdly tall, faceless man in a business suit. Pictures were Photoshopped and posted, and stories began to emerge as if the invented legend of the "Slenderman" were true. One of these participants was Troy Wagner, a film student at the University of Alabama. The discussion sparked the inspiration to start a horror series based on an investigation into the Slenderman. Under the handle MarbleHornets on both YouTube and Twitter, Wagner began the story of his fictional counterpart, Jay, looking into the disappearance of his friend and fellow film student, Alex Kralie. Alex had been making a student film entitled *Marble Hornets* in the summer of 2006, but halted production unexpectedly after suffering what seemed like a complete personality shift. Left with all of Alex's raw footage, Jay begins to sort through the tapes and upload his findings to his YouTube channel—and things start to get chilling from there, until Jay's life spins out of control entirely.

Today *Marble Hornets* is still ongoing, and has garnered a huge internet following of fans. It has set the standard for Slenderman mythos stories—of which there are many—and keeps its audience engaged through interactive elements. For instance, Jay communicates with the audience via Twitter, posting updates and occasionally answering questions. There is an organic quality to this medium, which helps to make the series so terrifying. With very little budget, its creators—Wagner, with friends Joseph DeLage, who plays Alex, and Tim Sutton, who plays another character with the same name—manage to capitalize on the fear that lies in anticipation. There is very little gore or violence, minimal special effects, and no Hollywood glaze of hair and makeup or elaborate sets. Because of this, there is an undeniable realistic feel to everything that happens. And since the story is told in real time, with each new update, the audience frets that it might be Jay's last.

Because the series is told on YouTube and Twitter, all of *Marble Hornets* is available for free. The series is now in its third "season," and the first two are available for purchase on DVD for those who might like special features and the chance to watch it on something other than a computer screen. The exposure has granted Wagner, DeLage and Sutton other opportunities, as well. For instance, the recently released indie PC game *Slender: The Arrival* boasts the trio as writers, as developers at Blue Isle Studios were heavily influenced by the *Marble Hornets* take on the Slenderman mythos. Most importantly, however, it was recently announced that there will be a Hollywood adaptation of *Marble Hornets*, bringing this internet phenomenon officially into the mainstream spotlight.

But again, here arises the question of translation. Much of what makes *Marble Hornets* work as a piece of fiction is its homemade quality and the freedom of its form. Can the scope of its vision be condensed into a finite quantity of screen time? And will the expectation of Hollywood fiction remove a layer of terror that works so well to its advantage as a story told on innocuous sites like YouTube and Twitter? Currently, there is no way of knowing. I'm personally both intrigued and hopeful, and at the very least consider this an opportunity for its creators to get the recognition they deserve for making something so unique and compelling in its original form. The question still persists, however, about the cost of adaptation, when one's initial success exists on an unconventional medium of online sources. This is likely just another pitfall of storytelling in a technologically advanced age: much like the never-ending debate of whether a book or its screen adaptation is superior, so the same discussion will be had about online mediums and their translations to a more "traditional" narrative model.

Embracing the Future

In conclusion, the publishing industry just isn't what it used to be in the pre-internet age, and it won't be returning any time soon. Writers, whether previously published or currently aspiring, need to approach the publication of their work in different ways. Whether seeking mainstream publishers or hoping to go the self-publishing route, exposure and self-marketing is key to an author's success. This can be accomplished in a variety of ways, from physically promoting a book like Christopher Paolini, to utilizing that most essential of all tools: the internet. One does not have to start out writing fan fiction, like E.L. James or Cassandra Clare, but an awareness of online fandom trends and savvy with social media can only help, not hinder. Whether one uses a personal blog site or hybrid storytelling with sites like YouTube, Twitter, Facebook and beyond, establishing yourself with an online presence is key. There are certainly common risks to the varying self-publishing methods: eliminating middlemen can make the process less complicated, but it also might compromise quality when it comes to copyediting or production value. Then there are the more abstract issues: when is a work so derivative the readers begin to doubt its literary value? In Cassandra Clare's case, many seem to care, but certainly not so much in E.L. James's. And does adaptation from an experimental medium to make a work palatable for mainstream consumption lessen the value of the work? David Wong's *John Dies at the End* suffers from this entropy in the leap from blog-based serial to novel, and it is still yet to be seen whether the do-it-yourself horror series *Marble Hornets* will experience it as well.

The best that can be taken from these trailblazers is that we as creators— regardless of our preferred medium—should maintain a sense of awareness. In a world where technology advances so rapidly the rest of humanity struggles to keep up, we need to remain hyper-vigilant and adaptable ourselves. There are more tools available to us than ever before, and we should learn to use them to our advantage in every manner possible, while striving to stay true to our original artistic vision for any particular work. This way, we can both put forth our creative best and help it reach its intended audience, through whatever means appropriate: major publisher, self-publisher, or somewhere in between.

*W*hether your book is self-published or published by a press, occasionally something is missing from your book launch: the actual, physical book. More and more books are published digitally, with no hard copy available. If your book goes this route, it can take some getting used to, but an electronic book is still a book. Read on for some ways to make yours a success.

Going Paper-Free: When Your Book is an eBook
by A.J. O'Connell

You hear it so often that it's almost a cliché: "I like the feel of a physical book in my hand."

When you've had your novel published as an e-book only, those words can seem like an indictment of your work, but do not despair. Readers love eBooks and an eBook is not all that different from a hard copy.

I sold my first book as an eBook. It was solicited by a publisher as part of an electronic-only series, and there was never any expectation that it would be sold in print. At first, this gave me pause: I wanted to see my book in print, rather than on a screen. Later, however, the book did go to print, and I realized something: Most of the people who were buying my book were buying the eBook; which was cheaper than the hard copy, instantly accessible, and easy to read anywhere. That shouldn't have been surprising; according to a 2012 report by the Pew Research Center, eBook consumption has been on the rise, and according to a 2013 report by the Book Industry Study Group, eBooks currently account for 30 percent of all books sold.

For me, publishing my books as eBooks has been almost exactly the same as publishing physical books. eBooks—like physical books—require careful editing, professional formatting and well-designed covers. Also, like physical books, eBooks need to be marketed and sold in person as well as online. There are a couple of differences, however. Here are some tips and cautions to help guide you through the publication process of your own eBook:

Print out the proof: When you publish a physical book, you receive a physical galley proof from the publisher to read through. When you publish a digital book, the galley proofs are digital. I've had a hard time catching errors on the screen of my computer or reader. It took me two books to learn to print out the proof that was sent to me and make my corrections on that.

You can still have a reading: Don't let the fact that you have an eBook keep you from getting your read on. You can and should schedule author events and signings. Thanks to the magic of the Internet, you can sell your book to smartphone and tablet owners who are listening to you read. And thanks to fabulous free services like Authorgraph, you can also sign those eBooks. In fact, since libraries now maintain eBook collections, a library is a better choice for an eBook event than a bookstore, which deals in paper books.

Or do an e-reading: I recently heard of an author who launched his book with an online event. He created a private Facebook group, invited friends, reviewers and readers and threw a party. Be creative and use online tools like Twitter, Google Hangout, Goodreads and YouTube to create events and connect with readers.

eBooks make sending ARCs to reviewers easier: It's a lot simpler to send an advance reading copy of your book to a reviewer when you don't have to pay for postage. Just make sure your email is neat and professional. Online book reviewers can be your best friends. In fact, some sites, which specialize in eBooks accept only eBooks for review. Read reviewers' submission guidelines carefully to see which review sites are best for you and your work.

There are still some e-book drawbacks: Some promotional tools (Goodreads giveaways, for example) can only be used by authors who are promoting physical books. Nielsen Bookscan, which provides point of sale numbers to the publishing industry, only tracks sales for physical books (which can make tracking your Amazon sales disappointing.) And of course, eBooks are still new. Some readers are technologically challenged and may not be willing or able to read your book. However, as eBook sales increase, I'm certain these things will change.

No matter how your book is published, and no matter what shape your publication takes, the road to literary success begins well before your first book even goes into production. Here are some things to do after your book is accepted for publication, but before it hits the shelves, to ensure that your work reaches as many readers as possible.

What to Expect When You're Expecting Your First Book
by Deborah Henry

Months of anticipation are finally over! Your first book is about to be born. The edits are done. The cover art is in the works. And, if you're like me, you begin to feel protective and passionate about your book as well as worried that it will be okay, that it will have a healthy life. Just as with a newborn, your instincts take over.

Other than my human children, I have never felt more passionate about anything than writing books. I won't give up on my babies or my books. I find it fascinating and curious that no one tells you what it's really like on the other side, maybe because it is so unique and each story is different. The difference between having a manuscript and a published book feels oddly similar to the great divide between a pregnant woman sweating it to get to the other side and a mother holding her newborn. But just like with a first baby, when you publish your first book, you might find yourself asking: Why didn't anyone tell me that bit? Why doesn't anyone tell us about that all-encompassing period from pre-birth to newborn book? Here's the inside scoop, the nitty-gritty details about the energy that goes into those early months of marketing your first book. One thing is certain: You'll have enormous passion, perseverance and moxie for your book during this joyous period, this special time in your book's life. You should: it is your baby. Here are some tips for making your book stand out. Welcome to the World!

Tips:

1. Get and stay involved as much as you can with the cover art. You know your work better than anyone else. There is nothing more distressing than holding your much anticipated book in your hands and hating the cover. Try to keep some control and exert input on the cover.

2. Make everyone on the publishing team as enthusiastic about your project as you are. Art is collaboration. Get along with those fantastic people who love your book. Listen to and respect them. They will be more likely to listen to your ideas. Read *Dale Carnegie's How to Make Friends and Influence People*. Collaboration can be trying. Carnegie's book has been a bestseller for more than sixty years and will give you great tips on how to understand your publishing team. You will learn techniques in handling people and ways to win people to your way of thinking.

3. Keep up your strength. This is not hard; it's your baby. If you have written a novel, when people ask you if it's fiction, and they will, just smile and say yes. There is not enough vodka in the world for all those people who look blankly at you when you tell them the name of your publisher, especially if it is teensy. It does not matter if your baby is born in a huge hospital or a small hospital. What matters is the care your baby receives. You are in control of that pre-publication.

4. Plan a budget. Publicity costs money. You want to provide your baby with the best start possible. It is the sad truth that without publicity, a good book, even a great book, will not become a bestseller.

5. If the budget is non-existent, the good news is the gate is wide open and getting wider every day to spread the word all over the Internet.

6. Go to Staples. Make Advance Reader Copies yourself if your publisher will not provide them. Send to all the trade newspapers and magazines four to six months in advance.

7. Make business cards with the book cover on it and essential information: email, social media sites.

8. For four months in advance of the book's birth and four months, at least, after the book arrives, find the news hook about your book and pitch to TV, radio, print and online.

9   Go to book parties, literary luncheons, readings, salons, writing conferences, talk with writers on your social media sites and exchange your stories. It is a turn off when all the blurbs are from your MFA mentors and all your publishing is through your MFA literary journal. Network well beyond your MFA friends and colleagues to gain credibility and develop a wider net.

10. I have been told that the average person must see your newborn book seven times before they will make a purchase. Continue to nurture real friendships with writers on Facebook and Twitter, and everywhere. Enormous opportunities will arise.

11. Become your own publicist. No one cares about your baby like you do. If it helps, make a timeline so you know what to expect next. Create a one-page press release about you and your book that you can send everywhere, including local venues.

12. Everywhere you go, the arrival of your book will be on your mind. Give a copy of your book to hotel sundry shops. Hotels love to buy books for their guests to enjoy by the pool. The clothing store chain Anthropologie sells books. Think outside the box.

13. On social media sites, post more about your authentic self. Yes, there is weather. Weather is fine, but unless it is extreme, go deeper into who you are. Share about your work. What makes you so passionate about this particular body of work? Interested reviewers will direct message you to receive a copy of your ARC.

14. Get trade magazine reviews and use as blurbs on your book.

15. Put all this progress on your website/blog.

16. Blog on Redroom.com and cross post on Facebook, Twitter, Linkedin.

17. People respond better to images than words. Make a book trailer.

18. NetGalley.com— Many thousands of people, reviewers, and librarians can download your pre-published PDF and spread the word everywhere, which leads to book clubs, more endorsements, eager wait lists at libraries and more buzz.

19. Ask your publisher to hire a publicist. It does happen if the publisher wants to make some noise and coin.

20. In general: Ask. Ask nicely. Be pleasantly aggressive. This is not the time to be humble or shy.

21. Ask 10 to 15 of your friends to spread the word verbally and also, ask them to post about your book on their social media sites. And not your friends from your MFA program. Diversify—or you will start to see the same five people liking what you say. Facebook/Twitter/ LinkedIn friends —ask these friends to also share with ten to fifteen of *their* friends.

22. Promote others. Authentically. Everything you do and say should be authentic. Even on the Internet, you can smell fake and it doesn't smell good.

23. Have a photographer take your author photo. Make sure of the copyright and know if this photo can be used internationally or only for North American rights.

24. Contact all satellite radio shows. Get on them linking your book to worldwide issues. If you wrote a novel or memoir, find the timely, non-fiction issues inherent in your work.

25. Promote discussions privately and online about art, literature, the writing process, film. The amount of writers who help new writers is astounding.

26. Many experts and top publicists share their tips on their blogs. Subscribe to them. Listen to their advice. For free.

27. Send your ARC to literary awards.

28. You have been preparing for this all your life. You are a writer. You know your material inside out. You know your characters. You have created this newborn book. So relax. Be confident.

29. Give back. If you can afford two margaritas and nachos, you can afford to buy someone's book after a book signing.

30. If you can afford two beers and a cheeseburger, you can also donate $20.00 to a literary cause, a library, whatever moves you. Authentically. You will feel good inside. And it will come back. Those same people will remember you and will interview you, suggest literary agents for foreign rights, offer readings. Be generous to your fellow writers.

31. Spread your wings. If you live a couple of hours from a major city, go in. You can meet a kindred spirit at an infinite number of events and places like the Center for Fiction and the Half King bar in New York City.

32. Write/email/direct message your favorite writers. Start a dialogue.

33. We live in a golden age. A full-page color ad in the New York Times Sunday Book Review, Price: $95,000. A banner on a cool website which gets thousands of hits daily can cost as little as $100.00 for one month.

34. Get on Summer Reading Lists. Start with schools you attended.

35. Get hundreds of pre-publication reviews. Lousy trade magazine reviews are painful because people are sheep and they listen to those trade reviews. The "general public" reviews can be lethal but you do not have to read them. Just get them up on Goodreads, Amazon— everywhere. If everyone loves your book, people will guess you are either a rock star like Keith Richards or that not enough subjective strangers are reading your book.

36. Almost everything is Googleable these days. Find your niche. If you wrote a thriller, for instance, try: The Big Thrill.org, Suspense magazine and newsletter, Banner versions on Ellery Queen and Alfred Hitchcock websites, Crime Spree Magazines, Thriller Fest Conference. Specialize.

37. Make an interesting Book Club Readers Guide for the back of your book.

38. Plan a book party, but first, do go to your doctor for anti-anxiety meds. You will have night sweats that only two people will show up and yes, one is your mother.

39. This will not happen. Your book party will be fabulous. Enjoy holding your new book and sign away.

40. When you receive mediocre or bad pre-publication reviews, remember this is subjective. Be thrilled that your book is getting a reaction and a review.

Chapter *11*

YOUR AGENT

edited by A.J. O'Connell

The previous chapter explores a select few of the many publication options available to writers today. Although author preferences in this area are clearly changing, many writers still prefer to follow a traditional path to publication. If you consider yourself and your work a fit for the traditional model and want an agent, don't despair: Your agent is out there. Learn what it takes and what to expect when searching for the right agent.

Although the hunt for an agent can be intimidating, there is no need to panic; there are ways to find someone to represent your work. This chapter lists some tips for finding the right agent for you, as well as a selection of resources to get you started. Also included are anecdotes from MFAs who've found agents, because scary as the search for an agent may be, it's important to realize that it's a task that many writers have accomplished, as will you. Each story is different because, at its root, a relationship with an agent is a relationship with another person, and every relationship is different.

How I Found My Agent
by A.J. O'Connell

Locating an agent, the person who will shepherd your masterwork through the maze of publishing routes we discussed in the last chapter, is probably the most daunting task an author will need to take on—that is, after actually writing the book itself. Here, four talented authors in different stages of their publishing journey describe how they each found an agent for their work.

Alena Dillon
Author of *I Thought We Agreed to Pee in the Ocean: And Other Amusings from a Girl Wearing Sweatpants*

Mine isn't a fairytale. It's a story of persistence, deep breaths, and realizing agents couldn't hear me cry so I might as well cut it out.

I'd heard that agents receive 400 queries a moanth and take on a new client maybe every other month. I didn't want to take my chances with 1/800 odds, so I submitted to as many appropriate agents as possible. A handful asked for the full manuscript, but it's a subjective business. One agent was more interested in the story that happened before the novel's timeline, and one wished it ended in a fantastical battle. I was open to revision suggestions, but not open to writing it into a different book. Months passed, and I was about to give up. Then I saw a listing on *Publisher's Lunch* announcing a new agent and I thought, well, I bet she'll need clients! She offered representation five weeks later. If I had given up, it would have been one submission too soon.

I'm too proud to admit how many queries I sent before being offered representation, at least not without a couple beers first. But I will say this, my success rate was way better than 1/800.

David Fitzpatrick
Author of *Sharp: A Memoir*

I met my literary agent, Richard Abate, the man who helped change my literary scope, my dreams, my possibilities, at an eighth grade basketball camp one summer. He was diminutive, but tough, and had a pretty impressive jump shot. We weren't best friends—he attended the rival middle school in town, but I think we respected each other's games. We stayed friends, and then spent a summer on Martha's Vineyard together with some guys, where he wrote some pretty decent poems, but also—and I never let him forget this—donned a large white cape that he wore around town. Rich called me throughout my time in hospitals, and then much later, six months before graduation from Fairfield for my MFA, he said, "It is my priority to see your book all the way through." Now maybe that's what all agents say, but I don't think so. He's so supportive and invested in me that it's a hell of a deal. So stay friends with all your early-teen buddies, because you never really know...

Stephanie Harper

Author of a recently agented debut novel featuring an agoraphobic graphic illustrator

The story of how I got my agent is not a particularly unique one. I began sending out query letters and sample chapters one year and one month before I received an offer of representation. Over the course of that year, I sent query letters to 128 agents. I know, because their names are forever emblazoned on a meticulously updated spreadsheet with which I tracked the entirety of my querying process. I received all manner of rejection letters, from a myriad of form letters, to the brief "thanks—not for me," to no response at all. Of those 128 agents, a total of 10 requested the submission of a full manuscript. I received some wonderfully kind and detailed rejection letters, all with seemingly disparate reasons for passing on the novel.

Finally, I received the email I'd been obsessively checking my inbox for. The stars had aligned and I'd found an agent who, despite seeing imperfections in a manuscript already read in full and rejected by three other agents in her own agency, wanted to work with me. I can't deny that the querying process was an emotionally rigorous one. I went through stretches where, as the ever-growing red splotches of rejection loomed from my oft-opened spreadsheet, I questioned my novel and my most fundamental abilities as a writer. Still, had I given in to that self-doubt, and to the disappointment that comes in the lonely periods of waiting to hear "thanks, but no thanks" 127 out of 128 times, I'd have never stuck with it long enough to hear that one resounding "yes."

Elizabeth Hilts

Author of the *Inner Bitch* series

I was in the incredibly fortunate position of having
the publisher of the now-defunct magazine *Hysteria*
suggest developing a book based on a short essay
about the Inner Bitch that had appeared in the
magazine. My colleague Jim Motavalli advised me
to get an agent to broker that deal and gave me the
contact information for the man who became my
agent—I called, explained the situation, and we've now
had a working relationship for 20 years.

The first step to a book deal in a traditional publishing model—as you've read in the stories earlier in this chapter—is securing an agent, or the circumstance and tenacity that leads you to an agent. Your agent is the person who will escort you and your book through the publishing world so that you can find the best home for your work and get the best contract possible. First, however, you and your book must catch the attention of an agent and then you must impress him or her. Read on for tips that will help you to snag the best agent for you.

How to Land a Literary Agent: Some Dos and One Don't
By Deborah Henry

There is something enormously satisfying about talking about your work with an interested literary agent. When they call you and say stuff like "Oh, on page 293, second paragraph, I think the Chevy would be red because they didn't make blue Chevys in 1963," you have landed an advocate who loves your work and will take it to editors they know well, whose tastes they know, and your book will be more likely to sell. Plus, a literary agent will act as a buffer and negotiate your publishing contract. When an insider in the publishing industry finds your work strong, and takes on your book, you jump a huge hurdle. Since your book is completely polished, you are also doing the job of pre-marketing your book at the same time as you search for the right agent. This is a twofold benefit: Showing marketing muscle helps land a literary agent and insures that your book will do well. Once the book takes off, your literary agent or your publisher will sell foreign, audiobook, graphic, merchandising and film rights. It is always best to have publishing experts on your team.

Do remember the old rule: Your literary agent is not your mother and she's not your friend. Pick an agent who calls you when she's got something to say about your book. You may become friends with your literary agent as your time together matures, but pick up on clues for what is best for your book as you make your selection. Is she talking more about her upcoming wedding than she is talking about your book? Cordial conversation is fine, but land an agent who is focused and professional.

Do remember there are thousands of shingles hung out there but only the top literary agents score deals repeatedly. You will notice the same literary agencies crop up in industry news continually. Go with the stars and the rising stars, too. Make sure you choose one that has intense credibility. No settling allowed.

Do remember you are not just selling your book. You are selling you.

Do get out of your comfort cocoon. Go to writing conferences but expand your reach. Order a drink at the bar by yourself. You will meet publishers, literary agents, and other writers.

Do cross your T's when emailing a literary agent. I do not appreciate getting typos in an email pass (I do not use the term rejection; I call them passes) from literary agents, but typos are unacceptable for a writer. This is a clear way to get a pass on your book.

Do tell the literary agent about your book and about you in one page or less. Less is more.

Do email your query early in the morning so she will see your email before her busy days gets overloaded with emails.

Do go to agentquery.com, querytracker.net, Agentresearch. com, writerunboxed.com, askaliteraryagent.blogspot.com, publishersmarketplace.com and all the other great sites listing agents and find out who they are, what type of work they represent, and what they are looking for.

Do remember that you should not believe everything you read on agent websites or anywhere else. Listen to your gut. Research the type of person the literary agent is. If the agent says no email queries, or no unsolicited submissions, email anyway.

Do multiple submissions if you do not hear back from your Number One and Two choices within 24 hours.

Do remember not to flood the agent world with your email submissions. It is very easy to press that send button, but if you do, you will be pressing your luck. They all know each other. You may be querying two agents while they are together checking their emails over lunch.

Do ask your writer friends—the ones that have similar writing styles to your own are best. Agents respect the opinions of those they represent.

Do network in person as well as online. Go to literary luncheons, seminars, readings at local events and in big cities near you.

Do begin the humiliating process of asking published authors for endorsements. Those blurbs will help you land an agent.

Do subscribe to blogs and newsletters written by literary agents, such as Book Marketing Buzz Blog. Many newsletters give awesome tips about finding a literary agent. Check out Johanna Penn and Cindy Ratzlaff's newsletter.

Do know the publishing industry by subscribing to Publishersweekly. com, Publishersmarketplace.com, Publisher's Lunch, Shelf-Awareness. com, newletter@pw.org, etc. The more you know, the more confident and interesting you will be during that initial telephone conversation with an interested agent.

Do know that some of this courting of a literary agent is subjective and out of your hands. Often, a literary agent will connect with your work because it resonates for her on a personal level.

Do know that if you are not getting positive feedback on your query or requested manuscript partial, it is time to review your work.

Do add your Facebook, Twitter, LinkedIn, and any important links to your email signature.

Do say thank you to all literary agent responses. Ask those who wrote friendly pass emails if they know any literary agents that might be the right fit.

Do not try to be cute or funny in your literary agent query. Unless you are really cute or funny. Just be you.

Do remember that there are loads of terrific university presses and independent publishers that work without literary agents. Query them directly.

Do put a Post-It note on your computer: "I am good enough and deserve everything." Because you are. This includes rejections. Suffering is part of life and definitely a part of the writer's life. Load up on lasagna, frozen garlic bread and extra mozzarella. Dark chocolate is a must-have in the house, too, along with the film *He's Just Not That Into You.*

Do remember to stay positive. A widely published Facebook friend told me to post on my computer: Beware "Beware 'Comparativitis'." You will get there. This is not a competition with other writers.

Don't let anyone tell you you're not fabulous.

$\mathcal{N}$ow that you've read up on some tips for scoring an agent, where do you start looking? Ashley Andersen Zantop explores some resources and provides some advice that will help you to connect with agents who are looking for clients. Don't let our list limit you, however. Keep your eyes open for any opportunity to meet agents, whether that opportunity arises at a convention that offers meetings with agents, or if an author friend of yours recommends her own agent, or even if you happen to meet an agent through a non-writing-related event or friend. Remember to do your own research as well. Finding an agent is important, but it is not impossible.

Agents: Decrease the Variables, Increase Your Chances
by Ashley C. Andersen Zantop

A needle in a really big stack of needles. Finding the right agent can often be as challenging as finding a publisher, and some of the same principles apply. You wouldn't waste a stamp or the time hunting for an email address to send a manuscript on modern home construction to a publisher of literary thrillers. Not if you've done your homework and want to be taken seriously. The same applies to literary agents. Agents often have specialties—categories of publishing within which they've developed a strong set of contacts or see potential for growth. These categories can be general such as literary nonfiction or commercial fiction, or they can be as specific as women's fiction or young adult memoir. Unless you've been asked to submit by an agent or recommended by a strong reference to an agent, save time and resources; don't send potential literary agents materials outside their acknowledged areas of interest or expertise (especially if they have taken the time to specify any). How do you know an agent's area of interest or expertise?

Do some digging.
Check a potential agent's website for a listing of his or her current clients. If you're not familiar with the names, do a quick online investigation of each author to determine their similarities

and differences. You'll get a feel for what types of literature the potential agent likes to represent, and where he or she may have openings or opportunities for new material. If your work is a fit, send your query. If you're not sure where to find the name or website of a potential agent, keep reading.

Read the boring stuff.
When you finish a book that speaks to you, makes you feel that any publisher that would publish such a title or agent who would represent such a title is right for you and your work, read the acknowledgements. Most contemporary authors rightly thank their agents in the acknowledgements section of one or more of their works.

Surf.
Thankfully, today there are a number of websites dedicated to listing literary agents/agencies and chronicling their areas of specialty. Often these sites are searchable by genre or subgenre. Below are a few to get you started, but do an open-ended online search for 'literary agent' every few months. More sites appear every year:

WritersNet: www.writers.net/agents

Poets & Writers: www.pw.org/literary_agents

QueryTracker.net: www.querytracker.net

AgentQuery: www.agentquery.com

Association of Author's Representatives: www.aaronline.org/DirLit

Scriptologist: www.scriptologist.com/Directory/Agent/Literary/Literary3/literary3.html

GalleyCat: www.mediabistro.com/galleycat/best-literary-agents-on-twitter_b17189

Literary Agent's Directory: literary-agents.regionaldirectory.us/

Find a Literary Agent: www.findaliteraryagent.net

Publisher's Marketplace (see the article *Associations, Memberships and Subscriptions for Writers* in Chapter 4): www.publishersmarketplace.com

http://www.writing-world.com

Agent Research & Evaluation: Agentresearch.com

Ask a Literary Agent: askaliteraryagent.blogspot.com

Chapter *12*

FROM COPYRIGHTS TO CONTRACTS: BUSINESS BASICS

edited by Jean M. Medeiros

The best way to protect yourself, your reputation and prevent costly mistakes and disputes: Know your rights. Understand your obligations. Intellectual property laws are much like traffic laws: if you break one (even unknowingly) and get caught, you're going to pay the fine. Protect your work and respect the rights of your colleagues and clients.

We are writers. Fiction, nonfiction, poetry, plays, screenplays, we put pen to paper (or tap to tablet) and conquer any and all genres. We craft words with the same care as a sculptor molds clay. But the jumble of words in a book or freelance contract? That's for businesspeople to decipher.

There is a gulf between art and business. Maybe it started with those aptitude tests we had to take that promised to evaluate our talents and personalities and point us in the direction of the perfect majors and careers. Maybe it was that magazine or online quiz that defined us as right-brained or left-brained after answering fifteen questions. The premise was that people fell in one of two camps based on the side of the brain they used more: creative and intuitive types on the right; the analytical and logical folks on the left. Scientists are now refuting that theory. It's time writers do, too.

That doesn't mean we trade in our MFAs for MBAs and law degrees. But we can educate ourselves and make more informed decisions about our rights and obligations.

This is the business of writing. And writing is our business.

ou've revised your latest short story for what seems like the hundredth time and think you may finally be able to find it a home. You send it to a handful of publications and wait. Your cousin, or neighbor, or yoga instructor asks if you're worried that someone will "steal" your story. You didn't worry, until now. Do writers need to copyright their works? What exactly does a copyright protect? Joe Carvalko breaks down the concepts and registration process for copyrights.

Basic Copyright
by Joseph R. Carvalko, Esq.

Overview

The moment an idea is reduced to a medium of expression, a property right in that expression is protected by copyright. For example, a copyright subsists in original literary works, musical works, pictorials, graphic works, motion and still pictures, sound recordings and choreographic works, and derivations and compilations of each of these. To use a copyrighted work requires permission from the copyright owner. There are rare cases, so called "fair use" exceptions, that permit the use of a work, but these typically do not apply to commercial use. Various periods of copyright exist depending on whether the creator is deemed an individual, corporation or an estate. To protect your interest in the things you create, always use the copyright notice.

What follows are some important topics related to copyright, but I suggest that you avail yourself to the United States Library of Congress, Copyright Office for further insight into the law, forms and the cost of copyrighting. See, http://www.copyright.gov/

What Does Copyright Protect?

Only an "original work of authorship" can be copyrighted. Copyright provides protection for the expression of an idea but not for the idea itself. For example, you might decide to do an advertisement featuring a dinner setting. Copyright in that advertisement would prevent others from copying it without your permission. However, copyright in that advertisement would not prevent third parties from creating an advertisement featuring a dinner setting, as long as such third parties either expressed the idea in a manner different from your expression or, if in a manner similar to yours, developed it totally independently from seeing your advertisement. Merely having access to a publication containing the advertisement might negate the presumption of independent development.

Examples of items that can be copyrighted include:

Books, manuscripts, screenplays

Advertisements

Instruction manuals

Art work

Photographs

Sound recordings

Computer programs

Teaching materials

Keep the following in mind: copyright protects only the manner of an author's expression in literary, artistic, or musical form. Copyright protection does not extend to names, word trademarks, titles, short phrases. That is the job of trademarks. So, a domain name is not protected by copyright. Nor does copyright protection extend to ideas, systems or methods. It does not protect the way something functions. That is the job of patents.

Protection under the copyright law (Title 17 of the United States Code, Section 102) extends only to "original works of authorship" that are fixed in a tangible form. "Original" means that the author produced the work by his or her own intellectual effort, NOT by copying a preexisting work. Contrary to popular belief, any potentially registrable copyright work does not have to be formally registered with the Copyright Office to enjoy protection under US law. However, registration affords proof of ownership and grants rights and privileges, such as statutory damages, in the event someone uses the copyrighted work without the owner's permission.

Although the duration of copyrights differ as between corporations, estates and individuals, "[A]s a general rule, for works created after January 1, 1978, copyright protection lasts for the life of the author plus an additional 70 years. For an anonymous work, a pseudonymous work, or a work made for hire, the copyright endures for a term of 95 years from the year of its first publication or a term of 120 years from the year of its creation, whichever expires first." http://www.copyright.gov/help/faq/faq-duration.html. To file for copyright registration, you must use the forms provided by the Copyright Office. You may register via mail or electronically. Different kinds of works or modes of expression in tangible form are filed using different forms. Send all forms for registration to: Register of Copyrights, Copyright Office, Library of Congress, Washington, D.C. 20559. If you are filing electronically, go to: http://www.copyright.gov/eco/notice.html

Name of the Copyright Claimant
The Library of Congress states, "pseudonym or pen name may be used by an author of a copyrighted work. A work is pseudonymous if the author is identified on copies or phonorecords, CDs of that work by a fictitious name (nicknames or other diminutive forms of one's legal name are not considered 'fictitious'). As is the case with other names, the pseudonym itself is not protected by copyright."

If you are writing under a pseudonym but wish to be identified by your legal name in the records of the Copyright Office, you should give your legal name followed by your pseudonym at the "name of author" (example: "Jane Doe whose pseudonym is Madam X"). If the author is identified in the records of the Copyright Office, the term of the copyright is the author's life plus 70 years.

If you do not wish to have your identity revealed in the records of the Copyright Office, you should give your pseudonym and identify it as such (example: "Clarence Darrow, pseudonym").

Useful Articles

Designs for useful articles, such as car designs, clothing, tool designs and household appliances and the like are not protected by copyright. Copyright protection will cover the pictorial, graphic, or sculptural features that exist independently of the utilitarian form in which they are embodied. Also note that ornamental features of artistic, industrial or commercial articles can be patented through what is referred to as a "design patent." The line between uncopyrightable works of industrial design and copyrightable works of applied art is not always clear. A two-dimensional painting, drawing, or other graphic work is still identifiable when it is printed on or applied to useful articles or other industrial designs or to fabrics, wallpaper, or containers.

Registration of Copyrights

As mentioned earlier, the registration of a copyright is not required to claim a copyright in the work. However, if you intend to sue for infringement, you first need to have a registered copyright. Registration also provides statutory damages in cases where it might be difficult to prove actual damages.

The Copyright Office issues forms on which applicants apply for copyright registration. You may file online or via mail.

See, http://www.copyright.gov/fls/sl35.pdf for a rundown of what is currently available online. Claims to copyright in either published or unpublished works may be registered. To apply for registration, send via mail or online the following material:

- A correctly completed application form (forms outlined below);

- A nonrefundable filing fee for each application. See, http://www. copyright.gov/docs/fees.html; and

- A nonreturnable deposit of the work to be registered, i.e. a copy of your book that won't be returned.

Manuscripts

A published or unpublished book or manuscript may be registered using Copyright Office Form TX for textual works. Form TX is used for registration of non-dramatic literary works including: fiction, nonfiction, poetry, contributions to collective works, compilations, directories, catalogs, dissertations, theses, reports, speeches, bound or loose-leaf volumes, pamphlets, brochures, and single pages containing text. Note that Form SE should be used for copyright registration for serial publications such as periodicals, newspapers, magazines, bulletins, newsletters, annuals, and journals.

To register a book or manuscript, send via mail or online:

- A completed application: http://www.copyright.gov/forms/formtxd.pdf;

- A nonrefundable filing fee for each application, See, http://www.copyright.gov/docs/fees.html; and

- A nonreturnable deposit of the work. The deposit requirements depend on whether the work has been published at the time of registration.

As is the case with collections when a work is registered as a collection, only the collective title will appear in catalogs and indexes. To have the individual titles appear separate, registrations must be made for each work.

Dramatic Works

Among the types of dramatic works either published or unpublished that may be submitted for registration in the Copyright Office are works prepared for stage presentation, such as choreography, pantomimes, and plays, with or without music, treatments, and scripts prepared for cinema, radio, and television.

Generally, dramatic works such as plays and radio or television scripts are works intended to be performed. Dramatic works usually include spoken text, plot, and directions for action. Because of misconceptions about copyright registration for radio and television presentations, the following points require emphasis:

- The title of a program or series of programs cannot be copyrighted;

- The general idea or concept for a program is not copyrightable. Copyright will protect the literary or dramatic expression of an author's idea, but not the idea itself.

- Registration for a particular script applies only to the copyrightable material in that script; "blanket" protection of future scripts or of a series as a whole is not available. (However, an unpublished collection of material may be registered with one application.)

Musical Scores

Musical scores and lyrics are also the subject of copyrights. Published collections of musical works and all of the copyrightable elements may be registered on a single form with a single fee if all of the compositions are owned by the same copyright claimant. See Circular 50, Copyright Registration for Musical Compositions, for details on the application form and specimen deposit requirements: http://www.copyright.gov/circs/circ50.pdf.

Unpublished collections of multiple musical scores can be registered on a single form with a single fee and deposit of one complete copy or phonorecord or CD if the conditions in "Collections of Music" in Circular 50 are satisfied. Registration of an unpublished collection of compositions extends to each copyrightable selection in the collection, but only the collection title appears in the Copyright Office catalogs and indexes. Note the Copyright Office advises: "A separate registration for each musical work results in a separate record of the individual title of work in the catalogs and indexes of the Copyright Office. A separate registration also may simplify identification of the work for purposes of licensing, transfer, permission, and distribution of royalties."

Phonorecords, CDs, etc.

Phonorecords, CDs or tapes are also registrable and specimens need to be submitted with the application:

- If the work is unpublished, one complete copy or phonorecord.

- If the work was first published in the United States on or after January 1, 1978, two complete copies or phonorecords of the best edition.

- If the work was first published in the United States before January 1, 1978, two complete copies or phonorecords as first published.

- If the work was first published outside of the United States, one complete copy or phonorecord of the work as first published.

- If the work is a contribution to a collective work, and published after January 1, 1978, one complete copy or phonorecord of the best edition of the collective work. See, http://www.copyright.gov/circs/circ56a.pdf

To apply for registration, send via mail or online the following material:

- A correctly completed application: http://www.copyright.gov/forms/formsr.pdf;

- A nonrefundable filing fee for each application. See, http://www.copyright.gov/docs/fees.html; and

- A nonreturnable deposit of the work to be registered, as indicated above.

Photographs

A collection of published or unpublished photographs also may be considered for registration as a unit on a single application Form VA, with a nonrefundable filing fee and a nonreturnable deposit of copies of the work, when certain conditions are met.

Two or more unpublished photographs may be registered as a collection if:

- The elements are assembled in an orderly form;

- The combined elements bear a single title identifying the collection as a whole;

- The copyright claimant in all of the elements, and in the collection as a whole, is the same; and

- All of the elements are by the same author, or, if they are by different authors, at least one of the authors has contributed copyrightable authorship to each of the elements.

Registration of an unpublished collection of photographs extends to each copyrightable element in the collection. A single registration may be made for all the copyrightable elements in a single unit of publication if the copyright claimant is the same for all elements. See Circular 40a, Deposit Requirements for Registration of Claims to Copyright in Visual Arts Material: http://www.copyright.gov/circs/circ40a.pdf.

To apply for registration, send via mail or online the following material:

- A correctly completed application: http://www.copyright.gov/forms/formva.pdf;

- A nonrefundable filing fee for each application. See, http://www.copyright.gov/docs/fees.html; and

- A nonreturnable deposit of the work to be registered, as indicated above.

Visual Arts

The visual arts category of copyrightable works consists of pictorial, graphic, or sculptural works, including 2-dimensional and 3-dimensional works of fine, graphic, and applied art, photographs, prints and art reproductions, maps, globes, charts, technical drawings, diagrams, architectural works, and models.

To register a work of the visual arts, send via mail or online the following:

- A completed application: http://www.copyright.gov/forms/formva.pdf;

- A nonrefundable filing fee for each application, go to: http://www.copyright.gov/docs/fees.html; and

- A nonreturnable deposit of the material to be registered. The deposit requirements will vary depending on whether the work has been published at the time of registration.

If the visual art is published, two complete copies must be provided as specimens. Identifying material may be deposited in some cases. If the visual art is unpublished, generally one complete copy is required. This copy must represent the entire copyrightable content of the work for which registration is being sought.

Identifying material deposited to represent the visual art shall usually consist of photographs, photostats, slides, drawings, or other 2-dimensional representations of the work. The identifying material shall include as many pieces as necessary to show the entire copyrightable content of the work including the copyright notice if it appears on the work. All pieces of identifying material, other than transparencies, must be no less than 3 x 3 inches in size, and not more than 9 x 12 inches, but preferably 8 x 10 inches. At least one piece of identifying material must, on its front, back, or mount, indicate the title of the work and an exact measurement of one or more dimensions of the work. (See, Circular 40a, Deposit Requirements for Registration of Claims to Copyright in Visual Arts Material) See, http://www.copyright. gov/circs/circ40a.pdf.

Choreography and Pantomime

Choreography and pantomimes are also copyrightable. Choreography is the composition and arrangement of dance movements and patterns usually accompanied by music. As distinct from choreography, pantomime imitates situations, characters, or other events. To be protected by copyright, pantomimes and choreography need not tell a story or be presented before an audience. Each work, however, must be fixed in a tangible medium of expression such as a video or pattern of steps from which the work can be performed.

To register a claim in a dramatic work, submit the following:

- A completed application: http://www.copyright.gov/forms/formpa.pdf;

- A nonrefundable filing fee for each application, go to: http://www. copyright.gov/docs/fees.html;

- If unpublished, one copy of the work; if published, two complete copies of the best edition of the work:

  - for a script, the copy may be a manuscript, printed copy, a film video recording, or a phonorecord;

  - for a pantomime, the work may be embodied in a film or video recording, or be precisely described in text or on a phonorecord;

  - for choreography, the work may be embodied in a film or

video recording, be precisely described on any phonorecord or in written text, or in any dance notation system such as Lab annotation, Sutton Movement Shorthand, or Benesh Notation.

Miscellaneous Works

Mere listings of ingredients as in food recipes, scientific formulas, chemical compounds or drug prescriptions are not copyrightable. Where a recipe, or formulae are embodied in, say, a book or other literary expression such as when there is a combination of recipes in a cookbook, there may be a basis for copyright protection.

To register the directions or instructions of a recipe or cookbook, send via mail or online the following:

- A completed application Form TX: http://www.copyright.gov/forms/formtxd.pdf;

- A nonrefundable filing fee for each application, go to: http://www.copyright.gov/docs/fees.html; and

- A nonreturnable deposit of the work. The deposit requirements depend on whether the work has been published at the time of registration:

  - If the work is unpublished, one complete copy.

  - If the work was first published in the United States on or after January 1, 1978, two complete copies of the best edition.

  - If the work was first published in the United States before January 1, 1978, two complete copies as first published.

  - If the work was first published outside of the United States, one complete copy of the work as first published.

  - If the work is a contribution to a collective work, and published after January 1, 1978, one complete copy of the best edition of the collective work.

Form of Copyright Notice

Although not placing a copyright notice on your work is not fatal to claiming ownership, the copyright notice should be included in a prominent place on the thing for which copyright protection is claimed.

The copyright notice may be placed on an article without formal US Copyright Registration.

A copyright notice should include the following elements:

- Copyright symbol: © or "C" or Copyright
- Year of publication: 1995, 2013, etc.; and
- Copyright holder: Your Name

Example: © 2014 YOUR NAME OR COMPANY NAME

Works by Independent Contractors

Every consultant, independent contractor, or service provider, whether they work on the premises, at home or for another company, must agree to assign their work to you where a possibility exists that they might create an original work. Unlike employees whose works are made for hire and the copyright automatically belongs to the employer, consultants and contractors must agree to transfer and assign the copyrights to their work to the company beforehand.

Need for License to Use Works of Others

In most instances, copyright gives the owner of the work the ability to prevent others from using the work without permission. A difficult question is when your expression of an idea infringes someone else's copyright. Literal copying is simple to determine. The problem gets progressively complicated when we create something that takes a fragment of another work, or borrows a non-literal similarity, or incorporates the look and feel of another work. If your idea was sparked by something specific, be careful how you express that idea. If the expression begins to look and feel like the original expression or you borrow a fragment of an expression, you probably need a license to avoid copyright infringement.

When Others Use Your Works

The following does not constitute legal advice specific to your situation, for only an attorney who learns the facts of you case can provide the necessary counsel. But copyright infringement is a serious matter, and we can benefit from knowing generally how to proceed in stopping the infringement and obtaining legal redress. Except for blatant copying, determining whether someone has actually infringed your work is complicated, because infringement and its defenses depend on many factors. These factors are specific to the type of work, so that infringement of a passage in a text might be analyzed differently from a work of art, a piece of software or music. But, if you believe that your work has been infringed, you might consider seeking out a legal professional or copyright organization that may assist in advising how to proceed.

Typically the first action in a potential copyright infringement case is to warn the accused infringer by certified letter explaining the circumstances. The letter needs to be carefully drafted to notify of the infringement, and to indicate that there will be further "legal consequences" without threatening to explicitly sue. This last point avoids being hauled into court by the infringer who may attempt to seek a declaratory judgment as to who is the rightful owner. Often, following the letter, there is an opportunity to discuss the matter with the potential infringer, and this may lead to a satisfactory settlement, where the person either stops, stops depending on some occurrence such as pulling the infringed article off the market, or obtains a license.

There are sites that may help mediate or step in to resolve a copyright violation occurring on the Internet (see, Facebook, Reporting Copyright Infringements; Takedown Piracy, at http://takedownpiracy.com/tips/; or Google, Removing Content From Google at https://support.google.com/legal/troubleshooter/1114905?hl=en.) There are other links found on the Internet, but to what extent these are effective is unknown. When sending a letter yourself or with the assistance of a free provider is ineffective, then you need to retain a lawyer versed in copyright law to seek redress.

Copyright infringement must be pursued in federal court (the infringement may also constitute a crime, which would be referred to the U.S. Department of Justice). However, before you can access the federal courts you must register the copyright with the U.S. Copyright Office. If a work is registered prior to infringement or within three months of publication, statutory damages will be available and payment of attorney's fees may be available, which serves to help in retaining an attorney within a realistic budget. Under special circumstances, e.g., anticipated litigation, the Copyright Office offers expedited processing of an application for registration of a claim to copyright for an additional fee. A registration made before or within five years of publication provides a presumption of the validity of the copyright and the facts stated within the registration certificate, which serves as a step up in proving your case.

The local or state bar association may recommend a copyright attorney, or you may contact the Volunteer Lawyers for the Arts or local law schools to assist locating reduced fee legal services. Lists of copyright industry organizations and author's organizations are available on the Internet.

Fair Use

The Library of Congress indicates, "One of the rights accorded to the owner of copyright is the right to reproduce or to authorize others to reproduce the work in copies or phonorecords". This right is subject to fair use limitations found in sections 107 through 120 of the copyright act (Title 17, U.S. Code).

Section 107 contains a list of the various purposes for which the reproduction of a particular work may be considered "fair," such as criticism, comment, news reporting, teaching, scholarship, and research. Section 107 also sets out four factors to be considered in determining whether or not a particular use is fair:

- The purpose and character of the use, including whether such use is of commercial nature or is for nonprofit educational purposes;

- The nature of the copyrighted work;

- The amount and substantiality of the portion used in relation to the copyrighted work as a whole; and

- The effect of the use upon the potential market for or value of the copyrighted work.

No guidelines truly exist that specify the number of words or pages that may safely be taken without permission. Acknowledging the source of the copyrighted material does not substitute for obtaining permission. However, the 1961 Report of the Register of Copyrights on the General Revision of the U.S. Copyright Law cites examples of activities that courts have regarded as fair use: "quotation of excerpts in a review or criticism for purposes of illustration or comment; quotation of short passages in a scholarly or technical work, for illustration or clarification of the author's observations; use in a parody of some of the content of the work parodied; summary of an address or article, with brief quotations, in a news report; reproduction by a library of a portion of a work to replace part of a damaged copy; reproduction by a teacher or student of a small part of a work to illustrate a lesson; reproduction of a work in legislative or judicial proceedings or reports; incidental and fortuitous reproduction, in a newsreel or broadcast, of a work located in the scene of an event being reported."

Public Domain

Eventually, works protected by copyright fall into the public domain. If works are in the public domain, it means that they may be used freely without infringing copyright or incurring liability for royalties. Government publications are generally in the public domain and free to use. Wikipedia and other such sites are regarded as in the public domain. A general guideline is that if the copyright notice on a work is more than 75 years old, the work is in the public domain. If the copyright notice is less than 75 years old be advised that the rules are quite complex. Examples of items for which permission may be necessary include:

- Advertisements

- Instruction manuals

- Art work

- Photographs
- Books
- Sound recordings
- Computer programs
- Teaching materials

International Copyright Protection

International copyright, as such, does not exist. But, you may still have protection under US and foreign treaties. The United States became a member of the Berne Convention on March 1, 1989. The works of an author who is a national of a country that is a member of The Berne or the UCC treaties may claim protection. There are no formal requirements in the Berne Convention. Under the UCC, the law may be satisfied by the use of a notice of copyright in the form and position specified in the UCC. A UCC notice should consist of the copyright symbol © accompanied by the year of first publication and the name of the copyright proprietor. This notice must be placed in such manner and location as to give reasonable notice of the claim to copyright. (See generally Circular 38a International Copyright Relations of the United States.)

Right of Privacy

Everyone should expect a degree of privacy in their lives, but privacy is not absolute. Under various circumstances, our lives can be made public and even used for commercial gain. Even though a copyright may not exist on someone's persona, using information about someone or a picture of someone's likeness for commercial gain is restricted and in instances of advertising a product or service prohibited, is often prohibited under various laws. Permission must be granted to use facts, photos, likenesses, and statements of other individuals unless it concerns a matter in the public interest--and commercial advertising is never considered in the public interest.

Fruits, labor and ideas of another cannot be used to further commercial gain unless permission has been obtained from their owner.

To use facts, photos, likenesses or statements of another or the fruits of another's efforts requires either a release from liability or a license that grants permission to use them.

2014COPYRIGHTCARVALKO

*A*fter years of writing and rewriting your memoir, you've finally landed the contract of your dreams. You're pretty sure it's the contract of your dreams, though the language in every other clause seems straight out of a foreign film with no subtitles. What does it all mean? Ashley Andersen Zantop, a publishing executive with more than 20 years of experience, helps us understand the basics of how to translate the language of contracts and highlights our rights and obligations.

Publishing Contract Basics
by Ashley C. Andersen Zantop

Raise your hand if you're more likely to read the works of Keats, Pound or Welty than you are Scalia, O'Connor or Rehnquist. Raise your other hand if, given a choice, you'd rather read the Father of English Literature than the Founding Fathers? (Assume you have to choose one.)

Now that you've had a good stretch, put your hands down and be honest; in your adult life, have you read the Constitution (or your country's bill of rights) in its entirety? What about the federal tax code? Do you make it your priority to stay informed about any changes or updates in your local traffic laws? If so, you can skip this article—I have little concern you'll fumble your author agreements. If on the other hand, you're more like the rest of us, read on; your art, your craft, your property, your rights are at stake.

So many of us complete sixteen to twenty years of schooling and yet we don't launch our adult lives with an explicit understanding of the contract, the legal rights and obligations, we enter into with our nation or even local government. The closest we're likely to come to understanding a fraction of our rights and obligations is in preparing for our driver's license test or our high school civics exam. And yet, in our lifetime, because of our obligations under this contract with our nation, we'll pay nearly one-third of every dollar we earn to our government. In some countries the figure is as high as half.

Imagine for a moment what that sum of money might be for you over the course of your lifetime (assuming you're reasonably financially successful). That's an expensive contract. Imgaine you had the good fortune to receive a single author agreement for that sum.

Can you see the figure? It would be a good idea to read that contract, right? You might even invest the money to hire an expert, like an intellectual property attorney, to help you interpret it. Surely it would be worth the expense.

Why don't we do that with our lives? After taking our very first job in a restaurant, coffee shop, store or factory, before we pay our very first tax bill, why don't we sit down with an expert on constitutional law to understand our constitutional rights and obligations? Why don't we sit down with a tax attorney and learn our rights and obligations under the tax code? They impact us for the rest of our lives. Aside from the bevy of small ones, two main reasons: expense and interest.

Expense. When we start our first job as an adolescent waiter, ticket-taker or cashier, we receive small sums and are responsible for paying out only corresponding small sums to our government. The stakes are at a relative low. The cost of expert counsel in comparison would be absurd. But we're not excused from the obligation. The same is true of publishing contracts. Your first contract is not usually large enough to justify hiring a professional to help you. Just as many of us learn to do our own taxes, repair our own homes (or at least parts of them) and cook our own meals one year, repair and meal at a time, we do the same with author agreements. Despite the profusion of experts and services available, we handle them ourselves because it doesn't make sense *not* to. But how well to we handle them?

"Take an active role in understanding your contracts and agreements. Read them with the same critical eye you'd use to edit your genre of choice."

That brings me to interest. We're allowed, even encouraged to say what is or is not "our thing." Not only do we identify with our intrinsic interests by articulating this, but we let ourselves off the hook when it comes to developing skills or disciplines we don't find interesting. How often have you heard, "Math's not my thing"? Yet, no one disputes the need to be able to do basic math to manage money and live your life. In all likelihood, if you have a job, you need to use basic math and mathematical logic at work in some way—even if you work in an English department. You may not be particularly interested in the physics of cooking or the biology of breathing, but both are good skills to have. Lawyers specialize in knowing the law so we don't have to. Yet, chances are you would not hire an attorney or even have an agent to review a $300.00 contract for publication of an essay. If you sign it, though, you are party to it and therefore responsible, regardless of whether you're intrinsically interested in the construction and interpretation of the agreement or not. For the sake of your work, your rights and your career, develop the discipline (if not interest) to take an active role in understanding your contracts and agreements. Read them with the same critical eye you'd use to edit your genre of choice.

> "Sir Arthur Quiller-Couch counsels writers not to be afraid to "murder your darlings." Well, don't be afraid to lease them out, either, but DO understand the terms of the lease."

Do not send contracts back to your publishers littered in editor's red marks eliminating run-on sentences and adverbs—as satisfying as that would be. Do decipher contracts with the same care you would apply to deciphering the arcane English in a work by Chaucer or Shakespeare. Consider interpreting legalese the same way you'd interpret work in an unfamiliar dialect. You need to synthesize meaning, be certain you understand what is stated and implied. Treat reading your contracts as the same challenge: decode the words, examine their intent, imagine the impact. Think of the worst possible scenario and interpret the language in those terms. Could you live with the outcome? How likely is the worst case scenario? When you understand the language, ask yourself: is what you give up, sell or lease worth the compensation? If the answer is yes, uncap your pen. Sir Arthur Quiller-Couch counsels writers not to be afraid to "murder your darlings." Well, don't be afraid to lease them out, either, but DO understand the terms of the lease.

What is a publishing contract?

Albert Greco, author of *The Book Publishing Industry; Second Edition*, describes an author agreement as "A contract . . . between an author and a publisher . . . This is a legal document; it contains (or at least should contain) clear information about fundamental issues so that all parties understand fully their rights and obligations under the agreement."

A publishing contract sets forth the complete understanding between the author and publisher concerning how the publisher will exploit the author's work (and you want your publisher to exploit your work and to pay you for it to the fullest potential you have allowed them).

Contracts can run anywhere from 1 to 75 pages, and the general rule of thumb is the more money at stake, the longer the contract. A longer contract may help cure your insomnia, but that's the one you'll want to stay awake for.

How to Read a Contract

Do treat close reading of your contracts as an exercise in translating an unusually ineffective dialect. This will help you with decoding, but it probably won't keep you awake, and there's more to it than that. Before reading any contract, remind yourself of the context. Contracts are not for when things go right. While publisher and author, alike, hope things go well, the only occasion you really *need* a contract is when things go wrong. If you're a glass-half-full person, you need to get into a different head space before you read a contract.

On the question of glass-half-full or glass-half-empty, someone I admire once told me not only is her glass half empty, she's pretty certain someone is going to steal it. She would have made a great corporate counsel. That's how you read a contract. Assume the worst case scenario.

How to Comment on a Contract

Once you've read a contract and interpreted it with the worst case scenario in mind, decide if the benefit is worth the risk. If the answer is yes, or mostly yes, you're ready to assemble any comments and questions you have.

Now is the time to strop fretting about your stolen glass and start considering what kind of juice is in it. Ask clarifying questions to be sure you understand the terms. Most publishing houses are happy to make sure you understand—this saves misunderstandings later for everyone. Suggest modifications to anything important that would make you feel more comfortable. Do not allow your comments or questions to paint you as paranoid wakco. You need to shift perspectives again and re-read your comments before sending or speaking them; Imagine yourself in the role of editor, counsel or coordinator receiving your comments. Convey your thoughts in polite, measured terms. Unless you know exactly how important your contract is to your publisher's business, don't overestimate your importance to your contracting party. If an editor can't see how he will get though a contract negotiation with you, let alone a manuscript, you're on you're way to finding a 'thanks but no thanks' email in your inbox. If on the other hand, you use this opportunity to show your publisher that you are smart, attentive, detail-oriented and reasonable, you've already begun to impress them before you even discuss your work. Claudia Suzanne, author of *This Business of Books* tells us "Look at an initial contract as the opportunity to launch a career, not retire from one."

TOP 10 PUBLISHING CONTRACT FUNDAMENTALS

The types and forms of contracts in the industry vary greatly. Depending on the type of work and type of publisher, you could see everything from a single page to a 90-clause tome. The following are the ten most important things to be sure you understand about the contracts you sign:

Rights

What rights are you granting, selling or leasing? Be sure you understand if the rights you are selling or leasing are exclusive or **non-exclusive**. If the latter, you may have the opportunity to sell the same rights to another entity during the time of the contract. Are you selling a combination of the two? For example, **FNASR**, or **First North American Serial Rights** means you are granting a publisher the exclusive right to publish your work in serial (periodical) form first. Only they can do this. After they've published in serial, you can sell that work to other types of publications.

Are you granting all rights, either as a **Work Made for Hire (WMFH)** or **Work for Hire** or for a limited duration? If you are selling your work as a Work for Hire, you are essentially relinquishing all right to the work. The entity you are selling to will file copyright in it's name and will take full control of the material. This is fairly common in the industry for certain types of publications. For instance, if a publisher asks you to write about their own intellectual property, or that of others, you'll likely need to do it as a Work for Hire. If you write about Mickey Mouse for Disney Publishing, they will insist on owning the right to that work, for good reason.

If you're selling or leasing your own original work you created on your own time inspired by your own creative process, you'll likely retain all the rights and simply lease some of them to one or more publishers. If you and your publisher co-developed the idea in question, you're probably beginning to tread in the gray area. You'll want to be sure you're comfortable that the consideration is fair and appropriate and that you expressly agree what rights are granted.

Copyright: Now that you've established who owns it, who's filing it—you or your publisher? Joe Carvalko draws a tremendously useful map of the initial steps to take in filing and understanding copyright. If you are lucky enough to receive a traditional publishing contract for your work, a publisher usually files copyright for all publications they produce, but read this section of your contract carefully to be sure this is detailed specifically. For any self-publishers: Beware; you *are* the publisher of your works, so be sure to file copyright.

Also, as Joe explains in his primer on copyright, pennames or pseudonyms are not protected by copyright, only the work you create is. If you use a penname you created and want to protect it, file a trademark. If you are under contract for a work made for hire and your publisher created the penname associated with the work, that name is the publisher's property and they will need to file the trademark to protect it.

Format

Your contract should specify in what form your work will be distributed and sold. Will it be a digital publication? A print publication? If so, what type? Are you selling or leasing all format rights such as hardcover, paperback, eBook, educational software, applications? That is more and more common, but it's something you need to know and understand. Find out what your publisher's strength is. If they ask for a format they don't currently sell, find out why. Will your work be part of a major new initiative to launch a new format? If so, that's good and should provide your work with lot's of attention. If not, it may not make sense for them to have the rights to a format they don't plan to sell. You want your publishers to exploit the rights you grant them as fully as possible, but you don't want to give up rights they have no plan for producing, either.

Territory

Territory defines the regions of the world in which the publisher has the right to market and sell your work. Generally, publishers ask for the territories they know they can sell into effectively, but it doesn't hurt to ask them about it if you're not sure. Like with formats, only give territories the publisher can actively exploit based upon its current sales operations, or make sure you are appropriately compensated for new territories if your work is part of a new initiative to expand. Your ability to do this will depend on how much leverage you have and how much you feel comfortable asking for, but you'll get a sense of that as you move through the negotiation.

Language

Define the language you are granting rights to. Are you only granting rights for English language sales or others? If you grant 'worldwide all rights', you've essentially granted rights to all languages, formats and territories, even though territories is the only term explicitly stated.

Term

Term defines the duration of the contract and rights sold or leased therein. If the contract is a Work for Hire contract, your term is perpetuity because the publisher owns all rights. If your contract has some other limited duration aspects or only grants limited rights, usually a section of the contract will cover what happens when rights revert to you, known as **Reversion**.

Scope/Delivery/Deliverables/Work

Usually a section of the contract describes what you are expected to deliver in order to meet the terms of your contract. Sometimes this section is a Schedule or other document that is officially attached to the contract and signed. This might specify the format in which you need to deliver your file, such as file type.

If there are specific page count or word count requirements, those items will be defined here.

Schedule

This section is fairly self-evident. If you see the phrase **Time is of the Essence**, take note. This term has legal meaning and basically conveys that the schedule is a material aspect of the contract, so if you fail to deliver something by the agreed to schedule, this might constitute grounds for breach and potentially a cancellation of the contract.

Compensation or Consideration

This section defines the compensation you will receive for your work. Make sure it's clear to you how much you'll receive and when. If a royalty is involved, be clear on how it will be calculated and how often it will be reported. We could dedicate an entire additional book to the various options and permutations in this area. The most basic and most important requirement here is that you understand how you will get paid, when you will get paid and how much you will receive. If you don't understand, ask polite questions until you do.

Subrights

Some contracts have clauses called 'subrights' for short or 'subsidiary rights.' This section of the contract spells out what types of rights your publisher has the option to license or 'sublicense' in this case, to another entity. Why would your publisher want to lease rights granted by you to someone else?

Assume for a moment that you have granted all rights to your work to your publisher for a limited period of time. This means they have all language rights worldwide, all format rights and possibly even media or entertainment rights. While your publisher themselves may not be interested in producing an edition of your work in Hungarian, their rights department (the team in the company responsible for selling subrights to other publishers) may know a Hungarian publisher who would like to do just that. Your publisher makes a deal with the Hungarian publisher. Your publisher retains part of the proceeds from that deal and you receive whatever is defined in your compensation and subrights clauses of the contract. Subrights sales are not always limited to languages, sometimes they include film, entertainment and other forms of media, consumer products licensing, and other more speciality forms of publishing.

Noncompete

If your contract requires a noncompete, be sure you understand the scope and are comfortable with it. A noncompete specifies those areas of content or the publishing industry you will not create material for during the term of the contract. Some noncompetes are very specific and not a challenge to live with. Some noncompete language is so general, if interpreted literally, it might prevent you from selling new work in other parts of the industry. The larger the value of the contract, the more likely it is to have a noncompete and the more broad the noncompete will be. If your contract has a noncompete clause, be sure you understand it and are comfortable with it before signing.

Not in the Top 10, But Should Be:

These items would be in the top 10 if this were like the Big Ten, where ten is somehow more like twelve or fourteen, and changeable as needed:

Marketing Commitment

If this is a big project, worth a significant sum of money and a material portion of time invested for you or your publisher, or both of you, it's not unusual to discuss and agree upon a basic marketing plan or commitment by both you and your publisher. Don't take this too far— if you insist on specifically naming every action and associated dollar your publisher will commit, you're essentially doing someone's job for them, and he won't enjoy or be nearly as invested in the project as he would otherwise be if able to help determine the most effective way to market the project. You want the entire staff of your publishing team to feel like your project is *their* project. The more they feel ownership of it, the more dedicated to its success they'll be.

Complete Understanding

Usually a contract of any material length specifies that the contract represents the only legal or binding agreement between you and your publisher. If your contract has such a clause, be sure everything that is important to you about your agreed transaction is in the contract. Imagine you have something documented outside the contract (in email, for example) that relates to the contract. If you have a complete understanding clause, that email may not be sufficient for enforcing your rights. If you find a complete understanding clause in your contract, if something you want is not in the contract, don't count on it.

Revisions

Some contracts specify what types of changes a publisher can make to your work if you are unwilling or unable to make requested revisions prior to publication. Be sure you're comfortable with the way this is described in your agreement.

Assignment

Assignment addresses the issue of what happens to the contract if either you or your publisher cease to exist in your current form. In your case, that would likely mean you died or became permanently incapacitated (remember, contracts are for situations involving stolen half full glasses). In your publisher's case, perhaps your publisher is bought by another company or declares bankruptcy. The Assignment clauses specifies whether your heirs or 'assigns' would automatically become party to the agreement and act on your behalf, or if you would each need to seek the other's permission before the agreement is assigned to another entity.

Negotiating as a First Time Author or with Little Leverage

Leverage. To make any material changes to an author agreement, you need sound reason for the request and some leverage. In a contract situation, the party that needs or wants the other party least has more of it. Don't despair. Life is a negotiation. Even if you are a first-time author, or have been offered a deal in which you have little leverage, you can still get something you want by giving up something the publisher wants. For example, if your publisher wants digital publication rights (assume they do—this is becoming standard now), why not suggest you would agree to grant all digital publication rights in exchange for book cover approval or review, if your cover means a tremendous amount to you? If your publisher is at all skilled in digital publication, you want them to publish your title in as many digital formats as possible any way. That only helps to better distribute your work.

Additional Cautions and Encouragement
If a contract does not contain or clearly imply, at minimum, each of these top ten key points, and you sign it despite potential ambiguity, be prepared to have your work potentially used or exploited in unanticipated ways. For example, if your contract grants very broad rights to the publisher but does not specifically address the issue of language, you could find your work translated into Polish the next time you're in Warsaw. If you clarify the intent of the contract in each of these ten key areas, you should have a good understating of how your work will be used.

Don't sign final hardcopies of your contract until you compare them with approved digital copies clause-by-clause. The larger the value of the contract, the more likely the signature copies are to be hardcopy, so get your game face on and your reading glasses out: You need to do a line by line comparison.

Heed 'notwithstanding.' If you see this term in your contract, pay close attention to what comes before and after it. It's commonly used in agreements and you'll grow accustomed to it, but until then, when you see this term, assign it the essential meaning of 'despite.' Be on the look-out for phrases such as "Anything in this agreement to the contrary notwithstanding. . ." or "Notwithstanding anything in this agreement to the contrary, . . ." Read these sections carefully, they are basically telling you that despite what the contract might say elsewhere about an issue, whatever the agreement defines in *this* section is what matters and will be used in interpreting the agreement's meaning.

Pay attention to all agreements you sign. Even contracts for relatively small works with small or no compensation can come back to bite you if you're not prepared or don't understand what you've committed to. If you grant total or partial rights of your work to a publisher for a period of time, don't resell those same rights in the same content to another entity during that time. Like speeding on the highway, even if it's accidental, you're still breaking the law. As a writer looking to build a career, you don't want to build a reputation for breaching your contracts instead.

Suggested Reading

If you're not completely terrified or in the deep slumber of article-induced narcolepsy and could stomach learning more about publishing contracts, the following is a list of useful resources:

Improving Your Book Contract, The Author's Guild; The Author's Guild (www.authorguild.org)

Rights 101, The American Society of Journalists and Authors, ASJA Contracts Committee (April 2003)

Pages 158–176 *The Book Publishing Industry; Second Edition* by Albert N. Greco; Routledge; (2005)

Pages 135–140 *This Business of Books: A Complete Overview of the Industry from Concept Through Sales* by Claudia Suzanne; WC Publishing; 4 Rev Upd edition (March 2004)

Pages 177 – 192 *Book Business: Publishing Past, Present and Future* by Jason Epstein W. W. Norton & Company; 1st edition (January, 2002)

*Y*ou've tried, but business is *not* your thing. Legalese works better than a glass of warm milk at bedtime. Yet, everyday, writers are forced to step out of the creative realm and into the worlds of business, law and marketing. Do not enter that territory without a GPS. Use this map to find the information you need to help make alien decisions about your writing.

Where to Go For Business or Legal Help
by Jean M. Medeiros

You've written your masterpiece and you want to protect your words. Maybe others love your work as well and you've reached your goal of getting that elusive book contract. Then you look down at that sheaf of papers, or more likely the e-mail attachment, written in legalese. You know the clauses are not Santa's family and that the royalty does not reside in Windsor Castle, but what really is the difference between a subsidiary right and a serial right? What if the publisher wants to copyright the work in its own name instead of yours? How much negotiating leverage do you have before the publisher decides to rescind its contract offer since you cannot agree on terms? Can a publisher even do that? You may have an agent who can try to explain it all to you, but you'll make better decisions on the business aspects of your writing if you can arm yourself with a hefty load of basic knowledge.

The information can come at no cost, a small fee, or as a benefit of membership, but help is out there. You just have to know where to look.

CHECK YOUR MEMBERSHIPS

Authors Guild: http://www.authorsguild.org/

For more than 100 years, the Authors Guild has been the backbone of legal advocacy for writers. If you've already published a book, have a contract or literary agent, or are a freelancer earning certain levels of income from writing, you may qualify for membership. Among the benefits are free reviews of book contracts and a copy of *The Authors Guild Model Trade Book Contract and Guide*, which provide explanations of standard contract language and negotiating tactics.

The Authors Guild website also provides useful (and free) information for non-members. For the scoop on copyrights, including a direct link to forms, check out: http://www.authorsguild.org/services/copyright-information/. For the ABCs of contract negotiation, see: http://www.authorsguild.org/services/legal-services/improving-your-book-contract/.

You can also find general information on e-book rights, freelancing writing for periodicals and articles discussing lawsuits involving authors and literary issues.

National Writers Union UAW Local 1981:
https://nwu.org/

In 1981, freelance writers joined together to form the National Writers Union, which later affiliated with the United Auto Workers. There are certain publication qualifications for membership, but the UAW sometimes accepts unpublished writers trying to get published.

UAW benefits include free contract reviews (but not legal advice) and grievance assistance with copyright or royalty problems.

The UAW website also offers non-members several "Tools and Resources" including downloads of articles regarding electronic publishing, copyright info for freelancers and contract negotiation. https://nwu.org/node/2426

Association of Writers & Writing Programs (AWP):
https://www.awpwriter.org/

AWP is best known for its annual conference, hosting more than 12,000 literary types (writers, writing students and teachers, MFA program reps, editors, publishers and readers) and providing three days of seminars, panels, readings and parties, in a different city every year. But AWP is also hard at work the rest of the year advocating for writing programs, teachers and students, and the craft of writing. (They also boast a "Guide to Writing Programs," a searchable database of information on writing programs all over the world, which is invaluable for anyone thinking of entering a formal writing program or later, for job search contact info.)

A benefit of membership is the *Writer's Chronicle*, a bimonthly print publication on the art, craft and pedagogy of writing. The website also provides a database of archived articles where you can search for interviews with your favorite writers, find out if you can use a snippet of a lyric in your essay, or get the latest news on censorship, as well as help for problems facing you as a writer. https://www.awpwriter.org/magazine_media/writers_chronicle_features

Volunteer Lawyers for the Arts (VLA):
http://www.vlany.org/

The VLA has provided legal and business advice to writers and other members of the creative arts community since the 1960s. Individual and organizational memberships provide discounts on publications, workshops and seminars, as well as access to MediateArt (a forum for negotiation and dispute resolution) and the invaluable VLA Legal Clinic.

The Legal Clinic gives all VLA members the chance to discuss their arts-related legal problems with volunteer attorneys at no cost. http://www.vlany.org/legalservices/clinic.php VLA also offers *pro bono* legal services to artists who meet certain income guidelines.

http://www.vlany.org/legalservices/probono.php

The VLA website also provides members AND non-members an

extensive list of resources, with links, where you can gather more information on contracts, copyrights, trademarks and forming a business. http://www.vlany.org/resources/index.php#bs

Mediabistro: http://www.mediabistro.com/

Mediabistro has long been the go-to website for media news and job openings, but it also offers a variety of online and on-the-ground seminars and classes. Courses in digital media, public relations, television and film, journalism and creative writing (including book proposals, contracts and legal issues) are available to non-members at varying costs, but members get a discount. http://www.mediabistro.com/courses/

HELP AT LOW OR NO COST

Poets & Writers (P&W): http://www.pw.org/

Now in its fifth decade, Poets & Writers has served as a literary font of information for all writing genres. You'll find articles on authors, the craft of writing, publishing, MFA programs and entire sections devoted to residencies, conferences, grants, awards, agents, journals and jobs. P&W magazine is available in print and online. The website offers online exclusive articles, as well as searchable access to a variety of topics including book contracts and copyright. A few dollars will also buy you the download of a "*Poets & Writers Guide to* ...." a variety of topics.

Access is free to the "Top Topics for Writers," basic tips and resources on writerly topics such as LitMags, agents, book publishing (including self- and vanity publishing) and promotion. http://www.pw.org/top10_faq

The online *Speakeasy* will let you chat with other writers and share info and angst in a variety of threads, or you can quietly lurk with a cup of coffee or an adult beverage. http://www.pw.org/speakeasy/

Writer's Digest: http://www.writersdigest.com/

Another long-standing print and online publication, Writer's Digest's print magazine focuses on craft and publishing, while the website offers up free articles (and some free downloads) on a variety of topics like protecting and selling your work, freelance rates and promotion. They also boast writing prompts, competitions and a bucket of advice.

For varying fees, they offer education in a variety of formats on a variety of subjects, including contract basics and other legal issues that sometimes stump writers. They also host annual Writer's Digest Conferences on the East Coast and West Coast.

U.S. Copyright Office (The Library of Congress):
http://www.copyright.gov/

If you've read this chapter, you already know the volume of important information available at the U.S. Copyright Office. But just because it's a government website doesn't mean it's all technical and stuffy. The basics are available on the FAQ page, but the Copyright people let you know that there's no truth to the rumor that you can copyright a story you've written by mailing a copy of it to yourself. http://www.copyright.gov/help/faq/

Also, in case you were wondering, you can't protect your sighting of Elvis. But you can copyright that photo you snapped of him in a diner eating a peanut butter and banana sandwich.

National Endowment for the Arts (NEA):
http://arts.gov/

The NEA is a proponent for all types of artistic expression, offering highly sought-after grants to individuals and organizations. The NEA also provides the contact info for regional and state arts' organizations. http://arts.gov/partners/state-regional

Most states have a "Council on the Arts" that focuses on the local arts community and encouraging information, education and participation. If they can't answer your question, they may be able to point you in the right direction.

IT DOESN'T HURT TO ASK

This is not a complete reference list and new opportunities for information are available every day. Google it and the answer will come.

Someone out there has struggled with your problem. Someone has needed the answer to your question. Like Stanley Kowalski in *A Streetcar Named Desire*, you may have a lawyer acquaintance. You may have colleagues who are writers, or friends in a writing group. You definitely have former MFA or other writing program classmates and faculty, maybe someone who could give you advice. You may prefer to go the membership or website route to find your answers. Just don't be afraid to ask the people in your life for help.

Chapter 13

TOP 13 THINGS EVERY WRITER SHOULD DO

edited by Ashley C. Andersen Zantop

Six writers and editors distill and share their list of writing imperatives for a successful writing life.

*W*hen you run low on inspiration, motivation or just need a quick jolt to zap you out of a persistent patch of writer's quicksand, browse through our editors' top 13 suggestions to help you stay engaged with your writing and create your best work.

DO

by Ashley C. Andersen Zantop, Michael Bayer, A.J. O'Connell, Erin A. Corriveau, Adele Annesi & Jean M. Medeiros

1. Write. Even bad writers write. There's no getting around it: You are not a writer unless you do it. Develop your schedule— you don't need to worry if it's not conventional. If you can write every day or if you write for three consecutive days once per month, it doesn't matter as long as it's a habit. You'll receive lots of advice on this topic: Write a minimum of so many words, pages or hours every day; write only on weekdays; write only on weekends. Try them all, until you find what works for you and then require it of yourself. *For more on how to keep writing and stay motivated, see chapters 5 and 6.*

2. Record. Keep a note-taking app on your phone or a small notepad with you to capture every spontaneous idea or important question. This will help you live better (and sleep better) when you're not writing. You can feel secure you won't forget your inspired thought before you have a chance to get back to your desk. *For more on technology aids for writers, see the end of chapter 5.*

3. Engage other writers. Isolation can seem like the defining characteristic of a writing life, but writers have a multitude of options for connecting with other writers. Be part of a writer's group, no matter how formally or informally you define it. Join a local writer's workshop. Keep in touch with other writers whom you trust, whether that means phone conversations, email exchanges or meetings. *For more on ways to connect with other writers and the writing community, see chapters 2, 3 and 4.*

4. Retreat! Retreat! Unplug regularly, whether on your own or with others. Good writing is exhausting. Just as you need to fuel up on experiences to electrify your writing, allow yourself some down time to relax and refresh. Consider the writer's retreat, or some kind of quiet time with your writing. This may seem like the commandment of contradiction, but it's important to spend time with other writers and it's important to spend time alone with your writing. You need to do both. And you need to spend some time away from writing entirely. *For more on writer's retreats, see chapter 5.*

5. Say "thank you." Contact authors to thank them for writing those books you love. They may receive your note or not. If they do, you are providing that feedback from a reader you hope one day to find in your inbox. You never know, you might even get a response. *For more on putting yourself and your work out there, see chapter 7.*

6. Publish your course work. Go back and take a look at it. Whether it's not as bad as you imagined or it's worse, you put thought (and likely some research) into it. You may or may not admire it in retrospect, but you graduated from your program with a portfolio of work. All artists have an early period; don't neglect yours. If you're short on inspiration for a while, browse your earlier unpublished work, like program requirements, and see if something sparks an idea for reshaping and submitting. *For more on making creative use of course work, see Chapter 1.*

7. Take risks. Inspire and challenge yourself. Write outside your usual comfort zone. Take on a new type of project. This can help you avoid manuscript fatigue with your usual work. Understand that your success will more likely come from the unexpected than the well-planned. Experimental projects may or may not succeed, but they will definitely stretch you in new directions. And, art is all about creating something new. *For more on taking creative risks, see the essay by William Patrick in Chapter 1.*

8. Revise. Write in drafts. Accomplished writers throughout time swear by pouring everything you have out into one awful draft. Get it all out of you onto the page. Then edit your work. After you finish revising, revise again. And again. Then see #9.

9. Use an editor. Everyone needs an editor. Even an editor. Whether you are one or not, you can't edit your own work. Ask someone from your writing group, a former classmate or a professional editor. Find someone you trust to give your words a fresh look and to offer useful suggestions. *For more on writing groups, writing buddies and writing partnerships see chapter 3.*

10. Vent. If you're frustrated with your writing, tell your therapist, your sister, or your spouse. Non-writers can offer good advice, or know when just to listen. After all, there are no new problems in the world. We just reinvent ways to have the same ones. Often, the best advice comes from somewhere outside the eye of the storm. The act of writing might be lonely, but a writer's life doesn't have to be. When you're done unloading, don't forget to return the favor.

11. Trust yourself. Trust your skills and the process of writing. But, write even when you don't. You'll get over it.

12. Read.

13. Live. Life is what inspires your writing and provides you experience to react to, to reflect on, to synthesize meaning from. Live life so your writing can explode with it.

Write, but live? Sound contradictory? It's a delicate balance, to be certain, and almost never perfect. Forgive yourself when life gets in the way of your writing. *For more on finding the balance between writing and life, see chapter 6.*

Chapter *14*

TOP 14 THINGS A WRITER SHOULD NEVER DO

edited by Ashley C. Andersen Zantop

A short list of the top proscriptions to help craft habits and for a successful writing life.

*S*ome of us respond best to positive reinforcement. For the rest of us, here is a list written in language we understand. A writer's life is some parts exhilaration, satisfaction, inspiration and some parts hard work, frustration and challenge. *Do not* make it harder on yourself than it must be. When you're stuck or just at an intersection, refresh yourself on these fundamental 'do nots' and make any necessary course corrections.

DO NOT

by Ashley C. Andersen Zantop, Michael Bayer, A.J. O'Connell, Erin A. Corriveau, Adele Annesi & Jean M. Medeiros

1. Write in endless isolation. You may have the literary muscle to power through long stretches of butt-in-seat-hands-on-keyboard, but you must emerge from the cave and test your work out on real live people with opinions that aren't yours. Writing in a vacuum can be productive if you measure success in word count, but you can easily loose perspective. Share your work with other writers and readers, if for nothing else than to recalibrate your compass to what readers enjoy and understand, what they don't and how effectively you deliver your message. Doctors seek second opinions for good reason; writers should, too. *For more on sharing your work with other writers, see chapter 3.*

2. Sign contracts without reading them. Seriously. Just don't do it. No matter how much they bore you, be the adult. Read the words. You wouldn't deposit a check without looking at who sent it. *For more on the basics of publishing contracts, how to read them and where to go for legal help, see chapter 12.*

3. Expect your books to be bestsellers. Your MFA or writing degree is not a golden ticket. It's not an automatic pass to the bestseller list or a full-time teaching gig. It is evidence of your dedication to craft and a step toward what you want to achieve. A big step. If you have real aspirations of writing a bestseller, writing isn't enough. Increase your chances by getting to know your industry. If you want a teaching gig, the same applies. *For more on your industry, see chapter 4. For more on tenure track teaching careers see chapter 9.*

4. Wait for readers to discover your work. You need to find and address your audience. Don't be shy about self-promotion. Tell people you're a writer and share what you write. Being good is not good enough if you want your work to be read. You need to put it in where people can find it. *For more on putting yourself and your work out there, see chapter 7.*

5. Beat yourself up. You probably have a list of things that you think a writer should do; maybe you haven't done them lately. Maybe you haven't done them at all. Don't waste your time on blame. Start now and move on. *For more on how to forgive yourself and keep writing, see chapter 6.*

6. Compare yourself to writers you know. Your friends or acquaintances may be driving the publishing fast track, with agents, acceptances and contracts. You're in the slow lane. Frustrated? Sure. Discouraged? Maybe. Envious and embarrassed to admit it? Try not to stay there too long. Negative comparison does nothing positive for you.

7. Always follow the rules. Show, don't tell? Sure, but sometimes telling works, too—or better. Trust yourself, your art, your instincts, and then find out if you're right. See #1.

8. Allow anyone to tell you what you can and can't do with your writing. Some of the most interesting and well-known literature of all time was considered taboo or unconventional when published. *For more on some rules to follow and break in publishing, see chapter 10.*

9. Give up. You've identified yourself as a writer by reading this book. If you struggle with doubt, frustration, inspiration, motivation or the time to write, the solution is to keep writing. You may need to take a short break, live your life, find an idea that ignites your need to write and then return to writing. *For more on how to stay motivated and productive, see chapter 5. For more on making ends meet while writing and careers for writers, see Chapters 8 and 9.*

10. Write only one draft. Don't edit while you write. Draft and redraft. Don't start your edits until draft two. See rule #1 to help keep you honest.

11. Expect that anyone else will be as invested in your work as you are. You are the only one who is ultimately responsible for your work and your writing life and career. *For more on getting to know your industry, understanding how to get an agent and publishing contract basics, see chapter 7, 10, 12.*

12. Write only for a paycheck. Your writing won't be as good if you aren't interested. Of course you can vend your craft as a writer, but if you are passionate about writing as well as skillful at it, make certain that a portion of your writing time is spent on subjects and genres that intrinsically interesting to you. *See chapter 7 on how to write for a paycheck and see chapter 8 on careers suited to writers. Pay special attention to Michael Bayer's essay on creativity in the workplace.*

13. Wear your roller skates near stairs. This one is borrowed from the 'don't' list for my four-year-old, but it's a relevant theme: Do not neglect yourself physically. A steady diet of coffee, cigarettes, Diet Coke, chocolate (or whatever your writing stimulant of choice) and backlit screen-time is not a good recipe for your health or the health of your writing. *For more on finding balance between your writing and life, see chapter 6.*

14. Take your loved ones for granted. You can forgive yourself when life gets in the way of your writing. You can not reasonably expect the reverse from your family on a daily basis. Supportive and forgiving family and friends are an invaluable treasure. You may need to prevail upon that forgiveness from time to time, but make sure you give back as much as you take

APPENDIX: ADDITIONAL RESOURCES

edited by Erin A. Corriveau

Online Resources for Writers by Category
by Adele Annesi

Author's Resources
Association of Authors' Representatives: http://aaronline.org
Audible: http://www.audible.com
Author Buzz: http://www.authorbuzz.com
AuthorAdvance: http://www.authoradvance.com
Authorlink: http://www.authorlink.com
BowkerManuscriptSubmissions.com: http://www.
    bowkermanuscriptsubmissions.com
Red Room: http://redroom.com

Blogging Resources
BlogCatalog: http://www.blogcatalog.com
Blogger: http://www.blogger.com
Brian Clark's CopyBlogger: http://www.copyblogger.com
Problogger: http://www.problogger.net
Successful Blog: http://www.successful-blog.com
Tumblr: https://www.tumblr.com
WordPress: http://wordpress.org

Book Clubs and Resources
African American Literature Book Club (AALB): http://aalbc.com/writers
Book Talk: http://www.booktalk.com
Children's Book Council: http://www.cbcbooks.org
Goodreads: http://www.goodreads.com
Reading Group Choices: http://www.readinggroupchoices.com
Reading Group Guides: http://www.readinggroupguides.com/content/
    index.asp

Book Trailers
Bookscreening: http://bookscreening.com
BookTrailers: http://www.book-trailers.net

Conferences
Algonkian Conferences: http://algonkianconferences.com
AWP Conference: http://www.awpwriter.org/conference
Backspace: http://www.bksp.org
BookExpo America: http://www.bookexpoamerica.com
Grub Street: http://www.grubstreet.org
Shaw Guides: http://www.shawguides.com
Writers Conferences and Centers: http://writersconf.org

Content Aggregators
About.com: http://beaguide.about.com
Christian Articles Resource: http://christian-topics.info
Helium: http://www.helium.com
Ping.fm: http://Ping.fm
Suite 101.com: http://community.suite101.com/join

Critique Sites
Fictionwritersreview: http://fictionwritersreview.com
Your First Page: http://yourfirstpage.blogspot.com

ePublishers and Resources
BookBaby: http://www.bookbaby.com
CreateSpace (Amazon): https://www.createspace.com
Cursor: http://thinkcursor.com
Digital Book World: http://www.digitalbookworld.com
E Is for Book: http://www.eisforbook.com
Kristen Lamb's Blog: http://warriorwriters.wordpress.com
Smashwords: http://www.smashwords.com

Forums
Absolute Write: http://www.absolutewrite.com/forums
P&W Shameless Plugs: http://www.pw.org/speakeasy
The Writer: http://cs.writermag.com/wrtcs/forums
Writer's Digest Block Party: http://www.writersdigest.com/forum/forums
Writing Forums: http://www.writingforums.org

Funding and Grants

Connecticut Arts Grants: http://www.cultureandtourism.org/cct/cwp
National Endowment for the Arts: http://www.nea.gov
Pen American Grants List: http://www.pen.org

Image Sites

Flickr Creative Commons: http://www.flickr.com/creativecommons
Fotolia: http://www.shutterstock.com
iStockphoto: http://www.istockphoto.com
Shutterstock: http://www.shutterstock.com
Sock.XCHNG: http://www.sxc.hu

Jobs and Markets

99designs: http://99designs.com
AllFreelanceWork: http://www.allgraphicdesign.com
Angela Hoy's Writers Weekly (free newsletter): http://writersweekly.com
Book Editing Associates: http://www.book-editing.com
Editor & Publisher Classifieds: http://www3.editorandpublisher.com/ep_jobs
Editorial Freelancers Association: http://www.the-efa.org
Elance: www.elance.com
Freelance Daily: http://www.freelancedaily.net
Freelance Success: http://www.freelancesuccess.com
Freelance Switch: http://freelanceswitch.com
Freelance Writing Jobs: http://www.freelancewritinggigs.com
Freelance Writing: http://www.freelancewriting.com
Guru: http://www.guru.com
International Freelancers Academy:
    http://internationalfreelancersacademy.com
IRE Job Center: http://www.ire.org
Jobs for Copy Editors: http://jobs.copyeditor.com
Journalism Jobs: http://www.journalismjobs.com
Media Job Market: http://nielsen.mobile.adicio.com/jobs
MediaBistro (free newsletter): http://www.mediabistro.com
MediaBistro: http://www.mediabistro.com
Odesk: https://www.odesk.com
PeoplePerHour: http://www.peopleperhour.com
Sunoasis Jobs for Writers, Editors, and Copywriters:
    http://www.sunoasis.com
Therenegadewriter.com: http://www.therenegadewriter.com

Travel-writers-exchange.com: http://www.travel-writers-exchange.com
Wooden Horse Publishing: http://www.woodenhorsepub.com
Worldwide Freelance: http://www.worldwidefreelance.com
Write Jobs: http://www.writejobs.com
Writerfind Jobs: http://writerfind.com/freelance_jobs
Writers Market: http://www.writersmarket.com
Writers-Editors Network: http://www.writers-editors.com

Legal and Government
International Standard Book Number Agency: http://www.isbn.org/
    standards/home
Legal Definitions: http://definitions.uslegal.com
LegalZoom: http://www.legalzoom.com/index1m.html
Lijit.com: http://www.lijit.com
U.S. Copyright Office: http://www.copyright.gov

Libraries and Online Research Resources
American Library Association: http://www.ala.org
Bibliomania: http://www.bibliomania.com
Internet Public Library: http://www.ipl.org
LibraryThing: http://www.librarything.com
Shelfari: http://www.shelfari.com
StumbleUpon: http://www.stumbleupon.com

Literary Agency Info and Query Resources
Agency Gatekeeper: http://agencygatekeeper.blogspot.com
Agent Query: http://www.agentquery.com
Agent Research: http://www.agentresearch.com
Allison Winn Scotch's Ask Allison: http://www.allisonwinn.com/ask-allison
Angela Booth's Writing Blog: http://www.angelabooth.biz
Betsy Lerner: http://betsylerner.wordpress.com
Bookends Lit Agency: http://bookendslitagency.blogspot.com
Buried in the Slush Pile: http://cbaybooks.blogspot.com
Guide to Literary Agents Blog: http://www.writersdigest.com/editor-blogs/
    guide-to-literary-agents
Janet Reid: http://jetreidliterary.blogspot.com
Nathan Bransford: http://blog.nathanbransford.com
Pub Rants: http://pubrants.blogspot.com
Query Shark: http://queryshark.blogspot.com

Query Tracker: http://querytracker.net
Rachelle Gardner: http://www.rachellegardner.com

Marketing and Sales
Children's Writer's & Illustrator's Market: http://www.writersdigestshop.
   com/Childrens_Writers_and_Illustrators_Market
Dianna Huff's B2B Marcom Writer Blog: http://www.diannahuff.com/blog
Grow Your Writing Business: www.growyourwritingbusiness.com
Market List: http://www.marketlist.com
NewPages: http://www.newpages.com
Publishers Marketplace: http://www.publishersmarketplace.com
Publishers Weekly: http://www.publishersweekly.com/pw/home
Spannet: http://www.spannet.org
Triberr (reach multiplier): http://triberr.com
Write and Publish Fiction: http://www.write-and-publish-fiction.com

Manuscript Services
Edit 1st.com: http://edit1st.com
Manuscript Editing: http://www.manuscriptediting.com

Online Communities
Next Big Writer: http://www.thenextbigwriter.com
Novelists, Inc.: http://www.ninc.com
OnceWritten: http://www.oncewritten.com
Writerspace: http://writerspace.com

Organizations for Writers (Including Those Offering Insurance)
American Christian Fiction Writers: http://www.acfw.com
American Copy Editors Society: http://www.copydesk.org
American Society of Business Publication Editors: http://www.asbpe.org
American Society of Journalists and Authors: http://www.asja.org
Americans for the Arts: http://www.artsusa.org
Association of Learned and Professional Society Publishers: http://www.
   alpsp.org/E-business/Home
Association of Writers & Writing Programs: http://www.awpwriter.org
Christian Storyteller: http://www.christianstoryteller.com
Christian Writers Guild: http://www.christianwritersguild.com
Council of Literary Magazines and Presses: http://www.clmp.org

Editor and Publisher: www.editorandpublisher.com
Independent Book Publishers Association: http://www.ibpa-online.org
International Women's Writing Guild: http://www.iwwg.org
Jewish Writer's Association: www.jscribe.com
JewishWriting.com: http://jewishwriting.com
Muslim Writers Society: www.oneummah.net
National Assembly of State Arts Agencies: http://www.nasaa-arts.org
National Writers Union: http://www.nwu.org
New England Science Fiction Association: http://www.nesfa.org
Pen American: http://www.pen.org
Poynter: http://www.poynter.org
Science Fiction and Fantasy Writers of America: http://www.sfwa.org
Society of Children's Book Writers and Illustrators: http://www.scbwi.org

Playwriting
Doollee.com: http://www.doollee.com
PlaywritingOpportunities.com: http://www.playwritingopportunities.com
The Playwrights' Center: http://www.pwcenter.org

Poetry
National Federation of State Poetry Societies: http://www.nfsps.com
Poem Hunter: http://www.poemhunter.com
Poetry Society of America: http://www.poetrysociety.org/psa
Poetry.net: http://www.poetry.net
Poets.org: http://www.poets.org

Public Relations
Bookwire: http://www.bookwire.com
Constant Contact: http://www.constantcontact.com/index.jsp
Google Alerts: http://www.google.com/alerts
Help a Reporter: http://www.helpareporter.com
PRLog.com: http://www.prlog.org

Publications—Online and Print
Arts & Letters Daily: http://www.aldaily.com
Booklist: http://www.booklistonline.com
Folio: http://www.foliomag.com
Poets & Writers: http://www.pw.org
Publishers Weekly: http://www.publishersweekly.com/pw/home

The Writer: http://www.writermag.com
Writer's Chronicle: http://www.awpwriter.org/magazine
Writer's Digest: http://www.writersdigest.com

Residency Listings
Alliance of Artists Communities: http://www.artistcommunities.org
Res Artis: http://www.resartis.org/en

Screenwriting
Final Draft: http://www.finaldraft.com
Screen Writers Guild: http://www.nndb.com/org
Screenwriters Federation of America: http://www.screenwritersfederation.
  org
Screenwriters Online: http://www.screenwriter.com
Screenwriters Utopia: http://www.screenwritersutopia.com
Screenwriting Software: http://www.screenwriting.com
Zoetrope Screenplay Contest: http://www.zoetrope.com/contests

Self-Publishing and Print on Demand
AuthorHouse: http://www.authorhouse.com
BookLocker: http://booklocker.com
CreateSpace: https://www.createspace.com
iUniverse: http://www.iuniverse.com
Lulu: http://www.lulu.com
Trafford: http://www.trafford.com
Xlibris: http://www2.xlibris.com

Software for Writers
MyWriterTools: http://www.mywritertools.com
Picnik: http://www.picnik.com
Story Weaver: http://storymind.com/storyweaver

Submissions Services and Information
Duotrope: https://duotrope.com
Qooid: http://www.qooid.com
Storiad: http://storiad.com
Submission Mission: http://www.shewrites.com/profiles/blogs/the-
  submission-mission-a-1
Submishmash: http://www.submittable.com

Teachers
Teachers and Writers Collaborative: http://www.twc.org

Technical Support
Nerds to Go: http://www.nerdstogo.com

Tradeshows
Book Fairs and Festivals: http://www.read.gov/cfb
Combined Book Exhibit: http://www.combinedbook.com

Warnings
Writer Beware: http://www.sfwa.org/for-authors/writer-beware/alerts

Website and ID Assistance
2CreateAWebSite.com: http://www.2createawebsite.com
Add to Any: www.addtoany.com
Bluehost: http://www.bluehost.com
Feedburner: www.feedburner.com
FriendFeed: http://www.facebook.com
Grader.com: http://grader.com
OpenID: http://openid.net
PayPal: https://www.paypal.com/home
Search Engine Guide: http://www.searchengineguide.com
Search Engine Journal: http://www.searchenginejournal.com
Search Engine Watch: http://searchenginewatch.com/seo
Site Meter: http://www.sitemeter.com
Technorati: technorati.com
Web for Authors: http://www.webforauthors.com
Website Ideas for Writers: http://www.sky-bolt.com/writers
Word Tracker: http://www.wordtracker.com

Writing Resources, Comprehensive
About Fiction Writing: http://fictionwriting.about.com
Daily Writing Tips: http://www.dailywritingtips.com
Every Writers Resource: http://www.everywritersresource.com
Fiction Factor: http://www.fictionfactor.com
Fictionaut: http://www.fictionaut.com
ForWriters.com: http://www.forwriters.com

How to Plan, Write and Develop a Book: http://
howtoplanwriteanddevelopabook.blogspot.com
National Novel Writing Month: http://www.nanowrimo.org
Preditors and Editors: http://pred-ed.com
Strongest Start Novel Competition on TheNextBigWriter: http://www.
thenextbigwriter.com/competition/strongest_start.html
TheNovelette.com: http://thenovelette.com
Wattpad: http://www.wattpad.com
Wired for Story: http://www.wiredforstory.com
Writers and Editors: http://www.writersandeditors.com
Writers in Touch: http://www.writersintouch.com
Writing World: http://www.writing-world.com

Workshops and Memberships: Making the Most of Belong

by Adele Annesi

Making the most of wherever you're a member, from the AAA to churches to writers unions to sports can be a great way to get a start at running (and charging for) a regular writing workshop. Doing workshops with unexpected groups like your local church or synagogue, or with local societies like the Audubon Society in Connecticut, or other museums can provide a valuable opportunity for you and organization patrons. Here is a list of possible writing and related organizations to market yourself and your workshop:

Alumni offices
Arts councils
Biographer
Book editor
Book stores
Career fairs
Career offices: High school, college, university
Conferences: Local, state, national, international
Continuing education
Corporate communications, including online, video and audio
Editor
Employment centers
Forums
Ghost writer
Grant writer
Guilds
Library
Lit agent
Manuscript evaluation
Marketing
Memoirist for others
Museums
Newspapers
Online, e.g.: About.com
Placement organizations

Platform, including: Nonfiction: Fields related to topic (e.g., social services)
Fiction: Fields related to theme (e.g., travel, parenting, etc.)
Proofreader
Public relations
Publishing jobs
Readers
Retreat centers
Salon: In-home (yours or someone else's) writers critique groups
Senior centers
Service Core of Retired Executives (SCORE)
Small Business Association
Societies
State and other writing groups and forums, such as: Connecticut Authors
and Publishers Association
Teaching: Preschool, elementary, middle school, high school, college, post
Work for hire
Writer

Places to peddle (advertise) your wares:
Acting studios
Americans for the arts
Art and writers supplies
Arts and culture, county
Arts foundations
Book groups
Bookstores
Cable TV
Chorale societies
City listings
Commission on arts, culture and tourism
Community centers
Concerts/happenings
County or regional writers groups
Cultural alliances/communities
Dance/conservatories/joy of movement
Education/classes
Farm art centers
Film societies

Friends of the library
Galleries
Graphic arts
Guild of artists
Historic sites
Historical societies
Illustrators
Libraries
Literary arts groups
Local writers groups
Magazines
Museums
Music and arts centers
Music studios/by style of music
National arts foundations
National arts marketing project
National endowment for the arts
National historic sites
New England foundation for the arts
Parks
Patch
Performing arts/artists
Playbills
Playhouses
Private schools
Productions for young people
Public schools
Publications
Radio stations
Reading circles
Regional arts foundations
Senior centers
State listings
Statewide writers groups
Symphony orchestras
Talk of the town
Theaters
Town listings

Visual arts/education
Writers
Writing as therapy
Yoga
Youth orchestras

THE PROGRAM THAT INSPIRED THIS WORK

edited by Ashley C. Andersen Zantop and Michael C. White

Writer Michael Bayer gives us a brief look at the writing program that inspired the creation of this guide.

The Program

by Michael Bayer

"Something very special happens here," says Dr. Michael White, director of the MFA in Creative Writing program at Fairfield University. "At the start of each semester, I hold a meeting with all the new students. I ask them to look around the room because these 'strangers' are about to become lifelong friends."

Having been one of those strangers in the summer of 2009, I can attest to the truth of those words and the special place that is the Fairfield MFA program. The entire experience was transformative, but there were very specific moments that have stayed with me the most. The chills when one of my mentors suggested the perfect change to my plot. The exhilaration of a workshop when everyone "got" my work. The lightening rush of my fingertips against my keyboard during a creative burst. Lying on a sunbaked lawn overhearing a conversation about Virginia Woolf. Even chatting with a poet while in line for the salad bar.

The vivid memories from our MFA program. We all have them. I cherished the feelings of inspiration and community I felt as a student. But why should this inspiration and sense of community have to fade once we've graduated? The MFA program should be just the beginning. It should be the spark that keeps your literary flame roaring for the rest of your life. Whether you aim for the pen to sustain you vocationally, spiritually, or both, the "writer's life" doesn't happen like magic. It takes knowledge, planning and quite a bit of discipline.

That's exactly why we created this book.

The Fairfield program is relatively young, and that may be why we're so proud of it, so proud in fact that we chose to compile and share our collective knowledge, insights and advice with MFA graduates and other serious writers. This supportive and collaborative spirit characterizes the Fairfield MFA experience. Some MFA programs are deeply traditional with entrenched ways of teaching and learning. Others are highly competitive. The Fairfield program is neither entrenched nor competitive. Fairfield writers work together. And we are thrilled by one another's success.

History

The Fairfield University MFA program was launched in 2009 after years of research, planning and preparation. The administration understood the unique value of an intense writing residency, so the program was designed to incorporate a low-residency model.

"The bonding and community that occur in a low-residency program are unmatched by any traditional program," Dr. White says. "One of the most important elements of any writing program, aside from the focus on craft and practice, is the inspiration gained from peers and faculty. Compared to spending a few hours per week in a classroom, there's no experience as inspiring as when writers eat, sleep, and socialize in close proximity for nearly two weeks at a time."

Venue

Fairfield MFA residencies are held on Ender's Island in Mystic, CT. Property of St. Edmund's Retreat, the island's eleven acres accommodate dormitories, meeting rooms, workspaces, the Chapel of Our Lady of the Assumption, and the main house, which comprises the dining room, kitchen, guest rooms, private reading rooms, and a stone fireplace—a popular gathering place during winter residencies. Surrounding the facilities are lush lawns, manicured flower gardens, stone pathways, sculptures, and towering trees, punctuated by a gazebo, a pergola and a seaside chapel. The entire island is encircled by a massive stone seawall, which protects the island from powerful storm surges and provides residents with solitude.

"On Ender's Island, we have an environment that feels like the perfect combination of an artist colony and a sacred place," says Elizabeth Hastings, Director

Michael C. White, Ph.D.

of Community and Lifetime Education for Fairfield University. "Many of the staff have worked here and been part of the local community for decades, and now they've become part of our MFA family."

Faculty

The Fairfield MFA faculty comprises some of the literary community's most renowned poets, novelists, essayists, and memoirists. Fairfield faculty boast diverse experience across genre, style and cultural background. They've published novels, memoirs, and collections through both major publishing houses and small presses. They've published stories, essays and poems in virtually every major literary magazine. They've won countless awards, prizes and fellowships. They are passionate writers and instructors.

"Fairfield MFA candidates possess a unique self-awareness as writers," says Baron Wormser, author, most recently, of the novel *Teach Us That Peace.* "Many of them arrive at their first residency with projects already underway and a keen sense of their writing objectives. As a mentor, I find tremendous fulfillment collaborating with writers who are eager to immerse themselves in the culture of writing and in a community of writers."

Curriculum

Fairfield MFA candidates select a genre focus in fiction, poetry, or creative non-fiction. If they choose, they may add a concentration in screenwriting, spiritual writing, or publishing. Applications are considered on a rolling basis, and candidates who are accepted begin their studies at either the summer or winter residency on Ender's Island. Each ten-day residency consists of morning workshops, afternoon seminars, and evening readings by faculty, students and guest authors in the chapel. Breaks, meals and social activities allow for plenty of personal writing, relaxation and bonding among attendees. Special guests and panelists typically include agents, publishers, and renowned authors; the program has welcomed Mark Doty, Wally Lamb, Rick Moody, Jayne Anne Phillips, Dani Shapiro, Anita Shreve and others.

Between residencies, the curriculum is rigorous. During the first two semesters, students work closely with their chosen mentors to develop their own creative work while reading and analyzing a variety of relevant literary works in their chosen genre. During the third semester, students conduct an intensive third semester project, typically an in-depth research paper or some form of work "in the field" with a publishing house, non-profit or writing center. During the fourth semester, students complete their book-length creative thesis, which requires review and approval by two selected faculty members. A formal commencement ceremony on Ender's Island celebrates each graduating cohort's achievement.

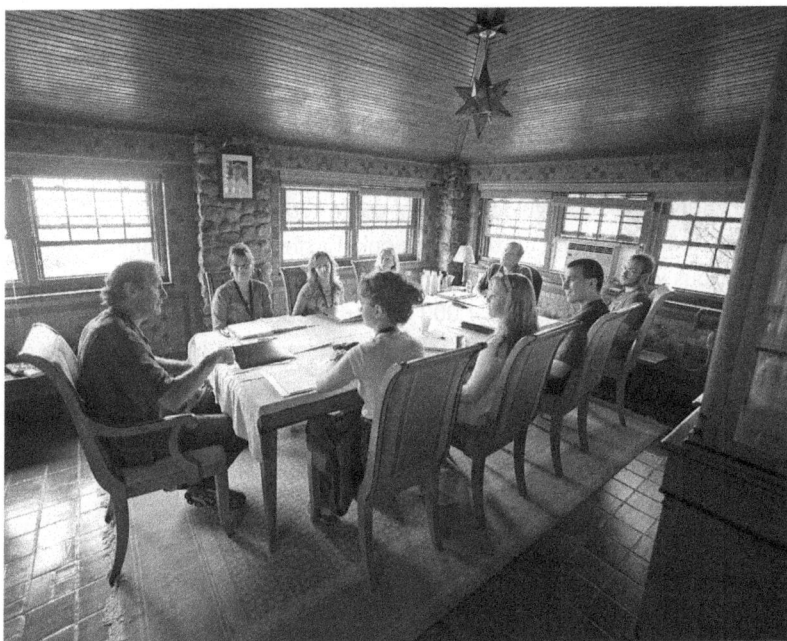

Students

Fairfield MFA candidates come from a wide variety of backgrounds and with a wide variety of writing goals. Students range from recent undergraduates to retirees, from published authors and accomplished teachers to entrepreneurs and career switchers. Similarly, graduates leave the program to pursue a variety of callings. Some enter teaching and academia. Some begin careers in publishing or communications. Some go on to Ph.D. programs. And some simply keep writing and publishing their work.

A major distinction of the Fairfield MFA experience is the vibrant alumni community, organized in part by the Fairfield University MFA Alumni Association (FUMAA). While many MFA programs maintain informal alumni communities online, few have alumni organizations with clear structure, consistent communication, and a variety of programs scheduled throughout the year.

Founded and managed exclusively by graduates, the alumni association's mission is "to provide lifelong community, opportunity and inspiration for graduates of the Fairfield MFA program, and to encourage maximum creative output and achievement for all alumni." Fairfield alumni benefit from a quarterly newsletter, an online networking community, an annual alumni-exclusive weekend residency, Alumni Day receptions every six months, and participation in a variety of local programs, projects and events. Association membership is free of charge.

The "Now What?" guide is one of those projects. It was concepted and created to help and motivate not only Fairfield's MFA community but serious writers everywhere, to keep living the literary life they want. Having committed more than 1,000 collective hours to plan, write, edit, produce, and distribute, it has been a labor of love. Just like writing itself.

For more information about the Fairfield MFA in Creative Writing program, visit the program website at www.fairfield.com/mfa or contact Elizabeth Hastings at EHastings@fairfield.edu or 203-254-4000 ext. 2688.